The Which? Guide to Employment

About the author

Ian Hunter was admitted as a solicitor in 1989 and is now a partner and employment law specialist at a City of London law firm. He is co-author of *Britain's Invisible Earnings* and a freelance journalist who writes for the national and trade press, including *The Independent* and *Sunday Business*. He has made regular television and radio appearances and lectures frequently on employment-related issues.

Acknowledgements

The author and publishers would like to thank the following for their help in the preparation of this book: Penny Christie, Pat Ghatauray, Rory Graham, Andrew Granger, Martin Harney, Elizabeth Lang, Jonquil Lowe, Karen Morris, Emma Murray, Lakhbir Purewal, Dennis Redgrave, Diane Rochester, David Rodwell, Sarah Tidswell, Virginia Wallis, Richard Ward, Mark Watson, Suzanne Whittaker. Consultant for Northern Ireland: Peter Lynch; Consultant for Scotland: Alistair Cockburn.

The Which? Guide to Employment

Ian Hunter

CONSUMERS' ASSOCIATION

Which? Books are commissioned and researched by
Consumers' Association and published by
Which? Ltd, 2 Marylebone Road, London NW1 4DF
Email address: books@which.net

Distributed by The Penguin Group:
Penguin Books Ltd, 27 Wrights Lane, London W8 5TZ

First edition September 1998

British Library Cataloguing in Publication Data
A catalogue record for this book is available from the British Library

ISBN 0 85202 735 4

For a full list of Which? books, please write to Which? Books, Castlemead,
Gascoyne Way, Hertford X, SG14 1LH
or access our web site at www.which.net

Cover and text design by Kyzen Creative Consultants

Typeset by Paston Press Ltd, Loddon, Norfolk
Printed and bound in Great Britain by Clays Ltd, Bungay, Suffolk

Contents

★An asterisk next to the name of an organisation in the text indicates that the address can be found in this section

Introduction

When you think about it, employment, or the lack of it, is a central consumer issue. Without a job the decision about which car to choose, holiday to select or pension plan to contribute to becomes, for the vast majority of us, one of academic interest.

Few areas of our lives have, in recent years, been subject to such constant change as that of employment. Since the 1980s the character of the job market has changed rapidly. The period has witnessed the rise and rise of part-time workers, the introduction of the job-share, increased use of fixed-term and fixed-task contracts, a growing number of service industry opportunities and a huge decline in the number of jobs in the manufacturing sector. All of this has been accompanied by technological changes and moves to globalisation which have transformed the job market.

New technology in the form of portable computers, mobile phones, the Internet and email have increased opportunities for home and flexi-working. The price has been the loss of jobs in some areas, as technology has reduced the demand for many traditional skills. Even the future of the typist, a familiar sight for almost a century, is threatened in the foreseeable future by the advent of voice-activated typing.

The changes in working practices and job opportunities have been accompanied by a steady flow of domestic and European Union legislation that neither employers nor employees can afford to ignore.

How European law affects employees in the UK

Since the United Kingdom joined the European Union (or European Economic Community as it was formerly known) it has become bound by the laws the European Union generates. In the employment sphere much of this European case law has centred on the issue of sex discrimination.

European law takes a number of different forms. First there is the Treaty of Rome, by which all member states of the European Union are bound, including the United Kingdom. This treaty includes a large number of provisions, among them Article 119, which upholds the principle that men and women should receive equal pay for equal work.

In addition to the treaty, the European Union has introduced a large number of laws known as directives, many of which relate to employment. These include the Equal Treatment Directive, the Working Time Directive, the Acquired Rights Directive and the Part-time Workers Directive. Once these directives have been adopted, the member states have a certain number of years within which to implement the directives into domestic legislation. For example, the UK legislative expression of the Acquired Rights Directive can be found in the Transfer of Undertakings (Protection of Employment) Regulations 1981 (TUPE) – see Chapter 8.

When UK domestic legislation is at odds with a European directive, the domestic legislation will be interpreted in accordance with the European directive – that is, European law will hold sway. This has occurred in a number of cases – for example, in relation to pension entitlement, where the Equal Pay Act 1970 was deemed to conflict with the Equal Treatment Directive. In addition, any European Court of Justice ruling on the interpretation of European law will be binding on the UK courts.

Developments in the UK

The issue of age discrimination seems set to achieve greater prominence. For example, a 1998 industrial tribunal held that the upper qualifying age limits for claiming unfair dismissal and redundancy payments contravened the Equal Treatment Directive (see Chapters 10 and 11). Other cases can be expected to continue to combat age discrimination.

The provisions of the Working Time Directive are likely to become part of UK law by the end of 1998. One of the more important provisions is that guaranteeing employees three weeks' paid holiday per year, rising in November 1999 to four weeks. Other provisions relate to average weekly hours of work, night-time working and daily and weekly rest periods.

The government has proposed a national minimum wage of £3.60 per hour for those aged 22 or over and a lower rate of £3 for those between the ages of 18 and 21 (this is expected to increase to £3.20 by June 2000).

The European Union's social ministers have also confirmed the intention to amend the current Acquired Rights Directive which impacts on, among other things, employees' rights on the sale of a business. One of the more interesting proposals is that member states will have the option of introducing legislation which will require the person acquiring the business to provide the transferring employees with pension rights comparable to those they received under their former employer. At present, those parts of an employee's contract of employment which provide rights under an occupational pension scheme do not transfer by law.

In its White Paper 'Fairness at Work' the government has set out its thoughts for the future, which include enhanced maternity benefits and better protection for sacked employees. These include reducing the qualifying period required before a claim can be submitted in respect of unfair dismissal and lifting the current cap on the level of compensation that can be awarded. In addition, as a result of the Employment Rights (Dispute Resolution) Act 1998 receiving royal assent, new rules about to come into force will change the way in which industrial tribunals (soon to be known as employment tribunals) are run.

Given the flurry of legislation in recent years, employment law issues have become increasingly complex. This has been reflected by a marked growth in the number of solicitors specialising in this area and in the number of employment law publications offering guidance to lawyers and human resources specialists. The same, cannot, however, be said for publications offering help to those outside this specialist field: the employers and employees most directly affected by the changes. Hence this book.

The Which? Guide to Employment does not attempt to provide a definitive statement of the law; nor has it been written with employment lawyers in mind. Instead, it aims to redress the balance by providing practical advice on the sorts of employment problem faced by someone somewhere every day, and explains rights and tactics in the workplace from the point of view of both parties in the employment relationship. Presenting the current law in a clear and user-friendly style, and indicating differences in Scotland and Northern Ireland where these exist, the book will enable its readers to find out where they stand – perhaps before seeking legal advice. While *The Which? Guide to Employment* cannot supply the answer to every problem, since all cases are different, its clarifications of obligations and its use of numerous real-life examples should go some way to helping people develop negotiating skills and achieve a satisfactory outcome in most situations.

Chapter 1

Employment *vs* self-employment

It could be said that parenthood is the only remaining job for life. After the massive upheaval in the UK during the recession of the early 1980s, when the country experienced rising unemployment coupled with a decline in its manufacturing base, the idea of working for the same employer year in, year out gave way to the reality of a much more flexible and fluid workplace. Employees are now expected to train and retrain with increasing frequency in order to ensure a regular pay packet.

Employment prospects in the traditional manufacturing industries, such as coal-mining and steel production, were dealt a severe body blow in the early 1980s. Central and local government and the National Health Service now out-source many activities, from rubbish collection to information technology (IT) support. Even the armed forces have not been immune from change and, primarily as a result of the end of the Cold War, have experienced manpower cuts and restructuring.

Yet as one employment sector diminishes in importance, others develop to absorb some of the slack. The service industries have undergone a period of sustained growth in contrast to the decline in the UK's manufacturing base. Financial services, information technology and leisure sectors of the economy have all enjoyed a boom and the voice of the customer has become far more potent, as result of which chain stores have taken to opening on Sundays, licensing hours have been relaxed and some banks now offer a 24-hour service.

These changes in the structure of the economy, coupled with technological advances and globalisation, have created a great deal more flexibility. Mobile phones, fax machines, email and portable computers now enable many employees to work from home or while on the move. New and imaginative working arrangements have become popular, even in traditionally staid professions such as law and accountancy. Part-time working, job-sharing, casual working, agency working and fixed-term contracts are increasingly challenging the idea of the 9 a.m. to 5 p.m. working day.

Employee or self-employed?

Despite the greater variety in the way people work, employment law recognises only two distinct types of worker in the employment relationship: **employees** and the **self-employed**. These categories cover every type of worker, from the managing director of a public listed company to the hod-carrier on a building site. In many cases the differences are not immediately apparent. For example, it is common for IT consultants to work alongside an employer's in-house IT support team, carrying out a broadly similar job. Similarly, contractors often hire self-employed electricians to work together with their own employees on a building site. However, despite outward appearances, significant differences exist between the two relationships.

Employees

- are usually entitled to statutory sick pay (see page 65), maternity pay and maternity leave (see Chapter 6), and legislation protects them if they are unfairly dismissed or made redundant (see Chapter 10), or if their employer decides to sell the business (see Chapter 8)
- typically receive perks such as holiday leave, season ticket loans, discounts on company goods and pension scheme membership. Senior employees may enjoy a company car, private medical insurance and permanent health insurance cover, while large companies often provide their workers with other corporate perks related to the company's performance in the form of share save and share option schemes.
- can claim back expenses – employers are obliged to reimburse travelling and hotel costs and other liabilities incurred by employees in the course of their work

- are not solely responsible for their actions – employers are vicariously liable for the actions of their employees, and can be sued as a result of careless or wrongful actions of employees, provided these are committed in the course of their employment. Note: this does not include actions carried out by employees on a 'frolic of their own' (see box below)
- come under the PAYE (Pay As You Earn) system, by which income tax is deducted at the point of payment and sent to the Inland Revenue. Employers are obliged to operate PAYE, and also to account to the Department of Social Security (DSS) for both employees' and employers' National Insurance contributions.

Employees who want to know more about the PAYE system can obtain a leaflet entitled *Pay as You Earn* (IR34) from the Inland Revenue.* Employers can consult the *Employer's Quick Guide to Pay as You Earn and National Insurance Contributions* (CWL3), also from the Inland Revenue.

A frolic of one's own

This term describes irresponsible actions which could not under any rational interpretation be considered to have been carried out by the individual while trying, however misguidedly, to do his or her own job. For example, a warehouse worker might borrow during his lunch hour a van which he is not allowed (or insured) to drive, and crash it into another car. This would constitute a frolic of his own, and his employer would not be liable for his actions.

The self-employed

- do not have the same statutory rights as employees (see above), or the same protection against their boss selling the business
- are usually responsible for their own expenses, unless there is agreement to the contrary
- are solely responsible for their actions – those who hire them will be responsible only if they themselves are negligent in the way that they recruit or allocate tasks to self-employed workers
- are responsible for their own tax returns and National Insurance contributions since they are not subject to the PAYE system (see

above). A useful leaflet is *National Insurance Contributions for Self-employed People* (CWL2) from the Inland Revenue.★

However, self-employed people:

- are allowed to set a much greater variety of expenses against income tax than employees
- are not subject to the same implied obligations (unwritten but mutually understood to be part of the employer/employee contract) as employees – e.g. the duty of good faith and loyalty (see page 71), which can restrict employees' ability to take on outside work without permission from their employers
- have greater freedom in how they carry out the work – and can, unless there is agreement to the contrary, subcontract that work to others since the relationship is generally not dependent on personal service: e.g. a self-employed electrician who agrees to complete some work for a customer would be entitled to send another colleague in his or her place. By contrast, someone employed as a receptionist would be required to carry out duties personally
- are considered the owners of any intellectual property rights, such as copyright or patents created in the course of the employment contract, unless agreement to the contrary has been reached (see Chapter 7). Clearly, this will be of greater importance to some than to others: a self-employed graphic designer or IT consultant might be anxious to retain ownership and control of any designs or programs developed during a contract, whereas a self-employed builder might be less likely to use innovative techniques which he or others might want to claim.

There is no legal definition of 'employee' or 'self-employed'. Each individual's status is subject to interpretation – especially by the Inland Revenue (see opposite).

In many cases it is obvious whether someone is an employee: for example, a production-line worker will almost always be an employee while the owner of a local newsagent will almost certainly be self-employed. However, other cases are not always so clear. What is the position, for example, of a non-executive director who holds the office of director in a company but is not involved in its day-to-day running and is restricted to an advisory role? Or of individuals who term themselves 'self-employed consultants' but who work for only one employer and are, save for tax and National Insurance purposes, treated identically to the employer's employee workforce?

First, what the parties involved call the relationship is not the deciding factor for PAYE or employment law purposes. In other words, just because *you* say you are self-employed it does not mean that either the Inland Revenue or an industrial tribunal will treat you as such.

- The **Inland Revenue (IR)** is interested in determining an individual's status for the purposes of deciding how he or she should be taxed. Amongst other things, this will determine what allowances and expenses the individual can set against tax.
- An **industrial tribunal** may also be concerned to establish the individual's status. This is because certain rights – such as the right to bring a claim for unfair dismissal (see pages 174–9), or a statutory redundancy payment (see page 191) – apply only to employees. Where a dispute exists as to whether someone is an employee, this issue must be resolved at the outset of the hearing because if the person is not an employee the tribunal will not have the authority to hear the case. (See Chapter 16 for more on bringing a case to an industrial tribunal.)

In exceptional circumstances, one worker was treated as self-employed by the Inland Revenue and as an employee by the industrial tribunal (see 'Phil' case history, page 17).

A number of different tests have evolved which provide some help. The purpose is to establish whether the individual is employed under a **contract of service**, or under a **contract for services**. There is an important distinction. The term 'contract of service' means that the individual retained is an employee. The term 'contract for services' means that the individual has self-employed status. People who are employed under a contract of service are entitled to all the obligations and benefits associated with being an employee (see pages 12–13). People who are employed under a contract for services are treated as being in business for themselves, and as such do not enjoy the same degree of protection afforded to an employee. Note that these definitions do not have to be contained in the job contract in order to determine a worker's status.

The tests to determine status include the following.

- **How much control does the employer have over the way in which the worker carries out the work?** Does the employee have to carry out precise instructions given to him or her, or is there flexibility as to when, and how, the job will be done? For example, a self-employed IT consultant devising new software might be given a free hand in a project with minimum interference from the employer, while a secretary might be more closely supervised and expected to work at set times. The greater the control, the more this suggests an employer/employee relationship

- **To what degree is the individual integrated into the employer's organisation?** Broadly, this means workers who are included in the day-to-day running of the employer's business. For example, individuals whose names appear on work rotas, who receive sickness pay and other benefits and work set hours are likely to be employees. So are those whom the employer is obliged to pay for on a regular basis as long as the individual is available for work, even if there is no work to do

- **Is the employment relationship personal to the worker, or can he or she hire someone else to do the work?** A contract of service requires a particular individual's service; a contract for services is primarily an agreement to complete a task which is not dependent on using the services of a particular individual

- **Is the individual in business on his or her own?** Does the person use his or her own equipment and pay workers out of his or her own pocket, keeping any profits and suffering any losses? Does the individual correct any faulty work in his or her own time and at his or her own expense? The greater the risks the worker assumes and the more independence he or she adopts, the less it is likely to be an employer/employee relationship

- **How flexible is the employer/employee relationship?** Is the worker obliged to accept any work offered by the employer, or can he or she pick and choose? Is he or she able to work for several employers at the same time? Is payment dependent on the completion of a particular project, rather than on simply turning up for work? The greater the flexibility of the relationship, the more it tends to suggest self-employed status.

It is, of course, possible for employees to have more than one employer, or to be employed in one place and self-employed in another. For example, an individual might work during the week as a freelance journalist – submitting articles to, and accepting commissions from, a number of newspapers – while being employed in the evenings as bar staff in a local pub. Likewise, someone might have several part-time jobs under different bosses, but which still require him or her to work for each particular employer at set times, signifying employee status.

The criteria opposite are those which a court may consider when looking at specific employee rights in a contract; the same principles will come under consideration by the Inland Revenue and an industrial tribunal (see page 15). These bodies almost always concur, although in one case they provided conflicting rulings on a worker's status (see 'Phil' case history, below).

CASE HISTORY: Phil

Phil, a factory sheet-metal worker, was offered the choice of treating himself as employed or self-employed by the company he worked for. He opted for the latter as it provided him with a tax saving of £500 per annum. The Inland Revenue similarly treated him as self-employed, even though he was paid the same hourly rate as other workers and worked the same hours. In addition, the company provided all his equipment. When Phil's contract was terminated, he claimed unfair dismissal, at which point the company argued that he was not an employee. The court to which the case was ultimately referred decided that, despite the fact that both the company and the IR had treated Phil as self-employed, he *was* an employee since he shared the same terms and conditions of employment as other workers, and as such was entitled to bring a claim.

CASE HISTORY: Laura

Laura was a dentist who was retained by a health authority to provide emergency cover once a week at a hospital. The patients were not from her own practice and she treated them using the hospital's equipment and medicine. Her pay, calculated on an hourly rate, was not dependent on the number of patients treated or the complexity of the work. Laura was under an obligation to find a replacement if she was not available for work. She did not receive holiday pay or sickness pay, and was responsible for her own tax and National Insurance. In addition, she did not have access to, and was not subject to, the hospital's grievance and disciplinary procedure. After Laura was sacked by the hospital, a court found her to be an employee despite the fact that considerations such as her self-employed tax treatment and lack of holiday and sickness pay suggested a self-employed relationship. In reaching a decision, the court had focused on the dentist's 'obligation' to turn up for work according to a regular rota system, and the hospital's duty to pay her for being available for work.

CASE HISTORY: John

As a freelance vision mixer, John worked for a number of production companies on short-term contracts. Although he used the companies' own equipment – which suggested employee status – he had no financial interest in the making of the films and programmes he worked on. He was registered for VAT and did his own paperwork from an office at his home. When the Inland Revenue attempted to treat him as an employee for the purposes of tax assessment, he appealed. The tribunal subsequently found him to be self-employed.

Different types of worker

A number of categories of worker exist who may be either employed or self-employed.

Homeworkers

It is now increasingly common for people to work from home. Typically this could include a solicitor updating a firm's standard documentation, an IT consultant developing software, an outworker sewing clothes, or someone stuffing envelopes or proof-reading. However, the fact that these individuals are working from home does not automatically mean that they should be treated as self-employed.

Working from home tends to suggest a greater degree of independence and flexibility, consistent with being self-employed. However, regardless of appearance other factors – such as whether or not the individual uses the employer's equipment – are significant: for example, an outworker may be provided with a computer, telephone, fax machine or other equipment to carry out the job. Even if the outworker does not have to work set hours, he or she may be required to work a certain number of hours a week and to submit timesheets to an employer. Obviously, other factors such as treatment for tax and

National Insurance purposes are relevant in determining whether or not someone is employed or self-employed. To establish which label is appropriate, the standard tests (see pages 15–16) should be applied.

Part-time workers

Part-time working (generally defined as less than 30 hours a week) is on the increase, particularly among women. About a quarter of employees in the United Kingdom work part-time, according to a Labour Force survey carried out in 1996. Ninety per cent of part-timers work in the service sector: many jobs in the retail and catering trade are part-time, and in most fields of employment part-time work has become a common arrangement. Women returning to work after having a baby will usually have the right to go part-time (see page 117).

The fact that an individual works part-time does not determine whether the person is an employee or self-employed; and in any case the worker's status may vary from one working relationship to another. The most reliable method of finding the correct label is to apply the tests on pages 15–16.

Equal rights for part-time workers

The government has recognised the importance of part-time workers to the British economy. It has agreed to adopt a European Directive relating to part-time workers, which will be introduced into UK law in April 2000. The purpose of this directive is to eradicate discrimination against part-timers and give them access, where possible, on a *pro rata* basis to the same benefits as their full-time colleagues. Employers will also be expected to smooth the way for part-time workers to progress within the organisation.

Workers with fixed-term and fixed-task contracts

Throughout a wide range of industries – for example, the IT sector, marketing and medical research – a growing number of people are being employed on fixed-term contracts (i.e. for a pre-arranged length of time), including workers providing maternity leave cover and teachers and academics. Doctors and solicitors often work on fixed-term contracts or fixed-task contracts (where employment ends on completion of a project), and construction workers are usually employed until a building contract is finished. Someone who works for a pre-determined period on fixed-term contracts may be either employed or self-employed, depending on the nature of the employment relationship. To check which term is likely to be appropriate, see the standard tests on pages 15–16.

Protection for workers with fixed-term contracts

Employees are sometimes nervous about accepting fixed-term employment contracts, believing that this arrangement offers less financial security than a permanent job. In reality, in many cases it offers greater security.

For example, an employee who has been offered a fixed-term contract for three years is better off than a worker who has a contract which can be terminated at any time on three months' notice. Although the first employee's contract will only last for three years, he or she has the security of being guaranteed employment for this length of time, and if he or she is dismissed before the end of the period, the starting point for calculating compensation will be by reference to the unexpired remainder of the contract. By contrast, the employee with the three-month notice period has only the security of that three-month period.

Any employee who has completed over two years' continuous employment (a limit which is likely to be reduced under current government proposals) has the right not to be unfairly dismissed. This applies even when the worker is employed under a fixed-term contract, unless he or she has contracted out of his or her rights to bring a claim (see page 178). However, this waiver of rights will only be enforceable where the contract expires at the end of the term. In other words, if the employee is dismissed before the end of the contract he or she might still be able to claim unfair dismissal.

Agency workers

Employment agencies offer employment to a wide range of workers, from accountants, solicitors and secretaries to other office staff, chefs, nurses and kitchen porters. Recruitment consultancies perform much the same task, although they tend to be more specialist and often deal exclusively with vacancies for senior staff.

Although these sorts of agencies have contracts with both the customers needing staff and the workers themselves (see box below), employees are normally expected to work under the direct control of the customer. The company generally pays a fee to the agency which, in turn, pays the worker an amount usually calculated at an hourly rate, while the agency normally deducts tax and National Insurance.

Types of employment agency contracts

Agency/customer contract This regulates the terms on which the worker's services are supplied. It will include the fee for the worker's services and a clause preventing the customer from employing him or her directly for a set period of time after the contract has ended. If the firm ignores this, it may be liable to pay compensation to the agency.

Agency/employee contract This sets out rates of pay and the procedure for returning authenticated time sheets. It does not normally entitle the agency worker to the same rights as a standard job contract (see Chapter 3).

In the past, it was always assumed that agency workers would never be employees of either the agency or the customer. These assumptions have since been challenged, as the case history below shows.

CASE HISTORY: Louise

After working as a 'temp' for an employment agency for several years, Louise was dismissed from her job. The court which heard her case found that she *was* an employee of the agency, despite the fact that the agreement between her and the agency clearly stated that she was regarded as self-employed and was not employed under a contract of employment. The reason for the court's decision was that the agency had, amongst other things, retained the right to dismiss Louise for misconduct and to deduct amounts from her hourly pay if she was late or adopted a difficult attitude – all of which suggested that Louise was in reality an employee, regardless of what the contract said.

People who are unhappy for any reason with the way they have been treated by an agency can contact the Employment Agency Standards Office★ helpline.

Consultants

Often, workers who wish to portray themselves as self-employed will style themselves consultants in order to aggrandise their professional status, and will also assume responsibility for the payment of their own tax and National Insurance. Some, in order to maximise the probability of the Inland Revenue accepting their status as self-employed, may arrange for their services to be provided to employers through a company which they have set up and wholly own. It does not involve a great deal of effort to set up a company – 'off-the-shelf' companies can be purchased for about £150 and are advertised for sale regularly in trade journals. The company set up by the consultant will then submit invoices for the consultant's services to the employer, and in turn will pay the consultant.

Despite outward appearances, by themselves arrangements of this type offer no guarantee that either the Inland Revenue, a court or an industrial tribunal will accept a consultant's self-employed status. The mere fact that the consultant has assumed responsibility for his or her tax and National Insurance contributions (even via a service company established by him or her) will not be sufficient to indicate self-employed status if everything else points to the relationship being that of an employer and employee (see pages 15–16).

CASE HISTORY: Ben

After working for 15 years for a firm of architects as a financial controller, Ben was dismissed by his employer. Owing to his long-standing service with the company, he was offered work as a consultant as part of the termination deal. Ben accepted and continued to do effectively the same job as before, the only difference being that his labour was now provided through a service company which he had established to bolster his status as consultant. However, for the purposes of assessing his employment status the relevant authorities would be likely to treat him as an employee because of the essentially unchanged nature of the employer/employee relationship.

Considerations for employers hiring workers

There are pros and cons associated with taking on either category of worker: employee or self-employed. Employers should think the issues through first.

Hiring employees

The advantages include the following:

- the employer can supervise closely employees' hours of work, behaviour and dress code. In addition, employees do not have the option of sending a substitute to do their job – a receptionist would be expected to provide personal service, for example, and could not send a friend in his or her place
- the unwritten obligations imposed on employees prevent them from working for competitors or poaching fellow employees or clients during their employment (see page 71)
- any intellectual property rights (such as any copyrights or patents) created by employees during the course of their employment will normally belong to the employer (see Chapter 7)
- cost-effectiveness: self-employed workers often charge higher hourly and daily rates, whereas employees can be required under the terms of their contracts to undertake unpaid overtime, and usually receive a lower rate of pay as a trade-off for the greater security of being an employee.

Disadvantages for employers who hire employees are:

- the employer must operate a PAYE system (see page 13)
- the employer is liable for statutory sick pay (see page 65) and maternity pay (see page 108)
- the employer is potentially liable for unfair dismissal (see Chapter 10) or a statutory redundancy payment when a contract is terminated (see page 191)
- the employer is obliged to pay the employees as long as they are available for work, even if there is no work to do.

Generally, employers are not obliged to provide employees with work, except in certain situations such as engineering or hairdressing apprenticeships, or solicitors' and accountants' traineeships, for which employees must be given on-the-job vocational training in order to complete their qualifications.

Employers may find useful a leaflet from the Inland Revenue* entitled *Thinking of Taking Someone On? PAYE Tax and National Insurance Contributions for Employers* (CWL3).

Hiring self-employed workers

Employers often take on self-employed workers to complete specific projects when they do not want to hire permanent staff. Employers that are in a position to choose could benefit from certain advantages associated with using self-employed workers:

- the employer does not have to operate a PAYE system, or pay National Insurance contributions (see page 13)
- the employer is under no obligation to provide statutory sick pay (see page 65) or statutory maternity pay (see page 108)
- the relationship has greater flexibility – staff can be hired (and laid off) more readily on certain projects (e.g. a building project that has fallen behind schedule)
- the employer is not liable for unfair dismissal (see Chapter 10) or a statutory redundancy payment (see page 191) when the contract is terminated
- the employer is much less vulnerable to being sued for any negligence or misconduct on the part of the worker.

Disadvantages for employers who hire self-employed workers are:

- usually, much less control over the workers and how they carry out their duties. This may not matter if the workers do not come into regular contact with the public (e.g. on night-time cleaning or security contracts), but when the job involves, say, operating a help-desk or promoting an employer's services they may require much closer management since their conduct could potentially affect the business. Clearly, even when workers do not have regular contact with customers, they would still be expected to carry out the tasks given to them to the required standard
- intellectual property rights such as copyright or patents created during the contract will not automatically belong to the employer (see Chapter 7)

- in the absence of a clear indication to the contrary, workers are free to work for competitors, use confidential information or poach clients or employees – either during the contract or after it is completed. For example, while converting a customer's loft for an employer, a self-employed builder could try to get further building work from the customer on his or her own account, without being obliged to refer the business back to the employer.

Before hiring self-employed workers, the employer will want to ensure that:

- the worker is responsible for his or her own tax and National Insurance, and will reimburse the employer if any demands are received from the Inland Revenue or DSS
- the agreement does not create an employment relationship – words such as 'employer' and 'employee' should be avoided. Typical alternatives such as 'contractor' and 'consultant' could be used
- the contract can be terminated immediately in certain circumstances (e.g. if the worker is incompetent or dishonest, commits a criminal offence, is ill for an extended period of time or becomes bankrupt). The exact circumstances will vary depending on the worker's role. For example, if the worker is a driver, a criminal conviction which leads to the loss of his or her licence will be more serious than for an IT consultant who works from home
- the length of the notice period is appropriate (see page 55). If the contract is terminated by the employer without notice or justification, the starting point for calculating the worker's compensation will be an amount equal to the payment that the worker would have received if the terms of the contract had been honoured
- benefits such as sickness pay or holiday pay are not provided
- if a fixed fee is paid, it is calculated by the number of hours worked or is subject to the completion of pre-determined tasks. The employer should ensure that the worker is paid only for the hours actually worked
- the worker is obliged to compensate either the employer or any of its clients for any losses suffered as a result of his or her faulty workmanship. One option is to require the worker to take out an insurance policy to cover any losses suffered – this is typically seen in contracts for professional services where sub-standard work may

result in the contractor suffering very significant claims for compensation from unhappy clients (workers to whom this might apply include IT consultants, surveyors, doctors, lawyers, accountants, bankers and architects)

- the worker provides his or her own equipment, where appropriate
- the employer owns any intellectual property rights (e.g. copyright, designs or patents) created by the worker while working for it – see Chapter 7. The employer should insist on protection of this type only if the contract on which the worker is involved merits it. If the worker is an engineer, an architect or an advertising executive involved in designing products, such protection may be very important. In the case of a hairdresser or a driver, such a clause would serve no useful purpose
- the worker is obliged to keep any information relating to the employer's business confidential (see page 71). He or she should also be compelled to return any property borrowed from the employer at the end of the contract (see page 58)
- (optionally) the worker is prevented from working for rivals while working for the employer. In certain circumstances, some contractors may not want competitors to be able to use the services of workers currently working for them – for example, to guard against rivals gaining access to confidential information such as customer lists and pricing strategies. In addition, if the reason for hiring the worker was to give the company a competitive edge, the last thing the employer wants is the worker using those skills to help its rivals in his or her spare time.

Considerations for the self-employed before starting work

Self-employed workers should ensure that any contract for services addresses the following points:

- the length of the agreement. They should make sure that they are guaranteed a certain period of work, ideally reserving for themselves the right to terminate the contract on short notice (see pages 45–6). The longer the notice the employer is required to give, the greater the financial protection
- the hourly or daily rate of pay for the job

- the number of guaranteed hours of work
- the frequency and method of payment
- the amount of assistance to be provided by the employer, e.g. use of equipment or access to secretarial or office facilities
- reimbursement of expenses such as travel and accommodation costs (see page 53). If undertaking a substantial project, setting up an office, flying regularly overseas or buying a large amount of materials and equipment, self-employed workers should insist on receiving an advance payment in respect of such expenses
- confirmation that VAT will be paid in addition on any invoices submitted, if necessary.

For more on the contract of employment, see Chapter 3.

Employers which fail to operate the PAYE system

This is a common occurrence, particularly in the building and catering trades, which often use casual labour. Employers simply inform the workers that they are self-employed in order to avoid paying employers' National Insurance contributions. Others tell their employees that they have deducted and accounted to the relevant authorities for tax and National Insurance, but instead pocket the contributions. It is important that employees ensure that the necessary National Insurance contributions are made on their behalf: their entitlement to a range of state benefits such as maternity pay and statutory sick pay will be prejudiced if the appropriate contributions are not made. The employer has a legal duty to make the appropriate payments.

Checking that contributions have been made

Employees are entitled by law to receive from their employer an itemised payslip which sets out the deductions made from their pay. Employees who are dismissed for asserting their right to such statements will have an automatic claim for unfair dismissal, regardless of their hours of work or length of service (see pages 181–2). If unwilling to rely on an employer's promise that the appropriate contributions have been made, employees can contact their local Contributions Agency,* which should be able to tell them what contributions have been made on their behalf.

Additional help

If there is uncertainty over someone's employment status for the purposes of tax and National Insurance, the problem should be resolved at
the outset: employers which fail to operate the PAYE system could
end up receiving demands from the Inland Revenue and the DSS for
payment arrears. Every tax district and local Contributions Agency
office now has a staff member assigned to deal with enquiries regarding employment status. A written decision on employment status can
be obtained from either the Contributions Agency★ or the Inland
Revenue,★ which have jointly produced a useful leaflet entitled
Employed or Self-employed? A Guide for Tax and National Insurance (IR56/
NI39).

Chapter 2

Gaining employment

For many people, the main worry is not whether they will be treated as employed or self-employed (see Chapter 1), but whether they will find a job in the first place.

Writing your CV

If you are applying for a job, whether in response to an advertisement or speculatively, you will want to maximise your chances of success by submitting a well-prepared application. The CV (*curriculum vitae*: 'course of life' in Latin) outlines the employee's abilities and achievements to the employer. From it, the employer should be able to discern the individual's aptitude for the job, level of motivation and ability to fit in. Many interviewers base the job interview on the contents of the candidate's CV, so prospective employees should ensure that their CV follows a logical progression when unfolding details of previous positions, responsibilities and skills.

To increase the chances of your application being noticed, you should:

- tailor your CV and covering letter to match the expectations of each new job and employer – avoid sending out an impersonal, identikit document
- do some research into the firm you hope to work for so you can personalise your application and demonstrate evidence of interest to the employer
- focus on what you have to offer in the future, not what you have achieved in the past
- develop key phrases describing yourself (e.g. 'experienced manager') and build them into positive career statements which incorporate the direction you plan to take

- address the recipient by name if sending a CV on spec (avoid heading your letter 'Dear Sir').

In order to write an effective CV it is necessary to learn what does not work. Traditional-style CVs laid out according to a rigid formula and recording dry chronological detail may fare poorly with employers. Employers are also liable to be put off by:

- over-long documents (two pages of A4 are quite sufficient)
- poor presentation (e.g. unprofessional printing or typing)
- gimmicks such as photographs, coloured paper and elaborate binders
- spelling, typographical and grammatical errors
- over- or under-writing: verbal excess or lack of detail
- structural disorganisation which makes it hard for the reader to obtain information or follow the chronology
- not enough detail about the candidate's achievements, at work or otherwise
- irrelevancy (e.g. giving the marital status of children).

When preparing your application, the most crucial points to remember are: be clear, be concise, focus on the organisation to which you are applying and emphasise the skills you can bring to the job. The most effective CVs do not just 'tell', they also 'show'.

The job interview

The job interview is an essential part of the job-hunting process. In many cases the decision on whether to employ someone is made on the basis of one interview, without further checking. Kitchen porters, construction-site workers and car-park attendants, for example, are often taken on immediately without the need for a reference, the thinking being that the only suitable qualification is proof that they can do the job for which they have been hired. The same situation applies in industries where qualified and/or experienced staff are in short supply: even at a high level, the job offer may be made on the strength of a single conversation. Sometimes these offers are made subject to suitable references being obtained (see pages 35–6).

Where particular skills or qualities are important – such as for marketing executives, bankers and accountants – candidates may have to undergo a battery of interviews and tests before an offer of employment is made.

Employers are entitled to ask employees about their work experience and qualifications in order to gauge their suitability for the job. However, in deciding whether to employ individuals they are not allowed to discriminate against them on the basis of sex, race or disability (see Chapter 5).

Psychometric tests

Employers are increasingly using psychometric tests as part of the job interview process. The purpose is to find out how a candidate thinks, and to assess how easily he or she will fit in to a particular environment. The tests usually involve a range of multiple-choice questions, which might be work-related or seemingly random.

Some candidates are inclined to over-react when asked to undertake this sort of test, because of an irrational fear that it will reveal some deep-seated personality defect. The reality is that individuals who raise an objection to undertaking such a test are more likely to be viewed with suspicion by the interviewer. In many cases, candidates will be offered the chance to discuss the test results with the prospective employer.

Negotiating terms at an interview

There is nothing to prevent the employer and the candidate negotiating different terms of employment at the job interview, or even following the job offer. This might involve the employer reducing the salary from the one advertised; likewise, the job candidate could bargain for more favourable terms. Once accepted by both parties, the terms will be binding on employer and employee. See Chapter 3 for information on how to negotiate the terms you want.

CASE HISTORY: Tony

Tony had worked in the catering trade for three months. He replied to a newspaper advertisement for an experienced silver-service waiter with pay at the rate of £7 per hour. The employer felt that he did not have the necessary experience but still offered to employ him at £6 per hour. Because Tony was keen to do the job, he agreed to accept employment under different terms to those advertised.

The offer of employment

A job offer need not be in writing to be binding on the employer. Ideally, no one should accept a job until he or she has received a written offer setting out in full the terms offered by his or her prospective employer. In reality, many people informally accept a job prior to receiving a written offer, and large numbers of employees never receive a written contract of employment. Yet the absence of a written contract does *not* mean that an employee has no rights. The crucial issue is that the terms of the offer should be clear, and that the job candidate should make it clear that he or she has accepted. The problem with agreements reached on a nod of the head or a handshake is that in the absence of any written proof of what the terms of employment are, it usually boils down to one party's word against the other. See pages 68–9 for details of the written information employees are legally obliged to receive about their terms of employment.

Obtaining written terms

Whenever possible, job candidates should ensure that the employer confirms the precise terms of the job offer in writing. *In extremis*, the candidate could force a recalcitrant employer's hand by writing a letter setting out what he or she believes are the terms of employment, for the employer to confirm or amend.

Considerations for employees before accepting a job

If your job application has been successful and you have reached the stage of discussing terms with a prospective employer, look before you leap.

- **Do not assume that a long contract is better** A long contract does not necessarily mean that you will be better protected, so do not be discouraged if the contract of employment consists of little more than a letter. The chairmen of Britain's leading companies and the City's highest-paid brokers are often employed on the strength of a two-page letter of appointment. Contracts of employment which run for pages and pages usually give the employer added protection in the form of elaborate clauses dealing with copyright and confidentiality, and include provisions which prevent the employee from joining competitors or poaching clients and employees once the employment has ended (see Chapter 7)

- **Do not sign any contract until you are satisfied with all the terms** Your main concerns in any contract will usually be restricted to the pay and benefits you will receive, the tasks you are expected to perform and the notice period to which you will be subject. Pressure to start work before issues such as pay, working hours, workplace, holiday and fringe benefits have been addressed should be resisted at all costs (see overleaf for what to do in this situation). All too often employees accept offers of employment in which the provision of benefits such as bonus, commission or pension arrangements have either not been settled or have not been properly recorded: employers may be able to exploit this uncertainty at a future date in order to argue that they are under no obligation to provide such benefits

- **Avoid agreements to agree** This warning is as relevant in employment situations as anywhere else. Basically, if you want to confirm that an offer is binding, ensure that it is nailed to the floor – and that nothing is left to be agreed or finalised at a later date (see box below).

'Agreement to agree' clauses

In employment contracts, this type of clause usually relates to obligations on the part of the employer to introduce bonus or commission arrangements, or set up a pension scheme. Typical wording might be:

- The employer agrees that it will at a future date put in place a bonus scheme for the benefit of the employee on such terms as the parties may agree between themselves

- It is the employer's present intention to put in place a pension scheme to provide the employee with such benefits as the parties shall agree.

In both examples, employees would have great difficulty in establishing an undisputed right to a pension or bonus because the arrangements are conditional on a future agreement being reached. In the second example, the employer has merely expressed a *present* intention to take steps at a future date; that intention can change at any time, so the employee has no legal right to receive those benefits at the outset of employment.

Actions for employees pressed to accept an offer before terms are finalised

Employees placed under pressure to accept an employer's offer when there are still significant points of principle outstanding should express willingness to spend however much time is necessary with the employer to resolve outstanding issues. If resolving these issues is likely to result in the employees clocking up legal fees, they should try to extract a written agreement from the prospective employer to pay these costs – even if they ultimately decide not to accept the job.

Job offers subject to conditions

The employee should not resign from his or her current job until any conditions imposed by the employer have been satisfied (see pages 35–41). If the offer is conditional on a medical examination, for example, the employee should not serve notice until the prospective employer has confirmed that it is satisfied with the results. If the offer is conditional on the receipt of satisfactory references, employees should find out from whom references will be required (see box, page 36).

Some employees – for example, sales and marketing executives and workers in professions such as law, banking and recruitment consultancy – have post-termination restrictive covenants contained in their contracts of employment. Usually, these impose a duty on the employee to continue to keep all of his or her old employer's affairs confidential. Similar clauses may also seek to prevent the employee from joining a competitor, working within a certain geographical area or poaching clients or employees (see page 135). Some prospective employers will not be concerned by the existence of such restrictions; however, if your prospective boss works for a competitor of your current one, the restrictions may dissuade him or her from offering you the job. It is always best, therefore, to address such problems at the outset.

If the prospective employer is still happy to take you on, but makes it clear that it wants you to disregard the post-termination restrictive covenants, you should obtain confirmation that the company will pay any legal or other costs that may be suffered by you if the old employer decides to sue. When weighing up the likelihood of this happening, it is worth remembering that restrictions which are very wide have little chance of being enforced – see pages 136–40.

Conditions the employer may impose

Before taking the employee on, the employer may make the job offer subject to the receipt of satisfactory references or the completion of a medical examination (or both). Once the candidate has been employed, the employer may impose a probationary period.

References

The way a reference is worded can instantly fix the reader's impression of a candidate's abilities and demeanour, as the examples below – featuring the same employee – demonstrate. If the allegations in the second reference were true, an employer would be justified in refusing to employ the individual.

Example A Mr Smith has been employed by the company in the position of service engineer for three years, during which time he has shown himself to be hard-working, honest and reliable. He will be greatly missed by the colleagues and customers with whom he has worked during his time with the company. We have no hesitation in recommending his services.

Example B Mr Smith has been employed by the company in the position of service engineer for three years, during which time his timekeeping has been poor. His technical competence has not reached the company's required level and we have on several occasions received complaints from both customers and colleagues regarding his surly and unco-operative manner. It was for these reasons that the company decided to terminate his contract of employment.

CASE HISTORY: Leslie

Leslie worked for a company selling financial services. When he applied to work for other companies, his ex-employer provided an unfavourable reference which suggested that Leslie kept the best leads for himself, had little or no integrity and could not be regarded as honest. This led to three prospective employers withdrawing their offers, at which point Leslie became suspicious. The case hung on whether Leslie's old boss owed a duty to him not to give a misleading reference. The court agreed that he did.

References: fact and fiction

Contrary to popular belief, employers are not obliged to provide departing employees with references. However, they *are* under an obligation to both the employee and the prospective employer to ensure that any references provided are accurate.

The employer cannot concentrate on a worker's positive attributes at the expense of the negative ones (or *vice versa*) if this creates a misleading impression. Workers can take action against former bosses who paint a false picture of their ability or character to prospective employers (see case history on page 35). If the employer considers a reference to be unsatisfactory, it is within its rights to reject a candidate – but cannot use this as an excuse for refusing to employ someone if the real reason is that its recruitment needs have changed (see page 41).

If you have applied for a new job and you are concerned that your present employer will not provide a reference – or you do not want to approach him or her – check that the prospective employer will be satisfied with a reference from an alternative source. Typically this reference could be provided by a former employer, client or, in the case of a young worker, a family friend or headmaster. A character reference of this sort should provide evidence of honesty and qualities such as a willingness to learn and work hard.

The precise form of the reference will vary depending on the employer's requirements. For junior employees, a character reference may suffice, while in other cases employers may have specific questions they require answering (see page 39).

Medicals

Professional sportsmen and women, members of the armed forces and the police are invariably asked to undergo a medical before starting a job. Increasingly, employers recruiting employees for highly paid or stressful jobs insist that the job offer is conditional on the satisfactory completion of a medical. It is becoming more common for employees in accountancy, banking and the law to have to have medicals.

The examination

Medicals are arranged and paid for by the employer and typically take place at private clinics. The purpose is to assess whether the employee is medically fit for the job for which he or she has been recruited. A standard medical will take about an hour; a more intensive medical might take much longer.

Checks generally cover blood pressure, cholesterol levels, liver and kidney function and the condition of the lungs. A number of blood tests may also be performed. The employee will be consulted about the findings at the end of the examination and his or her permission should be sought before the test results are released (see below). The clinic will then tell the employer whether any of the tests have high-lighted areas of concern that may deter the employer from taking on the candidate.

Medical examinations of this type are not covered by the **Access to Medical Records Act 1988**. The Act requires that the employee's consent to the release of medical records held by his or her own doctor must be obtained, but this is not so in the case of results of an independent medical examination carried out by a doctor appointed by the employer – although in practice, the employee's permission is usually sought.

Employees' and employers' rights following a medical

If a prospective employee were to refuse to be medically examined and it stated in the job offer that employment would be conditional upon the completion of a medical, the employer would be entitled to withdraw its offer of employment, because the candidate would not have complied with its terms.

Probationary period

The purpose of a probationary period is to give the employer the opportunity to assess the worker's performance and, if the performance is not satisfactory, to terminate the employment on short notice. Employees offered internal promotion, subject to a probationary period, might want to negotiate the right to return to their old jobs if they fail to complete the probationary period satisfactorily.

The probationary period: uses and abuses

Probationary periods are most often arranged when the employee will be entitled to receive a long notice period – three months or more – after the probationary period ends. They are not strictly necessary in other cases, for example if the employee is subject to a short notice period (e.g. the statutory minimum notice period of one week during the first two years' employment which the employee is entitled to after one month – see page 65), as this means that the employee can be dismissed at any time on one week's notice without the employer having to give a reason (written explanation is required only after the employee has completed two years' continuous employment).

The length of any probationary period imposed is entirely at the employer's discretion. Clearly, if the period is too long it may deter an employee from accepting an offer of employment. In practice, probationary periods usually last between three and six months, but may be subject to extension if the employer wants further time for assessment.

Considerations for employers when making a job offer

When making a job offer, your prime concern as an employer should be to ensure that the offer is conditional upon all points of concern being satisfied. Any offer of employment should state what these conditions are.

References

Employers should make clear that the offer is subject to the receipt of satisfactory references – see page 35–6. References can be obtained by any means – they do not have to be in writing. However, many firms still send out formal requests for references along the lines of the sample letter opposite.

Example of an employer's request for references

Dear

We have offered [Name] the position of [Position] with this firm. The offer is subject to receiving satisfactory references and your name has been given as a referee.

I should be glad of your comments on the following: honesty, integrity, professional knowledge and technical competence, relationships with colleagues, peers and clients.

In addition could you please tell us anything else which you believe to be relevant and confirm that you are not aware of any factors which might prevent us from proceeding with the applicant.

Your reply will be treated in the strictest confidence and I have enclosed a prepaid envelope for your use.

Yours sincerely

Medicals

Candidates should be told that the job offer is conditional upon a medical examination, if this is the case (see pages 36–7). If the employee refuses to be examined, the employer may be justified in withdrawing the job offer – or dismissing an existing employee.

Probationary period

Even if the employee satisfies all or any conditions attached to the job offer, the employer should still consider making the offer of employment subject to a probationary period (see pages 37–8). The job contract should state that the employee can be dismissed at any time on short notice during the probationary period. If the employer fails to do this and merely states that the employee is subject to, say, a six-month probationary period, the risk is that it will be unable – save in cases of gross misconduct or gross negligence – to dismiss the employee before the end of the six-month period without being liable to pay compensation. This is because a court or industrial tribunal may decide that such wording effectively guarantees the employee six months' employment.

Professional qualifications

Employers are entitled to see, and ask for, credentials. If employees need certain qualifications in order to carry out their duties at work, the job offer should be conditional on these requirements being fulfilled. For example, people employed in financial institutions – such as brokers – are often required to be members of self-regulatory bodies, such as the Securities and Futures Authority (SFA).

Clearly, if an employee does not have the necessary qualifications, he or she will be unable to perform satisfactorily the duties he or she was appointed to fulfil. In addition, if it is discovered that a candidate has lied – for example, a nurse claiming to be fully qualified or a researcher turning out not have the qualifications claimed at interview – the employer should either dismiss the individual immediately or at the very least be wary of keeping the person in employment. If the employer decides to dismiss the person, this should be done ideally within two to three weeks of discovering the deception and on the completion of any other investigations necessary to establish the truth. The danger is that once all the facts are known, a delay may be taken as evidence that the employer is happy to keep the person on, even in the absence of the appropriate qualifications.

The signing of a full contract of employment

Employers may want to make the job offer conditional upon the signing of a full job contract, in which case this intention should be stated in the offer letter. The alternative is to forward to the employee a comprehensive contract of employment at the outset, plus all documents mentioned in the contract which will be binding upon him or her (for example, staff handbooks, pension scheme documents). One danger for employers is that if someone starts work without signing, or having had sight of, the main terms governing his or her employment – such as restrictive covenants, intellectual property or confidentiality clauses (see Chapter 7) – he or she may, when the job comes to an end, be able to argue that they are not bound by those terms.

Work permits

If an employer offers a job to an overseas national who needs a work permit and Home Office approval in order to work in the UK, the offer should be conditional on both requirements being attained.

It is a criminal offence to employ someone who does not have a legal right to work in the UK, so the employer must be able to prove that the employee has this right. The employer will have to apply for a work permit for the employee: it should be made clear in the offer letter that if the work permit is not granted, the offer of employment will immediately be withdrawn. See Chapter 14 for more on employing overseas nationals.

Contributions to professional fees

If the employer is prepared to make a contribution to an employee's legal, accountancy or other professional fees, the contribution should be subject to a cap and in no circumstances should the employer make an open-ended commitment to meet all costs.

Withdrawal of a job offer

This might happen for a number of reasons.

Candidate's reference

Any employer which supplies a reference is under an obligation to ensure that it accurately portrays the employee's abilities and character (see page 36). However, the test as to whether or not the reference is satisfactory is subjective. This means that if the reference in some way raises a question mark about the employee's character or conduct, however small, a prospective employer would be justified in refusing him or her a job – even if nine out of ten other employers would be undeterred.

An employer is expected to act in good faith, however. If, during the time between making a job offer and taking up references, the employer finds that its requirements have changed and the employee is no longer needed, it cannot simply argue that the employee's references are not satisfactory in order to wriggle out of the job offer already made. In such circumstances the employee could sue for breach of contract (see page 191).

False or misleading information

An offer of employment can be withdrawn at any time before the employee has accepted it. An employer may be able to subsequently withdraw an offer if it becomes clear that the employee has provided false or misleading information – for example, lying about qualifications or experience. In this case, the employer would be within its rights to reject the candidate. For example, if an employer makes clear that it is a requirement of the job that an employee has maths and English GCSEs, and it subsequently comes to light that the worker has lied and does not have such qualifications, the employer would be entitled to withdraw the job offer, provided he or she acts within a reasonable period of time (see page 40).

Withdrawal of a job offer after it has been accepted

This may happen if an employer has failed to make a job offer conditional on the satisfaction of any outstanding requirements, but then finds that the employee is unsuitable. It can also occur when the employer decides that he or she no longer wants or needs the employee during the gap between the employee accepting the offer and starting work. In both these circumstances, if the employer withdraws the offer it will be in breach of contract.

The extent of the financial exposure depends on the terms of the contract. The starting point for calculating damages is a sum equal to the value of the net salary and fringe benefits the employee would have received during the notice period provided for in the offer of employment. Generally speaking, the longer the notice period contained in the offer of employment (see page 45), the greater the employee's claim for compensation. If the employee is subject to short notice during a probationary period (see page 38), any compensation will obviously be small.

Chapter 3

The job contract and terms of employment

Every contract of employment is different. A contract's content will depend on the strengths and weaknesses of the employer's and employee's positions. However, in most cases the employee has only limited scope for amending a contract. The sample contract on pages 59–62 is one example of the type of contract that many employees are asked to sign.

Considerations for employees when negotiating terms

Every employee, regardless of status or line of work, can turn the job contract to his or her advantage by approaching it the right way.

Assess the strength of your position

From the outset, it is crucial to assess how much scope there is to change the terms of any offer to your advantage. Some candidates are well placed to bargain for the deal they want, particularly those who have been head-hunted or have specialist skills. It is unlikely that you will be able to negotiate changes to the employer's standard job contract if you have been unemployed for some time or are going for a junior post.

Focus on your main concerns

Job candidates have different concerns depending on their age, circumstances and aspirations. For some, financial security is important; others seek job satisfaction or good training and experience.

As for any negotiation, it is worth drawing up a list of objectives with the intention of conceding some as part of the bargaining process. However, you should be wary of alienating a prospective employer by raising every point of detail. Remember, an offer of employment can be withdrawn at any time before it is accepted (see page 41). Employees who appear petty or lacking in commercial sense may cause a potential employer to have second thoughts.

Do not demand preferential treatment

When applying for a job, it is normally inadvisable to request concessions which are not granted to other employees. For example, if a company runs a pension scheme which you can join, it will probably be unwilling to discuss any modification of the rules, particularly if the scheme has a lot of members or Inland Revenue approval – although senior employees may be able to negotiate top-up arrangements. Likewise, if your prospective boss has a policy on company cars, he or she will probably be reluctant to make an exception for a particular member of staff through fear of alienating the remainder of the workforce.

Tips for successful negotiation

- **Remain flexible** For example, if the employer says that it is unable to offer a higher salary, you could explore improving conditions or fringe benefits (see pages 48–53).
- **Find out as much as possible about the employer** Knowledge is power. If possible, speak to existing or former employees about your prospective boss. Will assurances given at interview be honoured, or is it necessary to record everything in detail at the outset? Find out, if you can, why your predecessor left.
- **Check the market rate for the job in advance** You should be able to obtain from recruitment consultants, careers advisers, trade unions or colleagues an indication of the type of salary and fringe benefits that the job offer should contain.

Shopping for the best deal

Before accepting any job offer, employees should take into account not only the salary, but also any fringe benefits such as holiday entitlement, pension schemes, private health care and season ticket loans. The contract of employment should cover all the points itemised on pages 45–54.

Salary

Ensure that the salary offered represents the market rate for the job (see box opposite). The contract should at the very least include a provision for an annual salary review, and if possible should guarantee a minimum increase in each year.

Notice period

After the first month, every employee is entitled to a statutory minimum notice period (see page 65); however, until the employee has completed two years' continuous employment, this is restricted to one week. The notice period to which employees are entitled usually plays a key role in determining the value of the contractual damages they can claim if dismissed without notice in breach of contract (see page 191); the starting-point for calculating damages is a sum equal to the value of the net salary and fringe benefits that the employee would have received during the notice period.

If you are concerned about financial security, you will want to negotiate for as long a notice period as possible – especially if you have been recruited to take on a new role or build up a particular department. You might be able to push for a longer notice period by arguing that this will give you sufficient security as you attempt to initiate changes: a long notice period can act as a brake on impatient employers who may, in the absence of such an arrangement, be tempted to dismiss employees before they have been given sufficient opportunity to prove their worth.

A typical clause providing a longer initial period of notice would read something like this: 'The employee will be entitled to three months' notice expiring on the first anniversary of the date of this agreement or at any time thereafter.' This notice period effectively guarantees the worker employment for 12 months, since the earliest date on which notice can be served is after nine months of employment and the notice period itself is three months.

By contrast, always try to ensure that you are required only to give a short period of notice to your employer, as this will provide you with the maximum degree of flexibility if you want to leave at short notice to pursue another opportunity.

Bonuses and commissions

These can take different forms. In some cases employees have the right to receive only a 'discretionary' bonus – in other words, the employer is not obliged to make any payment and it is entirely up to the company whether it pays workers extra for particularly good performance.

However, in many cases bonuses or commission payments form an important element of employees' pay packets. For example, recruitment consultants, sales personnel and estate agents are usually paid low basic salaries which are topped up by means of a percentage of the sales income they achieve. The higher the sales income, the greater the amount they receive. The same system is used to reward City of London brokers, some of whom receive annual bonuses well in excess of £1 million.

It is vital to ensure from the start that the bonus structure is clear. If possible, ask your boss to provide a worked example of how the bonus will operate in practice. You should be clear about when payment will be made, and if terms such as 'profits', 'revenue' or 'turnover' are used they should be explained in a way that is clearly understandable.

Beware of any clause stating that the commission or bonus is payable only if you are still employed by the employer at the time of payment, and not under notice. This type of clause has become very popular with some employers because it acts as a method of deterring workers from leaving through fear that they will lose the right to the bonuses they have already earned. Clauses of this type also give cynical bosses the opportunity to dismiss staff just before the bonus or commission becomes due in order to avoid having to make the payments.

Often, employers are not in a position to pay bonuses or commission immediately after a sale is made because they have to wait for payment from the client or customer. For example, firms of recruitment consultants often fail to receive full payment until the job candidate they have placed has completed six months' employment, while estate agents do not get paid until the sale of the property has been completed – which frequently does not happen until some time after contracts have been exchanged. You should therefore be prepared to wait for bonus or commission payments – but ensure that the job contract makes it clear that you will be paid as soon as the employer receives payment from the customer. This payment should be made regardless of whether you are still working for the employer.

Sick pay

You should check what your prospective employer provides in the way of sick pay. If the contract of employment or staff handbook does not cover this, sick pay may be assumed to be restricted to the statutory provision (see page 65). As this is unlikely to be sufficient to meet most employees' outgoings, if entitled only to statutory sick pay you should try to negotiate a more generous entitlement, if this can be accomplished without arousing the employer's suspicions (see box below). Note that entitlement varies from employer to employer and it is difficult to define a norm – contracts providing full pay for four weeks and half pay for a further four weeks in any period of 52 weeks are not unusual, while some schemes (particularly those operated by financial institutions) are more generous, providing full pay for up to 26 weeks in any period of 52 weeks.

Your ability to negotiate alternative arrangements will obviously depend on the strength of your position (see page 43); senior employees are usually better placed to bid for favourable terms. In most cases, employers with an established sick pay policy will adopt a 'take it or leave it' attitude.

You should ask your employer to clarify that the right to sickness benefit is not restricted to pay, and that you will continue to receive all fringe benefits such as use of a company car and pension contributions (see pages 48–53). If you are concerned about long-term absence due to illness, you may wish to try to negotiate membership of a permanent health insurance scheme (see page 49).

Sick pay: an unhealthy interest?
Employers are likely to smell a rat if an employee enquires pointedly about sick pay provision, or makes any attempt to negotiate significantly better arrangements. Either may suggest that the employee is either in poor health, or anticipates so being.

Fringe benefits

Common types of benefits offered by employers are listed below. It would be unusual for any employee to be fortunate enough to have access to all, or even the majority, of them.

- **company car** Employees have different attitudes to company cars: some consider the company car an extension of their right arm and attach a deep significance to it, while to others it is merely another benefit. Running your own vehicle might be cheaper: employees pay tax at 35 per cent on a company car's purchase price, which may be reduced according to their earnings, the age of the car and the annual amount of business miles. If you regard the company car as a key part of the employment package, ensure that the contract provides for a particular model or one within an agreed price range, and for the car's replacement on a regular basis. You may also wish to negotiate the right to top up the employer's contribution in order to buy a car outside the price range available. If this option were exercised, you would not have ownership of the car: instead, the contribution would count towards private usage and reduce taxation. Make sure that your contribution is taken into consideration as and when the employer eventually sells the car. It is also important to get your employer to confirm that it will be responsible for the costs of taxing, insuring and servicing the car as well as paying for all petrol used on business trips. Some employers will, if pushed, pay all petrol costs, even private usage – note, however, that fuel for private use is taxable. Be alert to clauses which allow the employer to have the car returned at any time (particularly if you become ill), or replaced by another model. Employees who do not want or need a company car should try to get a car allowance in its place – which is just an increase in salary by other means. A useful leaflet from the Inland Revenue* is *Income Tax and Company Cars* (IR133)

- **holidays** The current position is that employees do not have a legal entitlement to holidays. This will change as a result of the European Working Time Directive (October 1998), which will entitle employees to three weeks' paid holiday in each year, rising to four weeks in November 1999. The average holiday entitlement of most employees in the UK is normally between 20 and 25 working days per annum in addition to the normal statutory and public holidays. Check your contract of employment to see whether you have the right to carry over unused holiday from one year to the next. Some employers allow workers to carry a limited number of days forward, while others say that the days will be lost if they are not taken by the end of the year. Many employers will pay workers in respect of holiday accrued but not taken when employment ends

- **life insurance** Some employers offer life insurance cover, also known as life assurance or death-in-service benefit. This sort of policy provides for the payment of a lump sum to employees' dependants or other nominees if the employee dies during employment. The lump sum payable is usually calculated as a multiple of the employee's salary

- **permanent health insurance** This guarantees the payment of a proportion (usually up to two-thirds) of the employee's salary during any period of long-term illness. Typically, schemes of this sort are offered by smaller employers which will negotiate rates for their workforce at a discount (group permanent health insurance). Participation is not dependent on undergoing a medical examination. The scheme is usually activated at any time after the employee has been seriously ill for more than six months, and payments continue to be made to the employee until he or she either retires or returns to full health, whichever comes earlier. Owing to the high cost of such schemes, this benefit is usually restricted to senior employees. However, your employer may be prepared to extend cover to more junior staff – there is no harm in asking. If you are not entitled to permanent health insurance, make getting good sick pay your priority (see page 47)

- **private medical insurance** More employers are offering their workforce private medical insurance, sometimes combined with dental insurance. As with permanent health insurance (above), employees do not have to give evidence of health. Ask for details of the scheme to ensure that it offers the level of cover and benefits you want. If you plan to join a scheme, ask whether it is possible to obtain additional cover for your partner and any children under the age of 18. The advantage is that employers can often negotiate group cover for employees at much lower levels than those available to individuals, so yours may be able to obtain discounted rates for your family. Note: you pay tax on this form of insurance. If the employer reserves the right to change the company which provides the cover, your contract should specify that the level of cover will remain the same, regardless of which organisation provides it

- **pensions** (see below)
- **share options** Many companies, particularly public companies listed on the Stock Exchange, run a variety of share incentive schemes for their employees based on the company's overall performance. Share options are worth asking about: if the company is doing well, they can be a very valuable benefit. Note: tax is payable on any gains when you exercise your option
- **interest-free and travel loans** Some employers are prepared to grant their employees interest-free loans to help them to buy their annual season tickets and make other purchases. These loans are usually repayable by means of monthly deductions from pay, and continue if you move jobs in the middle of paying one off. You will be taxed if you borrow over a limit of £5,000 in any one year
- **telephone, fax and modem** If you need to maintain contact with the office when working at home, your employer may be prepared to pay the cost of at least the line rental, and possibly of all calls as well
- **luncheon vouchers** Many employers provide meal vouchers for their staff. Employees are not taxed on the first 15p per working day of luncheon vouchers, provided these are non-transferable and used for meals only
- **other benefits** Other typical perks include mobile phones, use of sports facilities and health club membership at reduced rates, plus crèche and nursery facilities.

For full details on your tax position, see *Which? Way to Save Tax*, also published by Which? Limited.★

Pensions

Any state pension you qualify for is unlikely on its own to provide an adequate income in retirement. Therefore, pension arrangements are one of the most important parts of your employment package.

Many employers operate their own pension scheme which employees are invited to join. Membership of a pension scheme can no longer be restricted to full-time employees; any attempt by an employer to do so is unlawful. However, employers *are* allowed to make membership subject to the employee completing a probationary period of employment (see pages 37–8) unless this is clearly discriminatory, and many employers make membership conditional on the completion of a certain period of service. This condition may exclude employees on short fixed-term contracts.

Membership of a pension scheme is usually restricted to employees. If you are a home worker or an agency worker, you should therefore find out from your employer at the outset whether you are considered to be an employee for the purposes of membership of the pension scheme. If you are not, you may want to negotiate a higher hourly rate of pay to reflect this.

Schemes can take various forms, but the two main types are:

- **final salary scheme** You are promised a given rate of pension and other benefits, such as widow/er's pension and life insurance (see page 49) based on the number of years you have belonged to the scheme and your pay at or near the time you retire (or leave the scheme, if this comes earlier)
- **money purchase scheme** How much pension and other benefits you get depends on how well contributions paid in for you grow, and the rate at which the resulting fund can be swapped for pension at retirement.

The employer sometimes pays the whole cost of the scheme (known as a **non-contributory scheme**). Alternatively, you might be required to pay something towards it as well (a **contributory scheme**) – say, 5 per cent of your salary. The amount the employer pays in is not limited, but the total you can pay in is restricted to a maximum of 15 per cent of your earnings (including the value of taxable fringe benefits). Where you are newly joining a scheme, there is also a cap on the earnings which can be taken into account (£87,600 in 1998–9).

Under normal circumstances, most employers will not be willing to negotiate the terms of pension scheme membership. However, if you are a highly paid employee or director of a firm, your employer might agree to setting up an executive pension scheme. This is a special type of employer scheme, usually covering just one or a handful of employees, with benefits largely tailored to each member.

If there is no formal pension scheme at work, your employer might be willing to contribute to your own personal pension plan. As an alternative to an employer scheme, some firms have now arranged a **group personal pension scheme (GPPS)** for their employees. Under a GPPS, each employee can take out their own personal plan with a particular provider (usually an insurance company) but the employer has negotiated some special terms – for example, lower charges or flexible contributions – which the employee would not normally get if taking out a personal plan independently. All personal plans, including GPPS, work on a money purchase basis (see page 51).

There is a limit on the amount you can contribute each year towards your own personal pension plan (including a plan you have through a GPPS) – see table below. Your employer is not obliged to pay into the plan, though some will, and anything the employer does pay uses up part of your contribution limit.

Where your employer offers a proper employer pension scheme, joining it will generally be a better option than taking out your own pension plan either independently or through a GPPS. With an employer scheme, your employer must by law contribute and may also pay the administration costs of the scheme; employees usually get a package of benefits, too, not just a retirement pension. With a personal plan or GPPS, administration costs tend to be higher and are paid out of your pension fund, your employer does not have to contribute and adding other benefits to the plan will mean reducing the amount available to provide retirement pension. However, personal plans and GPPS can be more suitable if you change jobs frequently because the plan is tied to you, not your job.

Both employer schemes and personal plans (including GPPS) are tax-efficient ways of saving for retirement because you get tax relief on your own contributions at your highest rate, gains and some of the income from invested contributions builds up tax-free, and part of the benefits can be taken as a tax-free lump sum. The pension itself will be taxable.

Maximum contribution to a personal pension plan or GPPS[1]

Age at start of tax year	% of net relevant earnings[2]
35 or under	17.5
36–45	20
46–50	25
51–55	30
56–60	35
61–74	40
75 and over	No more contributions

[1] Plan started on or after 1 July 1988. Different limits apply to plans started before this date

[2] Broadly, all your pay including the taxable value of fringe benefits. Only earnings up to a maximum (£87,600 in 1998–9) can be taken into account

Example   A man aged 43 at the start of the tax year, earning £50,000 a year, would be able to pay up to 20% × £50,000 = £10,000 into his personal pension plan that year. If he were a higher-rate taxpayer, contributing the maximum £10,000 would cost him only £6,000 because he would get tax relief of 40% × £10,000 = £4,000.

Expenses

Although the employer is under an obligation to refund employees for any work-related expenses, employees who regularly incur heavy expenses should consider asking for a float (expenses payment on account), or the use of a corporate credit card. Anyone who travels a great deal or entertains clients regularly is likely to need to address the issue of expenses.

Place of work and mobility clauses

These clauses are included in employees' job contracts in order to give the employer sufficient flexibility to relocate their place of work and/or require them to work or travel anywhere in the UK or abroad.

It would be unusual to see such a clause in a junior worker's contract, or in the contract of an employee whose work is clearly confined to a particular geographical area (for example, a factory worker). If you are happy to accept a mobility clause, ensure that if you are required to move home and live abroad a suitable relocation package is provided which covers items such as removal expenses and estate agents' and solicitors' fees. If an employee is forced by the employer to relocate in the absence of a mobility clause, he or she may have a claim for constructive dismissal (see page 169).

Confidentiality clauses

Employers use these to prevent employees from disclosing confidential information after the employment has ended. If your contract contains this sort of clause, make sure that the obligation not to reveal details does not extend to a requirement that you prevent other people from disclosing information (see Chapter 7).

Restrictive covenants

These clauses sometimes appear in job contracts to prevent the employee from working for a competitor of the employer, say, or poaching clients (see Chapter 7). If faced by this sort of clause, you need to decide whether in principle you are prepared to accept such restrictions. An employer may be suspicious of an employee who is particularly hostile to this type of arrangement. When considering whether you will agree, it is worth remembering that there is no guarantee that any restrictions will be enforceable, especially as the law in this area is subject to constant change.

Description of duties

Employers tend to make the description of duties (job description) as wide-ranging as possible – see pages 56–8. Details are usually confirmed in the job contract, but may be provided during or after the interview. You should ensure that the job description does not require you to do anything inconsistent with your status – for example, a salesperson who specialises in selling a specific product should not be expected to sell another product with which he or she is not familiar, particularly if the salary is measured by the number or value of sales achieved.

Outside business interests

It is usual for workers' contracts to state that the employee must devote him- or herself fulltime to the employer's business. Some employees have outside business interests such as writing, helping to run a family firm, or part-time jobs. If you are in this position, in order to avoid any disagreement at a future date, obtain confirmation that your boss is happy for you to continue to pursue these external activities. This right to pursue outside business interests does not, however, extend to working for a competitor of the employer (see page 71).

Considerations for employers when negotiating terms

Regardless of the size of the company, all employers will want to address certain issues in the job contract, especially the following.

Notice period

Normally, it is in the employer's interest not to grant a long notice period owing to the compensation the employee may be entitled to receive as a result of dismissal without justification. For details of the statutory minimum notice period, see page 65.

Fringe benefits

The key here is for employers to ensure as much flexibility for themselves as possible, to ensure that they are not committed to providing benefits at a specific level.

- **company car** If you operate a company car scheme, you should require the employee to keep the car in good condition. Most employers restrict any petrol allowance to business use; some also require the right to have the car returned at any time (particularly if the employee is ill), or to replace it with another model
- **private medical insurance** If you provide employees with medical and/or dental cover, try to reserve the right to change the organisation which provides the cover in order to be certain of getting the best price. Employees should not be seriously alarmed if the contract contains wording of this type, provided that the contract makes clear that the cover shall be of a pre-agreed standard, regardless of which organisation it is provided by.

Place of work and mobility clauses

Employers may want to ensure that they have the necessary flexibility to move employees from location to location as required in order to meet their business needs: for example, the launch of a new branch of a retail chain may require the services of an experienced manager from another area. Clearly, this type of clause will only be appropriate for certain types of employee – see page 53.

A mobility clause must be operated reasonably; in other words, even if you, as employer, have the right to move the employee from London to work in Edinburgh, you must give him or her reasonable notice of the need to move. You cannot expect an employee to relocate his or her family at the drop of a hat. If you make unreasonable demands, you will be in breach of contract and the employee may – in serious cases – be able to treat him- or herself as having been dismissed without justification and therefore entitled to claim compensation.

Confidentiality clauses

Some employers want to ensure that the contract requires the worker to keep all information acquired during the course of business confidential during and after the end of employment. In the absence of such a clause, his or her obligation to withhold information will end once the employment finishes (see Chapter 7). In principle, employees cannot really object to clauses of this type, unless the employer expects them to prevent other people from revealing details as well. It is reasonable for the employer to want to protect its confidential information.

Restrictive covenants

Sometimes employers impose restrictive covenants in order to prevent employees from working for a competitor or poaching clients or employees after the employment comes to an end. Normally, obligations of this type should only be included in the contracts of people who are responsible for fostering and maintaining business relationships with clients, or whose departure is potentially likely to cause the employer serious difficulties (see Chapter 7). Restrictive covenants would not, for example, normally be appropriate in a lorry driver's or a receptionist's contract.

Description of duties

It is common to provide a description of the employee's duties (job description). Details are usually confirmed in the job contract, but are sometimes provided during or after the interview. These descriptions are often very widely drafted in order to give the employer maximum flexibility – see the example of the marketing manager, below – or because a loosely worded description is more appropriate for particular types of jobs.

Sample job descriptions

Example

You are employed as a marketing manager and you will perform all acts, duties and obligations and comply with such orders as may be designated by the Firm which are consistent with that position. The Firm may require you to undertake the duties of another post, either in addition to or instead of the above duties on the understanding that you will not be required to perform duties which are not reasonably within your capabilities.

Example

Job title: Warehouse supervisor **Responsible to:** Warehouse manager

Responsible for: Stores assistant **Job purpose:** To ensure that efficient service of goods inwards/outwards is maintained at all times.

Main duties:

(1) Supervise the control, movement and secure storage of goods.
(2) Maintain an up-to-date stock control database for all goods.
(3) Supervise the delivery and collection of goods, including payments, to other locations as necessary.
(4) Administer all aspects of the import and export control of goods under customs regulations.
(5) Ensure mechanical handling equipment is routinely checked and in good working order.
(6) Supervise and train new and existing members of staff within the department.
(7) Ensure warehouse area is clean and tidy and that all departmental health and safety procedures are followed.

Comparison of job descriptions

If given a job description similar to the first example, the employee may want to have the duties more narrowly and concisely defined. This would depend on his or her line of work and whether a specific list of duties would constrain whatever scope the post offered. The responsibilities are more clearly delineated in the second description because it is easier to identify the precise ambit of the warehouse supervisor's responsibilities.

Appropriateness of duties

However vague the job description, the employer can only make demands upon the employee which are reasonable and consistent with his or her position – for example, a managing director would not expect to be asked to do the photocopying or sort the mail.

Return of all company property to employer

During their employment, workers often have the use of their employer's property – typically, documents and computer disks as well as tools of the trade such as personal computers, cars, mobile phones and dictaphones. Employees should be obliged to return all of this property once they finish working for the employer. A well-drafted contract will also require the employee to return copies of any documents belonging to the employer. Strictly speaking, this means that the employee cannot keep copies of any useful manuals or documents that belong to the employer. In reality, of course, most employees do, and few employers object, provided the information is not seriously damaging to their business interests.

Drawing up a contract

When preparing a contract of employment, employers should consider taking legal advice if they want to impose complex clauses such as bonus schemes (see page 46) or restrictive covenants (see Chapter 7).

Sample job contract

The following contract is a typical, standard-form contract issued to all but the most senior employees. It is not unduly weighted in favour of either employer or employee and contains the particulars required to be given to employees in accordance with section 1 of the **Employment Rights Act 1996**.

CONTRACT OF EMPLOYMENT

This agreement is made on [Date] between:

(1) Newco Limited (a company registered in England and Wales under No 1234567) of [Address] ('we', 'us' or 'the company'); and

(2) John Smith of [Address] ('you').

1 **Job title**

   We will employ you and you will work for us as a sales manager or in such other position as we may decide.

2 **Commencement of employment**

   Your employment will begin on [Date] and your period of continuous employment with us will also commence from that date.

3 **Location**

   Your normal place of work will be at our premises at [Address] but we reserve the right to change such a place to any other place as we may decide within the UK. You will work and travel abroad as we may reasonably require.

4 **Hours of work**

   Your normal working week will be Monday to Friday 9 a.m. to 5 p.m. with an hour's lunch break each day. You are also required to work additional hours as are necessary for the proper performance of your duties – when necessary, in excess of 48 hours per week. We reserve the right to alter your working hours according to our business needs. Your employment will be full-time and you will not undertake any outside business interests or activities without the prior written consent of a director of the company.

5 **Pay**

   Your salary is £XX,000 per annum payable monthly in arrears by direct credit to your bank account on or before the last day of each calendar month. If at any time we make overpayments to you we shall be entitled to make deductions from your salary in respect of such overpayments.

6 Holidays

The holiday year runs from 1 January to 31 December. In addition to bank and other public holidays, the holiday entitlement is 25 days per annum, three of which must be taken between Christmas and New Year. If you start or leave your employment during the holiday year, your holiday entitlement for that year will be calculated on a *pro rata* basis. No holiday may be carried over from one holiday year to the next. No payment will be made in lieu of holiday accrued and not taken except in the year when you leave our employment.

7 Sickness and injury

Without prejudice to your right to statutory sick pay, you are entitled to full pay during the first 10 days of absence due to sickness or injury in any calendar year and thereafter such pay as we deem appropriate.

Absence through illness or injury must be reported to your manager immediately, i.e. on the first day of your absence. If you are absent from work due to sickness for more than three days you must complete a self-certification form and send it to the human resources department when you return to work.

If you are still ill after seven calendar days you must obtain a doctor's certificate, which must be sent to the human resources department and renewed regularly as necessary. If, from the start of the illness, your doctor feels that you will be unable to work for more than a week you will be given a certificate on the first day. The human resources department will calculate how much statutory sick pay you may be entitled to and this will be paid in the following month.

8 Medical examinations

We reserve the right to ask you to be medically examined by a doctor of our choice at our expense. In addition, a medical questionnaire is enclosed which must be returned to our company doctor within five working days of your receiving this contract, using the enclosed self-addressed envelope.

9 Life insurance/private medical insurance

We will during your employment, at our own expense and on such terms as we may decide, provide for you the following benefits (subject always to the rules governing such insurances in force from time to time):

(a) life assurance cover at a rate of four times your basic annual salary; and

(b) private medical insurance.

10 Pension

No contracting-out certificate under the Pensions Act 1993 is in force in relation to your employment.

You will be entitled to a state pension but otherwise you will be expected to make your own pension arrangements.

11 Notice and trial period

Your employment will initially be for a trial period of six months. During your trial period we or you may terminate the employment by one week's notice in writing. You will be informed by your manager if you have successfully completed your trial period. At any time during your employment you may be dismissed immediately in the case of gross misconduct (for example, dishonesty, gross negligence or assault). If your employment is confirmed at the end of your trial period the period of notice to be given in writing by you to us or by us to you to terminate your employment shall be not less than three months.

12 Confidentiality

You must not at any time during (except in the course of your duties) or after your employment disclose or make use of your knowledge of any of our confidential information. Confidential information includes, without limitation, all and any information about business plans, maturing new business opportunities, research and development projects, product formulae, processes, inventions, designs, discoveries or know-how, sales statistics, marketing surveys and plans, costs, profit or loss, prices and discount structures, the names, addresses and contact details of customers and potential customers or suppliers and potential suppliers (whether or not recorded in writing or on computer disk or tape), which we treat as confidential.

13 Intellectual property

You will promptly disclose to us and keep confidential all inventions, copyright works, designs or technical know-how conceived or made by you on your own or with others in the course of your employment. You will hold all such intellectual property in trust for us and will do everything necessary or desirable at our expense to vest the intellectual property fully in the company and/or to secure patent or other appropriate forms of protection for the intellectual property. Decisions as to the protection or exploitation of any intellectual property shall be at our absolute discretion.

14 **Disciplinary/grievance procedures**

If you are dissatisfied with any disciplinary decision relating to you, or have a grievance about your employment, you should make an application to your department head in writing who will involve the manager and/or human resources department as appropriate and, if you wish, the union representative. Please note that your right to be represented does not apply during your trial period. A full copy of the disciplinary rules and grievance procedure is set out in the company handbook.

15 **Collective agreement**

There is no collective agreement which directly affects your terms and conditions of employment contained in this agreement.

Signed for and on behalf of
Newco Limited

Signed ....
Position ....

Signed ....
JOHN SMITH

Contract commentary

Clause 2   Occasionally, the start date and the commencement of the period of continuous employment do not always coincide (see page 69).

Clause 3   This clause provides the employer with the right to move the employee around the UK and to require him or her to work abroad. Since a relocation package is not provided for, the employee may want to negotiate financial assistance. See page 53 (employee) or page 55 (employer).

Clause 4   The employer has reserved the right to require the employee to work additional hours without being paid overtime, and in order to comply with the Working Time Directive requires the employee to work in excess of 48 hours per week when necessary. (In certain circumstances, employees may be able to negotiate overtime in excess of the 35-hour week.)

Clause 5   The employer has included the right to deduct any overpayments made to the employee from the employee's salary. Typically this would cover payments such as season-ticket loans or overpayments of salary.

Clause 6   This clause is weighed in the employer's favour. No holiday can be carried forward and no pay is made in respect of holiday not taken in the holiday year.

Clause 7   The employee will only receive full pay for the first ten days of sickness in any calendar year. After this the employee will only be eligible to receive statutory sick pay (see page 65).

Clause 9   Although the employer is providing valuable benefits, it is reserving the right both to change providers of the private healthcare and the scale of the benefits provided. See page 49 (employee) or page 55 (employer).

Clause 11   During the trial period (or probationary period) the employee can be dismissed on one week's notice. The longer period of notice takes effect only at the end of the probationary period (see pages 37–8).

Clause 15   Collective agreements are negotiated by trade unions on behalf of employees (see page 272). They do not apply to most people's contracts. The inclusion of this section meets the requirements of section 1 of the Employment Rights Act 1996.

Chapter 4

Rights and obligations at work

Even in the absence of a written job contract, employer and employee are bound to each other by a mish-mash of statutes and common law (see below). Throughout the relationship – from the submission of the employee's CV to the issuing of Form P45 – these impose rights and obligations on both parties. (For more on the contract of employment, see Chapter 3.)

Employees' statutory rights

Certain entitlements and duties are implied into every contract, written or unwritten, either as a result of conduct (for example, getting paid – see page 67); by Acts of Parliament, usually referred to as 'statute law' or legislation; or by legal tradition established by legal cases, known as 'common law'.

Every employee has the right not to be discriminated against on the basis of race, sex or disability (see Chapters 5 and 6). This protection covers every step of the process, from submitting a CV to the job interview and taking up service with an employer. The **Employment Rights Act 1996** provides employees with additional rights, the most important of which include:

- the right not to be unfairly dismissed (see Chapter 10)
- the right to receive an itemised payslip (see page 67)
- the right to receive written reasons for dismissal (see page 182)
- the right to receive and give a statutory minimum period of notice (see opposite)

- the right to receive statutory maternity pay, take maternity leave and/or maternity absence (see Chapter 6)
- the right to receive statutory sick pay (see below)
- the right to receive a Statement of Particulars of employment (see page 68).

Statutory minimum notice

After the first month of employment, employers and employees are required to give each other not less than one week's notice at any time. After the completion of two years' employment, the employee is entitled to one week's notice for each year of employment, subject to a maximum of 12 weeks' notice. The employer continues to be entitled to receive only one week's notice. So an employee who has been employed by the same employer for 18 months is entitled to one week's notice and an employee who has been employed for six years is entitled to six weeks' notice, while an employee who has been employed by the same employer for 18 years is entitled to a statutory maximum notice period of 12 weeks.

If the job contract specifies a different length of notice period, this does not matter. The period in the contract will apply provided that it is not shorter than the statutory minimum notice.

Employees who do not have a written contract of employment may, as an alternative to relying on the statutory minimum notice period, assert their right to 'reasonable notice' (see overleaf).

Statutory sick pay

The right to receive statutory sick pay (SSP) is dependent on the employee having worked for the employer for three months continuously and having made adequate National Insurance contributions. The employee must meet the lower earnings limit to achieve this (£64 per week in 1998). SSP, for those eligible to receive it, is not very generous: in 1998–9 the maximum weekly amount is £57.70, subject to the deduction of tax and National Insurance contributions. The employee is not paid for the first three days of absence. SSP is payable for up to 28 weeks in any three-year period.

> **The right to time off work**
> Employees are entitled to time off work in a number of circum-
> stances: for example, to do jury service or carry out trade union
> activities. Pregnant women must be given time off for antenatal
> care (see page 104) and employees who have been given notice of
> redundancy must be allowed time off to attend job interviews.

Employees' non-statutory rights

Employees also have certain common-law rights.

The right to reasonable notice

As well as a statutory minimum period of notice (see page 65), and
in the absence of a stated notice period in the contract of employment, common law implies that the employee is entitled to 'reasonable notice'. What is 'reasonable' depends on the employee's
seniority and the norm in the particular industry or profession. For
example, a managing director of a fully listed company may be able
to argue that he or she is entitled to a minimum two years' notice,
whereas a general manager, salesman, secretary or solicitor may be
able to argue for an entitlement of between one and three months'
notice.

The issue of how much notice employees are entitled to is often of
importance in calculating the compensation to which they are entitled
if they are dismissed without notice in breach of contract. The starting
point for calculating such compensation (excluding reductions) is an
amount equal to the value of the net salary and fringe benefits that the
employee would have received during the notice period.

Example John, a sales executive, has worked for his employer for
over eight years. Under his contract of employment, his employer is
obliged to give him one month's notice. However, as he has
completed eight years' employment the statutory minimum notice
period is eight weeks.

Example Charles is a marketing manager. His colleagues all have
contracts of employment which give them three months' notice:

Charles does not have a written contract. Under statute, Charles is entitled to a minimum notice period of eight weeks; however, as there is no express notice period in his contract he is also entitled to reasonable notice. Charles should have a good case for arguing that 'reasonable notice' in his case should be three months, the same as is granted to his colleagues doing similar jobs.

Notice in Scotland

In Scotland, reasonable notice does not apply. The statutory minimum notice period will apply if the contract does not specify a notice period. However, in a contract for services or self-employment (see page 15) an absence of notice provisions means that the contract can be terminated immediately.

> **Statutory notice vs contractual provision**
> Where the employee's contract clearly states the notice period, but the statutory minimum notice period exceeds what is provided for, the statutory minimum notice period will apply.

Rights established by conduct

Employees should be able to establish the existence of certain contractual rights from the employer's conduct. For example, if the employer consistently pays the employee at the end of each month and issues a payslip to support it, this will provide sufficient evidence of the rate of pay the employee is entitled to receive.

The right to receive an itemised payslip

Every employee has the statutory right to an itemised statement listing: gross pay; variable deductions (e.g. income tax, National Insurance); fixed deductions (e.g. pensions); and where parts of the net figure are paid differently, the amount and method of each part-payment.

A leaflet entitled *Itemised Pay Statement* (PL704) from the DTI Publications Orderline* explains how complaints about payslips are settled.

Salary is not the only benefit that can be established by conduct. The same principle applies when establishing the right to receive perks such as private medical cover, luncheon vouchers or a season ticket loan. In addition, documents such as staff handbooks may refer to issues such as sick pay, disciplinary and grievance procedures and holiday entitlement. *Just because the document is not officially called a contract of employment, it does not mean that it does not give the employee legally enforceable rights.*

Rights established by custom and practice

Some obligations may be implied by custom and practice. This means that a practice consistently carried on by an employer and widely known to its employees is capable of creating a contractual right.

Example   It is widely known throughout a company that every Christmas without fail the employer pays its employees a bonus equal to one week's wages.

If the employer should decide *not* to make the payment one year, the employees would be able to argue that because of the previous history of payments, they have a legal right to receive the bonus – and would be able to sue the employer to recover it. Certain additional annual holidays granted by the employer on a regular basis might be another example.

What new employees must be told in writing

Section 1 of the **Employment Rights Act 1996** states that employees should receive certain information within the first two months of starting employment. This document is known as a Statement of Particulars. All contracts of employment should, in theory, provide this information as a minimum (see sample contract on pages 59–62).

The Statement of Particulars should include:

- the names of the employer and employee
- the name and address of the place of work
- the date when the employment began
- the date on which the employee's period of continuous employment began – see box below
- the job title
- the salary

- the intervals at which the employee will be paid (e.g. weekly or monthly)
- any terms and conditions relating to hours of work
- any terms and conditions relating to:
    holiday entitlement (including public holidays)
    holiday and sickness pay
    pensions
- the length of notice required from either party
- if the employment is temporary, how long it is expected to continue
- any disciplinary rules to which the employee may be subject.

Where the employee is required to work outside the UK for more than a month at a time, it should also cover:

- the period of work outside the UK
- the currency in which payment will be made
- any additional pay and benefits to be provided by reason of the work being outside the UK
- any terms and conditions relating to the employee's return to the UK.

See Chapter 13 for more on working overseas.

Calculating the period of continuous employment
This is usually, but not always, calculated from the employee's start date. If the employee has previously worked for a related employer, the date will be the day on which he or she started work with that employer. This information can help when assessing claims for unfair dismissal or calculating entitlement to statutory redundancy payments – see Chapters 10 and 11.

Many employees fail to receive a full statement of their particulars of employment. In part, this is because the sanctions for employers who fail to comply with this statutory duty are not very onerous. The only option for employees who do not receive a statement of full particulars is to apply to an industrial tribunal (see Chapter 16) for a ruling as to what should be included in their Statement of Particulars. Very few employees take advantage of this right, however.

Alterations to the Statement of Particulars

If the employer alters any detail of the Statement of Particulars, the employee must be informed of the change in writing within one month. If it is a significant change the employer should have obtained the employee's agreement, otherwise it may be exposed to a claim for constructive dismissal (see page 169). *Contracts of Employment: Changes, Breach of Contract and Deductions from Wages* (PL810), a booklet from DTI Publications Orderline,* outlines workers rights.

Rights not granted to employees

There is no general obligation on employers to provide employees with work. Exceptions to this rule include employees who need training or work experience in order to maintain their skills, such as apprentices, trainee solicitors or trainee accountants.

Employees currently have no right to holiday or holiday pay, even on public and statutory holidays. However, employees may be able to challenge this if they can show that employees have habitually received paid leave in the past. For example, if an employer normally gives its employees three weeks' holiday per year, an employee who was denied similar treatment could argue that he or she had a contractual right to receive the same amount of leave (see page 68). When the European Working Time Directive is implemented into UK law (October 1998), employees will be entitled to three weeks' paid holiday, rising to four weeks in November 1999.

Pay rises

Many job contracts provide for an annual pay review (see page 45). However, there is no statutory requirement for automatic pay increases. This will change when the government introduces the minimum wage in so far as those receiving less than the minimum wage will be entitled to pay rises bringing them into line with that level of pay.

There is nothing to stop employees asking for a pay rise: success depends on the strength of the negotiating position. If applying for a rise, make an appointment with your boss in advance to avoid interruptions. Ascertain the market rate for the job and stick to realistic objectives. Be prepared to broadcast your achievements to justify a rise – this is no time to be modest. If the employer will not comply, consider asking for alternative benefits such as longer holidays, shorter hours or a better company car.

A leaflet entitled *Individual Rights of Employees: A Guide for Employers and Employees* (PL716) is available from DTI Publications Orderline.★

Employees' obligations

The key obligation is the so-called duty of good faith and loyalty. This slightly old-fashioned phrase covers a wide range of issues (see pages 71–3).

Competition during employment

Broadly speaking, during office hours employees are expected to devote all of their time to their employer's business – i.e. they should not be using office time to conduct their own business, or to pursue activities such as buying a house, selling a car or searching for a new job. Outside office hours, employees' time is largely their own.

There is one qualification to this general rule. Workers should not be involved in any activities which might conflict with their boss's business activities. For example, a hairdresser who worked five days a week for her employer would be in breach of contract if she worked without permission for a competing hairdresser in the evenings.

Confidentiality

Employees must not reveal any confidential information relating to their employer's business. Clearly some jobs such as law, banking or marketing entail a high degree of exposure to such information. In such jobs, leaks of information may be treated very seriously.

Typically, confidential information may relate to the employer's clients, suppliers, sales performance, price lists or marketing strategies, and the duty of confidentiality generally ends when the employee leaves. However, it may continue after someone has ceased to be employed if he or she has encountered a narrow band of highly confidential information known as trade secrets. For more information, see Chapter 7.

The duty of confidentiality should not be confused with the **Official Secrets Act**, which was passed in 1909 to safeguard sensitive government information and today applies to all kinds of workers in local and central government. Breaches of the Act may lead to criminal prosecution. By contrast, a breach of the employee's common-law duty of confidentiality is not a criminal offence, but may lead to dismissal without compensation. The employee could also be sued for compensation by the employer (see page 131).

Disclosure of information

Employees must pass on to their employers details of inventions and discoveries created at work. Generally, anything created during the course of their employment belongs to the employer (see Chapter 7).

Doing the job properly

It is not sufficient for employees just to turn up for work. When they are there, they are expected to do their jobs properly. This means, in theory, that if an employee is grossly negligent the employer could sue him or her for any loss suffered as a result. For example, a public transport worker might fail to follow procedures set in place by the employer to protect the travelling public. If a passenger was injured as a result and sued the employer, the employer could in theory sue the employee for any loss suffered as a result of the passenger's claim. In practice, however, employers usually rely on the employee's poor performance to justify dismissing him or her without compensation.

Duty to account for secret profits

This means that workers must not make money for themselves at their employer's expense. Typically, an employee responsible for ordering equipment for a business might accept a bribe from a supplier in return for placing a lucrative order with him. The bribe could be cash, a holiday, a free sample or some other payment in kind. A common variant is for an employee to sell off the employer's property at a discount in return for a secret payment – for example, a car-park attendant allowing a customer to stay in the car park all day in return for a backhand payment, or an estate agent introducing buyers to property in return for a secret commission. Depending on the circumstances, this sort of behaviour may lead to criminal charges.

Honesty

Employees are expected to be honest. This obligation is widely interpreted and goes beyond the narrow confines of not stealing or not committing fraud – see case history below.

CASE HISTORY: Raymond

Raymond worked for an engineering firm and was also a trade union official. He was allowed access to one directory of the firm's computer system in order to carry out his engineering duties, but other parts of the system were off-limits to him. Hoping to obtain some confidential information for the trade union, he appropriated another worker's password and used it to gain unauthorised access to certain stored information he was not entitled to view. He later used the knowledge in a manner that was hostile to the interests of the company. When this behaviour was discovered, Raymond was found to be dishonest and was dismissed for gross misconduct.

Obeying reasonable instructions

Employees are also expected to comply with reasonable instructions given to them by their employers. What is considered 'reasonable' obviously depends on the circumstances and the employee's position. However, it would never be reasonable for an employer to ask an employee to do anything illegal or to lie on its behalf.

Personal service

Employees are obliged to carry out themselves the job they were employed to do. For example, a chef employed by a restaurant cannot send a colleague to do his job on his behalf. Employees should also be willing and ready to work. For example, those who fail to turn up for work when they are fit and able would be in breach of contract. A typical example of this is employees claiming to be sick when they were perfectly capable of making it in to work.

Employers' obligations

In accordance with common law, employers must observe certain obligations towards the people who work for them. They must:

- pay their employees, as long as those employees are available for work. This means that even if employers have no work for their staff, they must still pay them. They cannot simply pick and choose the days on which there is work to do
- refund employees for expenses incurred at work
- ensure that employees are safe while doing their jobs. This general duty has been supplemented by a battery of statutes, regulations and European laws. It will vary depending on what the employees do: e.g. construction workers should be issued with hard hats, machines should be safe and fitted with guards where necessary, and workers handling dangerous chemicals should have adequate protective clothing. Employees are not expected to pay for protective gear out of their own pockets; employers must provide whatever is necessary. See Chapter 15 for more details
- act reasonably towards their employees. They are obliged to do this under the so-called duty of mutual trust and understanding, which can be construed in many different ways: actions such as imposing unilateral pay cuts and humiliating, harassing or demoting employees represent typical breaches of this duty. Such behaviour may enable employees to sue for damages for breach of contract, or, in more extreme situations, treat themselves as having been sacked without justification. This procedure is known as constructive dismissal (see page 169).

Recent decisions by the courts have suggested an extension of employers' implied obligations.

CASE HISTORY: Northern Ireland Health Service Trust

Through oversight, the Northern Ireland Health Service Trust failed to draw to its employees' attention the opportunity to enhance their pension entitlement by making additional pension contributions. The employees succeeded in bringing a case because the court decided that there was an unwritten obligation on the employers to let their workers know about such opportunities. As a result, the trust was successfully sued.

CASE HISTORY: Sarah

Sarah was a member of her firm's permanent health insurance scheme. Under this type of scheme, if an employee is unable to work as a result of illness or injury for a long period of time, usually over six months, he or she has the right to receive a proportion (usually two-thirds) of his or her normal salary until he or she fully recovers or reaches retirement age. When Sarah became absent from work due to sickness, she claimed benefits from the scheme. She was then dismissed by her employer and lost the right to receive payouts from the policy. The court to which she appealed ruled that if an employee is absent due to long-term sickness and is receiving benefits under the employer's permanent health insurance scheme, if it is a condition of that scheme that benefits are payable only while the employee remains employed, the employer is under an obligation not to dismiss the employee. If the employer breaks that obligation, as in this case, it will be liable to make up the value of the benefits lost by the employee as a result of being dismissed and having to leave the scheme. The amount of compensation could potentially be enormous.

Because court decisions are reached on the particular facts of each case, it is often difficult to predict whether judges will take the view that the precedent set by a particular ruling is a suitable one to follow in every future case. The general rule is that the more senior the court, the greater the weight that can be attached to the ruling.

Chapter 5

Discrimination at work

Discrimination is alive and well in the workplace, despite the fact that legislation was introduced in the 1970s to eradicate it. For example, although over 43 per cent of the working population are women, according to the Equal Opportunities Commission (EOC),★ women receive on average only 79 per cent of the salary their male counterparts earn. Meanwhile, the Commission for Racial Equality (CRE)★ found that in 1995 the average hourly earnings of full-time employees from ethnic minorities were about 92 per cent of those of white employees.

Statutory protection against discrimination

Five main Acts of Parliament aim to eliminate discrimination at work. The main thrust of the legislation is to ensure that people are not discriminated against on the basis of their sex, racial origin or disability — either in terms of pay or by any other means.

- The **Sex Discrimination Acts 1975 and 1986 (SDA)** and the **Equal Pay Act 1970 (EPA)** aim to eliminate discrimination on the basis of gender. These Acts receive additional support from European law in the form of the Equal Treatment Directive and the Treaty of Rome.
- The **Race Relations Act 1976 (RRA)** aims to eradicate racial discrimination.
- The **Disability Discrimination Act 1995 (DDA)** aims to eliminate discrimination against disabled people.
- The **Trade Union and Labour Relations (Consolidation) Act 1992** makes it unlawful for an employer to treat trade union members less favourably than non-members, and *vice versa*.

Types of discrimination which remain legal

No legislation has been passed to combat discrimination on grounds of religion or age.

Religious discrimination

Apart from in Northern Ireland, the UK has no legislation to prevent discrimination against employees on the basis of their religion. In Northern Ireland, legislation covering religious and political discrimination is contained in the Fair Employment Acts of 1976 and 1989, and the Fair Employment Commission* offers support to those who suffer religious and/or political discrimination. The ambit of the Race Relations Act extended to the province in 1997.

Age discrimination

Unlike in the United States, there is – to date – no protection for employees against age discrimination. This means that it is still legally acceptable to place advertisements for jobs which specify an upper or preferred age limit; or alternatively to require a certain number of years' experience. However, some advertisements stipulating a particular age range have been found to amount to indirect sex discrimination. For example, an advertisement requiring candidates aged between 18 and 35 could arguably indirectly discriminate against women, since these are the years in which women are most likely to have children and therefore fewer women than men are likely to be able to satisfy the age requirement. It has also been made clear by one industrial tribunal that selecting an employee for redundancy because of his age is not 'a fair reason'. In this case, the employee succeeded with a claim for unfair dismissal (see Chapter 10).

Similarities between the RRA and the SDA

The RRA and the SDA have very similar provisions and because of this are usually read the same way by industrial tribunals. Cases decided under one Act have been used as authority for cases brought under the other. This is because both Acts came into being within a very short time of one another and as a result have very similar provisions and aims.

The RRA and SDA protect all employees irrespective of age or status, whether they work full-time, part-time, from home or with an agency, on fixed-term, temporary or permanent contracts. They apply to large and small employers, to trade unions and to employers' organisations such as the CBI (Confederation of British Industry).*

Protection for the self-employed
Unlike much employment-related legislation, the RRA and the SDA both extend protection to self-employed workers as well as to employees.

The SDA and RRA attempt to deal with:

- direct discrimination
- indirect discrimination
- victimisation.

Direct discrimination

Direct discrimination takes place when an individual is given less favourable treatment than another employee because of his or her race or sex: for example, if an applicant were refused an interview because he was Irish or West Indian, or a woman were turned down for a job because she was female, even though she was clearly better qualified than the successful male candidate.

In cases of direct discrimination, the aggrieved employee does *not* need to show that the employer intended to discriminate. The only issue is whether the employee actually suffered discrimination.

CASE HISTORY: Paul

Paul applied for a job as a carpenter. When he went to the building site for an interview, the foreman told him, 'Sorry, we don't tolerate blacks here as we find they don't fit in.' The tribunal found that the employer had discriminated against Paul.

CASE HISTORY: Keith

Keith managed a pub in an inner-city area that was troubled by racial violence. When he advertised for bar staff, he rejected one job candidate's application on the grounds that employing her would have caused problems because of racial tension in the area, and that customers would object to her race. He was subsequently found liable for racial discrimination, even though he had not intended to discriminate against the woman but merely wanted to avoid aggravating local sensitivities.

Indirect discrimination

Indirect discrimination arises in situations where all employees appear to be treated alike on the surface, but, on closer examination, members of a particular racial group or gender are found to be discriminated against.

Both the RRA and the SDA define indirect discrimination as occurring when:

(1) the proportion of the group to which the individual belongs that can comply with the condition or requirement is considerably smaller than the proportion of the remainder of the population who can do so;

(2) the employer cannot show that the condition or requirement is justified; and

(3) the affected worker suffers a detriment as a result of the condition or requirement.

All three conditions must be satisfied at the same time for a claim to succeed.

Example   A woman returns from a period of maternity leave and wants to work part-time, but her employer insists without justification that all posts must be full-time.

This is indirectly discriminatory because women are statistically more likely to need to work part-time for family reasons. Therefore, the number of women who can comply with the requirement that they work full-time is considerably smaller than the number of men who can conform – which satisfies the first point. Secondly, the employer cannot show that the employment is required to be full-time; the failure to justify this requirement objectively satisfies the second point. Finally, the requirement is detrimental to the female employee's employment prospects in that she must leave if she is not prepared to work full-time, which satisfies point 3. (For more information on maternity rights, see Chapter 6.)

Example As a condition of employment, an employer requires all employees (one of whom is a Sikh) to wear a hard hat – even though there is no health and safety reason why they should.

The number of members of the Sikh community who could comply with this sort of demand is potentially considerably smaller than the remainder of the population, since they are compelled to wear a turban for religious reasons. This satisfies point 1. Point 2 is met as the employer cannot show why the condition is justified; point 3 would be satisfied if a Sikh could show that he was refused employment or promotion because of his inability to comply with the condition.

Example A firm imposes a requirement that employees work full-time in order to have access to membership of a company pension scheme.

A considerably higher proportion of the part-time working population in the UK is female, and as such the full-time working requirement is indirectly discriminatory to that proportion of the population – which meets point 1. Furthermore, the employer cannot justify restricting membership of a pension scheme to full-time staff, which satisfies point 2. Point 3 would be satisfied if a part-time employee could prove that he or she had suffered financially through not being allowed to participate in the scheme.

CASE HISTORY: Alison

Alison, a train driver, had a young son. When the shift system was altered she was unable to comply with the changed times because they were incompatible with her childcare arrangements. The train company suggested that she could be a train driver or a mother, but not both. Alison then left her job to care for her son. She was found to have been indirectly discriminated against because the shift pattern, which required drivers to work early and late, affected women far more than it did men. This is because it created difficulties for people who were responsible for children, and many more women than men were in this position.

CASE HISTORY: Alan

A firm in Liverpool made clear when advertising a job that it did not want applicants from the city centre whose friends might hang around the shop and discourage customers. Because of this, Alan, a black applicant who lived in one of the prohibited central postal districts, was refused an interview. A tribunal found that the company had indirectly discriminated against him since 50 per cent of the population in his postal district were black, as opposed to two per cent throughout Merseyside as a whole. The condition that no job applicants be recruited from a particular postal district unjustifiably excluded a significantly larger number of black than white applicants, and therefore amounted to indirect discrimination.

Employer's defence

An employer will have a defence if it can show that any condition imposed is justifiable. This amounts to a balancing act between the employer's need to impose a particular condition and the extent of the discrimination that would result as a consequence of that condition – for example, it would be more justifiable to ask a Sikh to wear a hard hat on a building site than in an office.

Once a case for discrimination gets under way, the burden of proof lies with the employer. In deciding whether the employer's requirement is justified, the industrial tribunal will balance the discriminatory nature of the requirement against the reasonable business needs of the employer. In other words, the more discriminatory and less conducive to business the condition imposed is, the more difficult it will be to justify.

Victimisation

This happens when an employee is singled out for unfair treatment because he or she has attempted to exercise rights under the RRA, SDA or EPA (see page 96), or has assisted others in enforcing their rights: for example, if an employee were to appear as a witness to support another employee's claim for discrimination and as a result suffered unfair treatment at the hands of the employer.

One purpose of the RRA and SDA is to ensure that employees are not dissuaded from bringing discrimination claims because of the fear of subsequent victimisation. If an employee is victimised because he or she has brought or supported a claim for discrimination, it does not matter whether it is actually established that any discrimination occurred. The important point is that the person who either brings or supports a claim should not be penalised as a result of bringing that action.

Example   When Employee A brings a claim for racial discrimination against his boss, Employee B (who is not in a racial minority group) agrees to give evidence on his behalf. Employee A's claim fails; however, as a result of supporting his cause, Employee B does not receive the pay rise he was due. In this case, Employee B would have a potential claim for victimisation.

Racial discrimination

Alone amongst its European partners, Britain has for many years had comprehensive anti-race discrimination legislation. The first laws date from as far back as 1965. Surprisingly, no European law addresses the issue of racial discrimination, despite the existence of comprehensive laws aimed at eliminating sex discrimination.

Section 1(1) of the **Race Relations Act 1976** states: 'A person discriminates against another ... if, on racial grounds, he treats the other less favourably than he treats, or would treat, another person.' Discrimination on racial grounds is, for the purposes of the RRA, defined as discrimination on the basis of colour, race, nationality, or ethnic or national origin.

A racial or religious issue?

Often, it is unclear whether an employee is a member of an ethnic minority. The RRA considers an ethnic group to go beyond race alone and may include any group which has a shared history or culture. Examples of ethnic groups include Jews, Sikhs and gypsies; however, other groups such as Rastafarians have been held not to constitute a distinct ethnic group because their shared identity is based on religion.

Therefore a Muslim may not be able to establish racial discrimination on the grounds of his religion, but may be able to establish that he has been discriminated against because of either his race or his ethnic background.

Exceptions to the RRA

The Act recognises that for certain jobs membership of a particular racial group can be a genuine requirement for the particular occupation. These include:

- entertainers, actors and actresses
- artists' and photographers' models
- waiters and waitresses, where it is a requirement of the restaurant that the employees are of a particular race (e.g. in a Chinese or Indian restaurant)
- personal welfare services which can be ministered most effectively by members of a particular racial group (e.g. a Bangladeshi social worker in the Bangladeshi immigrant community).

Racial harassment

The RRA does not provide any definition of racial harassment. What counts as harassment will vary depending on the circumstances.

Harassment is merely another form of direct discrimination. The term spans persistent and open racism, such as verbal or physical bullying or intimidation, as well as more subtle forms of harassment such as racist jokes, banter or graffiti. It also includes shunning people, excluding them from conversation or picking on them unnecessarily because of their race, colour, nationality or ethnic background. Industrial tribunals have consistently taken the view that there is no acceptable degree of banter or abuse.

CASE HISTORY: Sean

Sean, an Irish builder, was subjected on a daily basis to derogatory Irish jokes from his colleagues. After being told by his employer to ignore them because they were 'just jokes', he was subsequently dismissed on the grounds that he did not fit in. The industrial tribunal concluded that Sean had been sacked because he refused to accept such abuse, and that the employer had tried to justify the dismissal by claiming Sean did not fit in. Sean was awarded £8,ooo in compensation.

CASE HISTORY: Prem

Prem, an Indian officer who worked for Nottinghamshire CID, faced constant racial abuse and unfair treatment. He complained to a senior officer and then to the Chief Superintendent alleging racial abuse, but was not satisfied with the treatment he received. Finally, he brought a claim to an industrial tribunal in 1990, which established that racist language was widely used throughout the force. Prem received £30,000 in compensation.

CASE HISTORY: Eddie and Derek

The PVC fabricating company where Eddie and Derek worked was regarded as informal and friendly, yet a couple of incidents against the two coloured employees led to a claim for racial discrimination. First, a notice entitled 'Application for Employment Minorities Division', which turned out to be fake, appeared at the factory. It was considered by the industrial tribunal to be 'the most offensive, insulting and degrading it had ever seen'. However, the foreman had treated it as a joke and done nothing. The second incident took place a week later when the two employees were handed a notice containing an offensively worded job description. The tribunal found this, too, to be an appalling case of discrimination. The employees were each awarded £3,250 as compensation.

Compensation in race discrimination cases

In its 1998 report, the CRE provided evidence that awards made by industrial tribunals are increasing. Discounting two exceptional compensation awards, in 1997 the average tribunal award for cases supported by the CRE was £7,405. This shows a rise of 62 per cent on 1996.

Sex discrimination

The **Sex Discrimination Act 1975 (SDA)** states that it is unlawful to treat someone less favourably on the basis of their sex: 'A person discriminates against a woman ... if, on the grounds of her sex he treats her less favourably than he treats, or would treat, a man.' This applies equally to women and men.

Like racial discrimination, sex discrimination may take place at any stage in the employment relationship – including recruitment and dismissal. For example, job advertisements which discriminate on the basis of sex or use words which imply that the employer wishes to recruit someone of a particular gender are unlawful. Likewise, at the job interview stage employers are prohibited from using discriminatory selection policies. It would be inappropriate, for example, to ask a woman whether she is likely to leave in the near future to have children, or whether she has children, unless it could be clearly shown that the same question was put to men in the same circumstances.

Marriage discrimination

It is unlawful to discriminate against married people. However, it is not unlawful to discriminate against single people in terms of the treatment they receive in comparison with married colleagues. Therefore, an employer could in theory give a married employee a better relocation package or car allowance than someone who is single. If an employer imposed a condition which discriminated against a considerably higher proportion of married than single employees – for example, requiring staff to work unsocial hours – this could constitute indirect marriage discrimination if a married employee was dismissed as a consequence.

Exceptions to the SDA

The main exceptions to the SDA where discrimination is permitted are:

- jobs which, for genuine reasons, must be carried out by someone of a particular sex (including dramatic performance or entertainment). Occupations requiring physical strength or stamina are not considered genuine exceptions
- privacy or decency require it (e.g. changing-room attendants)
- accommodation is provided but it is not practical to provide separate sleeping accommodation for both sexes (e.g. a nurses' home housing female nurses)
- jobs which involve work in a country whose laws or customs require the individual to be of a certain gender (e.g. Iran, Saudi Arabia)
- single-sex hospitals, prisons or care centres

- personal welfare services which are better performed by one sex than another (e.g. some probation officers).

Sexual harassment

Sexual harassment is a direct form of sex discrimination. As for racial harassment (see pages 83–4), there is no statutory definition of sexual harassment. It is, however, defined in the European Code of Practice as amounting to 'unwanted conduct of a sexual nature, or other conduct based on sex affecting the dignity of women and men at work.' This can include unwelcome physical, verbal or non-verbal conduct in the form of body language, emails or letters; it may also include unwelcome sexual attention and suggestive or over-familiar behaviour. If someone indicates that sexual favours may further career prospects, this counts as sexual harassment. Less obviously it may include behaviour that creates an unpleasant working environment in which women or men feel uneasy, perhaps involving the display of pornographic pictures or the use of crude sexual language.

A survey carried out by the Industrial Society★ in 1993 showed that 45 per cent of the 1,727 working women approached had been victims of sexual harassment, and that 58 per cent of those harassed were in the 25–34 age group.

In sexual harassment cases, the important point is to establish that the treatment received by the victim would not have been meted out to someone of the opposite sex – see case histories below.

CASE HISTORY: Anna

Anna was a cleaner whose job involved cleaning the office toilets. She noticed more men than usual using the toilets when she was working. In order to avoid embarrassment, her policy was to knock on the toilet door and call, 'Is there anybody there?' before entering. On one occasion, on hearing no reply, she opened the door to find a man urinating and another man apparently masturbating. Anna made a number of complaints to her employer, who took no action. Eventually she was dismissed for failure to sign out on completion of her work. The industrial tribunal decided that she had been subject to direct sex discrimination because a man cleaning male or female toilets would not have been subjected to the same treatment.

CASE HISTORY: Lucy

Lucy suffered from anorexia and was exceptionally thin. Her colleague Mark made some unpleasant and offensive comments about her body which included references to the size of her thighs and bottom. Distressed by these comments, Lucy complained but was then dismissed, at which point she claimed sex discrimination. The claim failed because the industrial tribunal decided that the comments made to her were not based on her sex – in other words, Mark might just as easily have made the remarks to another man.

Sexual harassment is entirely distinct and separate from any romantic or flirtatious relationships that may develop between employees. It is often unclear what amounts to sexual harassment, although the context is often crucial. For example, suggestive remarks made by a male 23-year-old office junior to a female secretary of the same age may not be unwelcome and oppressive, whereas they could be were they made by a 55-year-old senior manager. A string of seemingly innocent or innocuous incidents can, on investigation, provide an entirely different picture which suggests sustained, if subtle, harassment. What is considered tolerable in terms of physical contact will vary between individuals and professions. However, some basic guidelines as to what is acceptable at work exist.

Sexual harassment guidelines

Acceptable	Potentially unacceptable	Unacceptable
handshake	two-handed handshake	hugging
	handshake gripping the arm	hand-holding
		bottom-/thigh-patting
		brushing leg/breasts

Excuses for sexual harassment (all unacceptable) may range from 'I'm only being friendly' and 'I thought you liked it' to 'It's just my personal management style' and 'I prefer to treat women like ladies'. However, there is no defence for offensive behaviour.

Employees who feel that they are suffering harassment should make a careful note of every incident, including the date and time on which it takes place. They should not be deterred from taking action simply because each incident viewed in isolation does not of itself appear serious, and should notify someone in authority at the earliest opportunity. If senior management take no action following an appeal, the employee could consider contacting the police, while being aware that this may alienate the employer. For more information on bringing a claim, see pages 94–5.

Relationship contracts

In the United States, some employers, in an effort to deflect possible claims for sexual harassment resulting from relationships between employees, have required workers to sign agreements stating that the relationship is mutually agreed and waiving their rights to bring such a claim if the relationship ends.

Such 'relationship contracts' are not common in the UK and an employer attempting to enforce one would face a number of legal and practical problems. Contracts such as this would be ineffective in preventing the individual from subsequently bringing a claim for sex discrimination as only in very limited circumstances can individuals contract out of their rights under the SDA.

According to an Industrial Society survey (see page 86), among people who filed a complaint or who took their case to an industrial tribunal, 78 per cent and 70 per cent respectively reported an improvement within one year as a result of taking such action. However, the Industrial Society also revealed that only 5 per cent of people who have been harassed take such a measure, for fear of being seen as a trouble-maker or receiving insufficient support or advice.

Actions for employers if racial or sexual harassment is alleged

In cases of both racial and sexual harassment, the employer should make it clear that the harassment will not be tolerated. Employees should be encouraged to report an incident at the earliest possible opportunity, and should be assured that any allegations will be treated in strictest confidence. Employers should fully investigate all allegations. In order to carry out this investigation effectively it may be necessary in serious cases to suspend the individuals allegedly perpetrating the harassment.

The employer should do everything reasonably possible to

encourage employees to give evidence freely. If necessary, disciplinary procedures should be activated in relation to the offending party. While protecting the party making the allegations, the employer is however expected to ensure that the employee accused of harassment is given a fair hearing. Failure to do so may lead to a claim for constructive dismissal on the basis that the employer has breached its duty of mutual trust and understanding (see page 74). Employers which fail to take action against employees guilty of harassment may find themselves on the receiving end of a sex or racial discrimination claim.

Harassment by the employer

On occasion, the individual guilty of harassment is the employer. In such a case, the employee's options for redress, short of indicating to the employer that he or she will take action against it and submitting a case to an industrial tribunal, are somewhat more limited. This is because going through an internal grievance procedure is unlikely to achieve the desired result. For information on bringing a claim, see page 94.

Rights of an employee falsely accused of racial or sexual harassment

The employer has a fine line to tread. Every incident must be fully investigated with the utmost discretion and a fair hearing afforded to both parties. If the allegation has no foundation the employer should consider taking disciplinary action against the person who made the allegation of harassment. False accusations of harassment would normally constitute gross misconduct and disciplinary action should be taken against any such employee making them.

It is not unknown for vindictive employees to submit claims of harassment against more senior colleagues which are completely without foundation. Failure by the employer to support a falsely accused employee either initially or in any subsequent disciplinary action may lead that employee to allege constructive dismissal on the basis that the employer's lack of support has led to a breakdown in mutual trust and understanding (see page 169).

Employers' liability for employees' discriminatory acts

Employers are liable for their employees' acts of discrimination when those employees are acting in the course of their employment. Unfortunately, this sometimes constitutes a grey area (see below). The issue of the employer's liability is usually one of immense importance for the employee alleging discrimination: although the worker may have a claim against an individual employee, the more significant claim is usually the one against the employer – which is normally much better placed to pay any compensation that may be awarded.

The question of when employers are liable for their employees' actions has been the subject of some debate. In the past it was always assumed that an employer was liable only when the employee was either carrying out some act authorised by the employer, or, if the duties were not actually authorised, was acting in the course of his or her employment. In other words, actions by workers which were clearly not authorised or justifiable would fall outside the category of acts for which the employer could be liable. The problem with this interpretation of the law is that employers could argue that certain forms of discrimination – such as harassment – would never be authorised by them; nor could it be reasonably argued that discrimination of this type was practised by the employees in an ill-judged effort to do their jobs. The case histories below illustrate this problem.

CASE HISTORY: Patrick

Patrick worked as a postman. While sorting mail he saw an envelope addressed to one of his neighbours, who was black. He picked it up and added some words with a drawing, both offensive, on the back of it. In this case the court judged that the Post Office was not liable for the discrimination because Patrick was held to be acting outside the ordinary course of his employment, and hence without authority.

CASE HISTORY: Michael

While working in a garage, Michael, a sixteen-year-old youth of mixed race, was subjected to verbal and physical abuse by two colleagues. It was held that the employer could not be liable as the abuse could not be considered to have been carried out by the employees during the course of their employment.

Judging by these two cases, many people might conclude that the worse the active harassment or discrimination, the less likely the employer is to be liable. The courts have tried to find a way round this loophole by suggesting that the test above is too literal, and that the employer should be liable for its employees' actions. In practice, industrial tribunals tend to avoid a very literal approach and instead take the view that employers *are* responsible for their employees' actions at work – even where their behaviour is, on occasion, outlandish.

Employees should be aware that the employer may use the argument above in order to claim freedom from liability. This should not deter an employee from submitting a claim.

Employers' liability for harassment by third parties

This type of harassment typically occurs in service industries such as hotels, pubs, parking control and public transport where staff are subject to abuse by customers. Neither the RRA or the SDA make employers liable for discriminatory acts by people who are not their employees. However, industrial tribunal decisions have made clear that employers may find themselves liable where they fail to protect their staff from harassment by a third party – see case histories below.

CASE HISTORY: Debbie and Sandra

While working as waitresses, Debbie and Sandra, who were both black, had to serve at a dinner attended by a famous comedian. The comedian directed some obscene racist comments at them and encouraged guests to join in. Debbie and Sandra succeeded with a case against their employer for failing to protect them from harassment by a third party.

CASE HISTORY: Natasha

Natasha worked for a company that provided children's parties on a commercial basis. During a party, she was subjected to sexual remarks by one of the male parents. When she left the party to complain, the company director sent her back and she was propositioned again. The employer was judged to be guilty of direct discrimination because it had failed to do anything to prevent the harassment recurring once Natasha had complained.

Employers' defence

In certain circumstances, such as those involving discrimination against an employee for pregnancy-related reasons (see Chapter 6), the employer is immediately liable. Other cases may hinge more upon what steps the employer has taken towards eliminating discrimination. Employers will have a defence against a claim for racial or sex discrimination if they can show that they have taken reasonable practical steps to prevent discriminatory behaviour by their employees (see 'The CRE and EOC codes of practice', below). The extent of the measures invoked will be taken into account when liability is considered.

Small employers are not exempt from the RRA and SDA, as they are from the Disability Discrimination Act (DDA) – see pages 99–102. However, the actions they might need to take to prevent discrimination are not likely to be as extensive as for large employers.

The CRE and EOC Codes of Practice

The Commission for Racial Equality★ and the Equal Opportunities Commission★ have both issued Codes of Practice (copies can be obtained from any CRE or EOC office).

It is not compulsory for employers to implement the Codes, but they can be used by industrial tribunals as evidence of good practice when deciding whether an employer's conduct is reasonable. If an employer can show that it has tried to implement the principles of either Code, a tribunal will take such actions as evidence that the employer has tried to do everything reasonably practicable to stamp out discrimination.

The CRE Code of Practice

The CRE Code identifies the major areas of responsibility for employers. It recognises that small employers have fewer resources and are therefore unable to put in place the same complex measures as, say, a major public company – and also acknowledges the fact that owing to their more intimate relationship with their employees, small employers do not need to institute such rigid procedures in order to eradicate discrimination.

The Code recommends that every employer should adopt, implement and maintain an equal opportunities policy for all employees and job applicants in order to guard against unlawful discrimination. To this end, it proposes:

- allocating overall responsibility for the policy to a senior member of management
- broadcasting the policy to all employees and job applicants
- providing training and guidance for staff
- carrying out regular reviews of existing procedures and criteria to ensure that they reflect the current state of the law
- implementing additional analysis of the workforce according to ethnic origin and monitoring it to avert discrimination.

The Code also identifies some potential areas of discrimination, including:

- **job advertisements** The Code warns employers not to confine advertisements unjustifiably to areas or publications which would exclude or reduce the number of applicants from a particular group. In addition, specific requirements (e.g. language or academic qualifications) should not be included where they are unnecessary
- **selection of job candidates** Employers should take care when giving instructions to schools or employment agencies that details of the types of employee required are neither directly nor indirectly discriminatory (see pages 78–81)
- **selection for promotion and training** Employers should afford employees equal access to opportunities for promotion, transfer or training and the selection process used should not be discriminatory (see above).

The EOC Code of Practice

The EOC Code of Practice covers many of the issues dealt with by the CRE Code of Practice. It takes a similar approach, although instead of racism it aims to eliminate sex discrimination in the workplace. Like the CRE Code, it recommends an equal opportunities policy to counter discrimination in recruitment, training and benefits.

Claiming racial or sex discrimination

The right to bring a claim in respect of racial or sex discrimination is not restricted to employees. Discrimination may occur at any stage of the employment process: from when an advertisement is placed to the interview stage and finally when the employee is selected for dismissal.

In cases involving sex or race discrimination an industrial tribunal has the power to make unlimited awards of compensation, although the awards are usually not substantial (see page 84). However, in some cases, particularly those involving embarrassing allegations of sexual harassment, employers may be prepared to settle out of court for much higher amounts than the industrial tribunal is willing to offer in an effort to avoid the adverse publicity associated with a high-profile case (see Chapter 12).

Time limits for submitting a claim

Claims in respect of racial or sex discrimination must be submitted to an industrial tribunal within three months of the date of the incident which caused the complaint to arise. Although the deadline is strict, it is not as rigid in unfair dismissal applications and the tribunal can admit late applications if it chooses to.

In some cases it will be clear when the discrimination occurred: for example, if a job candidate's application is turned down or an employee is sacked for racially motivated reasons. Sometimes the situation may be less clear: for example, if an employee is continually turned down for promotion on racially motivated grounds or is subject to constant racial abuse. In such circumstances, the discrimination is ongoing and the time limit will continue to run. Note: employees should not be deterred from complaining to the employer after the time limit has expired.

Actions for employees suffering discrimination

Sometimes employees fear that bringing a claim for discrimination may alienate their employer. However, the bottom line is that individuals have a choice: they can either live with the discrimination and do nothing or challenge the employer to rectify matters. Remember, if the employer penalises the employee for taking action, the employee will have a potential claim for victimisation even if the claim for discrimination ultimately does not succeed (see pages 81–2). Employees should however take care to avoid damaging relations with colleagues and management; not jumping to conclusions, using emotional language or volunteering unfounded opinions, for example.

The employee should, in the first instance, attempt to resolve the issue through the employer's internal grievance procedure. In cases of sexual harassment the employer may have a procedure dedicated solely to resolving issues of this type. The employee should however keep in mind the three-month time limit for submitting a claim to an industrial tribunal (see above), and should not delay submitting an application just because the internal grievance procedure has not been exhausted. Otherwise, the employee risks his or her application becoming time-barred. The employee can always withdraw an application at a later stage if the matter is satisfactorily resolved. For more on applying to an industrial tribunal, see Chapter 16.

As with so many employment law–related cases, providing evidence is crucial. If you are being discriminated against, follow the steps below (see box).

Gathering evidence of discrimination

- Make a careful note of all incidents and of who said what on what occasion. It may be worth attempting to record conversations or to find witnesses who can support you.
- Keep copies of all potentially incriminating documents, save all relevant emails and make a note of any attempts to stop the discrimination that the employer ignores – e.g. a verbal or written protest on the part of the employee.
- Consider contacting other former employees if you believe they left because of discrimination. Your case will be stronger if you can show that the employer has a history of discrimination.

Additional help

Help in preparing applications can be obtained from Citizens Advice Bureaux,★ local law centres or trade union officials (see Chapter 17). Although legal aid is not available for bringing a claim to an industrial tribunal, employees may be eligible for initial free advice under the legal aid 'green form scheme' operated by some solicitors (see page 276). In cases of racial discrimination, the CRE★ will consider applications for assistance from applicants: the necessary forms can be obtained from any CRE office or from the Racial Equality Council.★ The EOC★ sometimes offers assistance to individuals in sexual discrimination cases.

Pay discrimination

The objective of the **Equal Pay Act 1970 (EPA)** is to ensure that women receive the same pay as men for the same, or comparable, work. Although the EPA talks in terms of attaining equal treatment for women, the same protection against sex discrimination over pay-related issues is also extended to men.

Female employees are assumed to receive equal treatment if their employment terms are no less favourable than those of their male counterparts. In order to bring a claim under the EPA, it is not enough for a woman to show that she has been treated less favourably than her male colleagues. In addition, her claim must meet certain requirements (see below) and she must be able to show that her work resembles that done by her male counterparts (see 'EPA categories', below).

Claiming pay discrimination

The female employee must ensure that whatever man she compares herself to is in the same employment. This means that the male counterpart must be employed by the same employer – or an associated employer. Note: the male employee need not be employed *at the same time* as the female employee, provided he was recently employed on similar work to that performed by the woman. For example, a female worker doing exactly the same job as a male predecessor for less pay would have a claim, as would a woman employed at a different branch office or factory from her male equivalent, provided the same terms and conditions of employment covered both locations.

EPA categories

The purpose of the EPA is to ensure that women are given the same treatment as men:

- who are engaged in **like work** in the same employment

- whose work is **equivalent–rated**
- whose work is otherwise of **equal value**.

In order for a claim to succeed, a woman must be able to prove that one of these definitions applies to her situation.

Like work

The EPA states that a woman and a man will be regarded as being employed on like work if their work is the same or of a broadly similar nature, and the differences between their tasks are not of practical importance.

Industrial tribunals do not normally take a pedantic approach when considering this test. What is relevant is what the employees actually do, as opposed to what is provided for under their contracts of employment. If there are differences between the employees' jobs, the tribunal will consider whether the differences are significant enough to justify the different terms of employment.

Equivalent-rated work

This term describes the situation where a woman's job has been evaluated and rated of equal value as that of a man in the same employment, but in spite of this she is still being treated less favourably over pay. This type of evaluation is typically carried out by large organisations such as local or central government bodies to grade employees according to their suitability to receive rates of pay, benefits and training.

In order to succeed with a claim under this heading, the woman must show that her job has been rated equivalent to that of her male counterpart under the job evaluation study. If such a study has not been carried out, the woman will only be able to succeed with a claim for equal pay by proving that she does like work (see above) or work of equal value (see below). If a job evaluation study has been carried out which shows the jobs of a male and female colleague to be of different value, an equal pay claim will not succeed unless the employee could show that the evaluation system itself was discriminatory – this would be the case if differences in pay were justified on the basis of physical strength, for example.

If the employer has carried out a proper job evaluation, it will have a defence against potential equal pay claims because it can rely on the job evaluation results to justify any differences in pay.

Work of equal value

The third route by which a woman can establish a claim for equal pay is to show that her work is of equal value to that of a man in the same employment. This type of claim often arises where an employer has refused to carry out a job evaluation and can prove the most difficult to resolve: industrial tribunals frequently request reports from independent commissions in order to clarify matters.

A woman who makes a claim under this heading must show that she is employed on work which is, in terms of the demands made upon her, of equal value to that of her male counterpart. The tribunal may determine itself whether the woman's work satisfies this criterion or may ask a member of a team of independent experts to prepare a report to assess whether the work is of equal value.

CASE HISTORY: Jane and Margaret

Jane and Margaret worked as speech therapists. They claimed that they were entitled to the same pay as male colleagues in comparable professions: clinical psychology and pharmacy. Because Jane and Margaret's work was rated of equal value, their case succeeded.

Employer's defence

An employer will have a defence if it can show that its reasons for paying one employee differently from another are genuine. In one case, for example, market forces were held to constitute a material necessity for paying one employee more than another. This type of situation may arise when there is a shortage of qualified candidates and the employer wants to attract a particular employee into employment.

Definition of pay under the EPA

Pay is not narrowly defined. It will include:

- fringe benefits such as private health care (see page 49) or the use of a car (see page 48)
- sick pay (see page 65)
- benefits paid out under an occupational pension scheme (see pages 50–53)

- redundancy or severance payments (see Chapters 11 and 12)
- the right to join a pension scheme (see pages 50–53).

Actions for employees suffering pay discrimination

Claims under the EPA must be submitted to an industrial tribunal either while the employee is still employed or at any time in the six months following the termination of employment. For more information, see Chapter 16.

Industrial tribunals have the power to demand the modification of any discriminatory term in the employee's contract in order to bring it into line with that of her male colleagues. In addition, the industrial tribunal will award a woman back pay where she is paid less money than her male colleagues. Where the employee has been treated less favourably in relation to a benefit in kind – such as the use of a company car or the provision of life assurance or private health insurance cover – an award of damages will be made. In either case, the industrial tribunal has the power to award interest on the compensation paid. However, any award made will be backdated only by a period of two years from the date on which the claim was made – see below.

Example If an employee received £100 a month less than her male counterpart without justification for three years, the actual loss suffered as a result of the pay discrimination would be £3,600 but the maximum compensation an industrial tribunal could award would be £2,400 (calculated over two years).

Disability discrimination

The **Disability Discrimination Act 1995 (DDA)** has been in force since December 1996. The intention of the Act is to provide protection against discrimination for, amongst others, employees who are classified as disabled.

Under the Act, anyone with a physical or mental impairment which has a substantial and long-term adverse effect upon his or her ability to carry out normal day-to-day activities is termed disabled. The disability can be physical, sensory or mental and, to be classified as long-term, must last, or be expected to last, for 12 months. Deafness, blindness and confinement to a wheelchair are considered disabilities. The Act also covers conditions which have a slight effect on day-to-day activities but are expected to become substantial. Conditions such as multiple sclerosis, asthma, ME, HIV and diabetes fall within the definition. Severe disfigurement is also classed as a disability.

> A survey conducted for the European Commission in 1995 showed that 54 per cent of disabled people suffered incidents of violence and harassment while 46 per cent suffered psychological abuse.

.The DDA provides that it is unlawful for employers to discriminate against a disabled person in relation to:

- the recruitment process (including advertising a job, the interview process, the terms of a job offer and the decision as to which applicant is offered the job)
- opportunities for promotion, training and transfers or other benefits
- dismissal or other treatment to the detriment of a disabled employee.

In order to succeed with a claim of discrimination, the employee must show that the employer has treated him or her less favourably than someone else for a reason which relates to his or her disability and, in addition, the employer must not be able to prove that the treatment was justified. It is also discrimination if the employer fails to make any reasonable adjustments to accommodate the disabled person (see below), and cannot show that this failure is justified.

Exceptions to the DDA
At present, only employers with 20 or more employees are prohibited from discriminating against disabled people. Also, the DDA does not apply to operational staff employed in the armed forces, police, prison service and fire service, or to anyone employed on ships, hovercrafts or aeroplanes.

Adjustments the employer should make

A disabled employee may demand from the employer some reasonable adjustments to help him or her do the job, such as being given special equipment which enables him or her to carry out the work in the same way as an able-bodied person. They may also include time off for medical treatment, or altering the employee's working hours.

The size of the employer, its resources and any effort it has made – such as finding out whether grants for equipment are available – will be taken into account by an industrial tribunal in deciding whether any failure to make reasonable adjustments is justified.

CASE HISTORY: Gail

When Gail's club foot began to cause her pain, she became unable to carry out her work as before. Gail's employer sought a medical opinion and advice on ways of alleviating her condition. A specialist advised the firm to purchase a special chair to help Gail. The chair was not expensive. However, the employer did not obtain the chair and the tribunal found that it had failed to make reasonable adjustments. Because of this, Gail succeeded in her claim for discrimination.

Protection against dismissal

There is no special protection against dismissal for disabled people for reasons which do not relate to their disability. If there are other reasons which justify the dismissal – for example, the worker has committed theft – the fact that the employee is disabled will not prevent the employer from treating him or her in the same way as someone else.

CASE HISTORY: Simon

Under the DDA, Simon – who had diabetes – was classified as disabled. However, his performance at work was generally unsatisfactory: he performed his work carelessly, was often late and was reprimanded on several occasions for other matters. Simon often took time off in connection with his diabetes for hospital appointments with his employer's permission. When he took time off in connection with his illness without giving advance notice, he was subsequently dismissed. Simon claimed his employer had discriminated against him on the grounds of his disability. However, the tribunal found that the reason for his dismissal was not his diabetes but his attitude and performance.

Making a medical condition known to the employer

If the employer is not aware of the disability, the obligations placed on it by the DDA will not apply. It may therefore be in the employee's best interests to advise the employer sooner rather than later. Provided the employer is large enough (that is, with 20 or more employees), the employee will be entitled to be treated no less favourably than anyone else. In addition, the worker may benefit from any adjustments the employer may make for him or her (see pages 100–1).

Actions for employees suffering disability discrimination

Workers being subjected to discrimination should monitor the abuse by following the steps on page 95. As in the case of racial and sex discrimination, they may make an application to an industrial tribunal (see page 99 and Chapter 16). If it is successful, the tribunal may make a declaration, a recommendation of any action it considers the employer should take and/or an award of compensation with no limit, including a sum in respect of interest and injury to feelings.

Additional help

People with special needs or who suffer from ill health can consult a Disability Adviser at their local Jobcentre.★ The Disability Alliance★ and the Royal Association for Disability and Rehabilitation★ (RADAR) have useful publications.

Chapter 6

Maternity rights

These statutory provisions are of inordinate complexity,
exceeding the worst excesses of the taxing statute; we find that
especially regrettable bearing in mind that they are regulating
the everyday rights of ordinary employers and employees.

Mr Justice Browne-Wilkinson (1982)

In short, this is a complicated area. Matters have not significantly
improved since this comment was made about the workings of maternity legislation. The reluctance of successive governments to overhaul
this legislative hotchpotch systematically is guaranteed to lead to continuing worry for employees and confusion for employers. This chapter
explains the rights of both parties and how the current law works.

In May 1998 the government produced a White Paper entitled
'Fairness at Work'. Among other aims, its intention is that legislation
to improve maternity benefits should be introduced in 1999.

Maternity rights: the legal entitlement

Maternity rights are contained in the **Employment Rights Act
1996**, the **Sex Discrimination Act 1975**, the **Social Security Act
1986** and the EU Pregnant Workers Directive. Maternity rights fall
into five categories:

- the right to paid time off work for antenatal care (see below)
- the right to maternity leave (see page 104) and, where applicable,
  maternity absence (see page 105)
- the right, where applicable, to receive pay and benefits while absent
  due to pregnancy (see page 106)
- the right to return to work after the birth of the child (see page 114)
- the right to protection against discrimination on maternity-related
  grounds (see page 118).

The right to paid time off work for antenatal care

All pregnant employees are entitled to paid time off for antenatal care. This means that they should not be unreasonably refused time to keep appointments with their doctor, health visitor or midwife. During any absence due to ante-natal care, employees should be paid at the normal rate.

The definition of 'antenatal care' is not restricted to medical examinations or check-ups; it can include relaxation classes and guidance lectures for parents. However, any appointments of this sort must have been made on the advice of a qualified doctor, midwife or health visitor.

If requested to do so, the employee must show her boss a certificate from her doctor or a registered midwife or health visitor confirming that she is pregnant, as well as an appointment card or some other evidence showing that an appointment has been made. This is to prevent the employer's trust being abused.

Form MATB1

The doctor or midwife will issue the woman with **Form MATB1** at about the 26th week of pregnancy. This confirms the pregnancy and states the expected week of childbirth (EWC).

The right to receive maternity leave and maternity absence

Two distinct types of maternity absence are provided for by statute: maternity leave and maternity absence.

Note: for the purposes of maternity legislation, and all calculations in this chapter, weeks are deemed to run from Sunday to Saturday inclusive.

Maternity leave

This is open to all employees, regardless of the length of service with the employer or the number of hours worked.

- The period of maternity leave is 14 weeks (three-and-a-half months). Under current government proposals this leave period will be extended to 18 weeks in 1999.
- The earliest date on which employees can commence their maternity leave is the 11th week before the **expected week of childbirth (EWC)** – sometimes called the 'expected week of confinement'. The EWC is confirmed in Form MATB1 (see box opposite).
- Maternity leave must begin no later than the EWC itself (or actual birth date, if earlier). In other words, the woman can work right up to the week the baby is due, but not beyond it, if she wants to maintain her statutory rights. If the woman wants to work after the 36th week of pregnancy, the employer can ask her to produce a letter from her doctor confirming that she is fit enough.
- Every employee is required by law to take at least two weeks' maternity leave immediately after the birth of the child.

Maternity absence

This is an extended period of leave which follows on from maternity leave. Only employees who fulfil certain requirements qualify.

- To qualify, employees must have completed over two years' continuous employment with the employer prior to the beginning of the 11th week before the EWC (see above). Under current government proposals this period will be reduced to one year in 1999.
- Maternity absence lasts from the end of the maternity leave period up until the end of the 28th week beginning the week after the week in which the baby is born.

Maximum entitlement to maternity absence

Employees who have completed two years' continuous employment for one employer can take the statutory 14 weeks' maternity leave followed by a period of maternity absence. The maximum period of combined maternity leave and maternity absence is approximately 40 weeks (10 months).

Breaks from work

If the employee has taken a sabbatical or a career break, she may still qualify for maternity absence as long as the employment was not terminated during the long break.

Maternity entitlement for self-employed women

Self-employed women and most agency workers are not covered by the maternity rights legislation because they do not have employee status. Self-employed women may be entitled to the lower rate of maternity allowance (see page 110) and may also be eligible for state help (see page 110). To determine employment status, see Chapter 1.

The right to receive pay and benefits

During the maternity leave period, all employees have the right to continue to receive all the usual benefits under their terms and conditions of employment except those relating to remuneration (see 'What is not covered by the maternity legislation', opposite). So if the employee normally received holiday leave, for example, that would continue to accrue during maternity leave. In addition, women should continue to receive fringe benefits such as:

- the right to participate in share option schemes (see page 50)
- reimbursement of professional subscriptions (e.g. to journals and clubs)
- the use of a company car, mobile phone or laptop computer
- permanent health insurance cover (see page 49)
- private medical insurance (see page 49)
- pension contributions by the employer (see pages 50–3)
- other perks such as membership of a health club.

However, at the end of the 14-week maternity leave period the employee ceases to have a statutory right to receive whatever benefits she might normally expect under her terms and conditions of employment (including fringe benefits) if she were working, unless she goes back to work at that stage.

The maternity benefits calculator on page 112 summarises the benefits which are due to workers who have been employed for varying lengths of time.

The right to normal terms and conditions

The employee retains various other rights during the time she is away from work:

- she continues to be an employee during maternity leave and maternity absence
- during both periods, she is protected against unfair dismissal (see Chapter 10) and maintains the right to receive a statutory redundancy payment (see page 191)
- both periods count towards a period of continuous employment for the purposes of assessing seniority, pensionable service and other personal length-of-service benefits.

Employer's refusal to grant what is due

The law on what happens when the employee gets passed over for a scheduled pay rise or promotion is not clear. However, the woman might be able to claim discrimination on pregnancy-related grounds (see page 118) if the employer withheld a benefit that was due to her during maternity leave or maternity absence – see case history below.

CASE HISTORY: Clare

While eight months pregnant, Clare had to attend an interview at the company she worked for in order to gain promotion. The interviewer considered her performance to be sub-standard and did not award her the position. When Clare took the matter to an industrial tribunal, it took the view that the reason she had not been promoted was related to her pregnancy and that the failure to promote her constituted an act of discrimination.

What is not covered by the maternity legislation

Employees are not entitled as of right to receive benefits relating to remuneration during maternity leave or maternity absence. The definition of 'remuneration' is not entirely clear, but it will definitely include normal salary and is also likely to cover payments such as bonuses and commission payments. Many employers do however operate arrangements whereby female employees continue to receive a proportion of their salary during the time they are away from work (see 'Contractual rights', page 119).

The right to receive maternity payments

Provided that the employee meets the lower earnings limit (see below), she will usually be entitled to either statutory maternity pay or maternity allowance, which is payable by the DSS (see page 110).

Statutory maternity pay

An employee is eligible to receive **statutory maternity pay (SMP)** from her employer if she has been continuously employed by that employer for at least 26 weeks by the 15th week – known as the **qualifying week** – before the EWC (see page 105), and her average weekly earnings are on, or above, the lower earnings limit for the purpose of National Insurance contributions (£64 in 1998).

Employees cannot claim SMP prior to the beginning of the 11th week before the EWC. After this, employees are entitled to receive SMP for an 18-week period. During this period, two rates of SMP are payable:

- the higher rate, payable for the first six weeks, is calculated at a rate of 90 per cent of the employee's normal earnings. When employees are paid weekly, normal weekly earnings are calculated by reference to the employee's average in the eight weeks prior to the last payday before the end of the qualifying week (see above). When employees are paid monthly, the weekly SMP rate is calculated by adding together the total pay received in the two months up to and including the last payday before the end of the qualifying week, multiplied by six and divided by 52.
- for the remaining period of up to 12 weeks, a lower rate is payable at a flat rate of £57.70 per week (1998). This rate is reviewed regularly.

How SMP is paid

SMP is paid to employees in exactly the same way as they normally receive their salary, and is subject to the deduction of tax and National Insurance. Though expressed as a weekly rate, SMP does not have to be paid on a weekly basis if this is not the employer's customary practice. The employer receives a full or partial refund of SMP payments from the state (see below).

Eligibility for SMP

Working women who earn less than £64 per week (the lower earnings limit for National Insurance contributions) are not entitled to receive any SMP. They may however be eligible for state help (see overleaf).

Leaving work

The entitlement to SMP is unaffected if the employee resigns or is dismissed once on maternity leave or maternity absence. The employer must continue to make payments to the woman for the appropriate length of time.

Returning to work

The employee has the right to receive SMP even if she does not intend to return to work after maternity leave or maternity absence, provided that she has completed 26 weeks' continuous service prior to the qualifying week (see opposite) and all notification procedures have been followed (see page 111). SMP ceases once the employee has returned to work for the employer.

Recovery of employers' SMP payments

Employers are usually reimbursed 92 per cent of the SMP they have paid out. This can be done by deduction from their next payment of PAYE and National Insurance contributions to the Inland Revenue. If the amount claimed is in excess of the payment due, the employer can carry it forward and deduct it from future tax liabilities.

> **SMP exemption for small employers**
> Employers whose gross National Insurance contributions amount to £20,000 or less in the previous tax year can deduct the total amount of SMP from payments made to the Inland Revenue, as well as an additional seven per cent.

Maternity allowance

Those employees who have not completed 26 weeks' service prior to the expected week of childbirth (EWC) – page 105 – are not eligible to receive statutory maternity pay. Instead, they can obtain a statutory **maternity allowance (MA)** if they have been employed – not necessarily with the same boss they will return to work for – and met the lower earnings limit (see page 108) in 26 weeks out of the 66 weeks up to and including the week before the EWC.

MA can be paid for a maximum of 18 weeks, as in the case of SMP. MA is payable once the woman has reached the 11th week before the expected week of childbirth.

Two rates of MA are payable:

- the higher rate is £57.70 if the woman was employed in the qualifying week (see page 108)
- the lower rate is £50.10 if the woman was not employed in the qualifying week.

> **How to claim MA**
> If you are eligible to receive MA, you should obtain **Form MA1** from your local Benefits Agency* or antenatal clinic. When you submit this with **Form MATB1** (see box, page 104) to the Benefits Agency, you will receive a booklet of weekly orders which can be cashed at a post office.

State help for those ineligible for SMP or MA

Women who are ineligible for either SMP or MA may be able to claim Sickness Benefit. Employees who do not qualify for MA are automatically considered for such benefit, and Form MATB1 is accepted as evidence of incapacity. Employees who cannot claim SMP or MA may also qualify for Income Support. This income-related benefit is subject to maximum levels which are set by the government each year. However, if the woman or her partner work for more than 16 hours a week or have savings in excess of £8,000, they will not normally be eligible for Income Support.

Notifying the employer

In order to take advantage of maternity leave and the right to SMP, it is important that the employee follows certain procedures. The woman must inform her boss about the pregnancy at least 21 days before she intends to start maternity leave, but is under no obligation to do so before then.

The employee must give the employer:

- written notice of the fact that she is pregnant, including confirmation of the expected week of childbirth (EWC) – see page 105
- written notice of the date on which she intends to begin her maternity leave – which may be no earlier than the beginning of the 11th week before the EWC
- the date on which she intends, if eligible, to start receiving SMP, which may be no earlier than the beginning of the 11th week before the EWC
- if she is eligible for maternity absence, written notice of the fact that she intends to exercise her right to return after this period. The employee may later change her mind (see 'Returning to work after the baby's birth', below).

Women who fail to comply with the notification requirements within the specified time limits may prejudice their right to return after maternity leave (or, where applicable, maternity absence), and SMP. The time limits can be extended only in exceptional circumstances where it is not reasonably practical to comply.

Early departure from work owing to illness

If the employee becomes unable to attend work due to a pregnancy-related illness before the date on which she has told her boss she intends to start maternity leave, the maternity leave period will start early. If she is absent from work for at least a whole day for a

Maternity benefits calculator

Length of service with employer	Entitlement
0–26 weeks by 15th week before the estimated week of childbirth	14-week maternity leave maternity allowance (subject to lower earnings limit) normal terms and conditions continue right to return to the same job no notification required prior to returning (unless returning before the end of maternity leave)
Between 26 weeks by 15th week before the estimated week of childbirth and two years prior to beginning of 11th week before the estimated week of childbirth	14-week maternity leave statutory maternity pay (subject to lower earnings limit) normal terms and conditions continue right to return to the same job no notification required prior to returning (unless returning before the end of maternity leave)
Two years prior to beginning of 11th week before the estimated week of childbirth	14-week maternity leave maternity absence statutory maternity pay (subject to lower earnings limit) normal terms and conditions continue only during maternity leave right to return to the same job or suitable alternative employment with the same employer notification of return required at least 21 days in advance must respond to any enquiry about intention to return from employer within 14 days

Entitlement to SMP or MA

-19	-18	-17	-16	QW	N1 -14	-13	-12
-11	-10	-9	-8	-7	-6	-5	-4
N2 -3	-2	-1	EWC	1	2	3	4
5	6	7	8	9	10	11	12
13	14	15	16	17	18	19	20
21	22	23	24	N3 25	26	27	28

Entitlement to maternity leave and maternity absence

-19	-18	-17	-16	QW	N1 -14	-13	-12
-11	-10	-9	-8	-7	-6	-5	-4
N2 -3	-2	-1	EWC	1	2	3	4
5	6	7	8	9	10	11	12
13	14	15	16	17	18	19	20
21	22	23	24	N3 25	26	27	28

QW Qualifying week

EWC Expected week of childbirth

N1 Earliest date to notify employer of maternity leave (or maternity leave and maternity absence)

N2 Latest date to notify employer of maternity leave (or maternity leave and maternity absence)

N3 Latest date to notify employer of return from maternity absence

Each square = 1 week

Period during which SMP or MA can be claimed (for up to 18 weeks)

Period during which 14-week maternity leave must be taken (all employees)

Time which must be taken as leave by law, if the child is born during the EWC

Extent of maternity absence (entitled employees)

pregnancy-related illness within six weeks of the EWC, maternity leave may be considered to have started on that date. These rules do not affect medical conditions that are unrelated to pregnancy.

Premature births

If the baby is born prematurely, maternity leave will be deemed to have commenced on the date on which the employee left work, and maternity payments will commence from the week after the birth takes place.

Late births

The maternity leave period for which all pregnant employees qualify is currently 14 weeks (but see page 105). If the mother does not give birth within the maternity leave period, the leave must by law be extended so that it does not finish until two weeks after the date of childbirth.

> If the baby is **stillborn** after the 16th week before the expected week of childbirth – i.e. from one week before the qualifying week (see page 108) – the woman is entitled to claim whatever maternity pay and leave would have been due to her had the pregnancy continued successfully. If the woman has a **miscarriage** before the 16th week before the expected week of childbirth, she claims statutory sick pay (see page 65). However, if the baby is born alive but subsequently dies, she will be entitled to the normal rate of maternity leave and pay.

Alternative maternity arrangements

Employers and employees are free to agree to a longer period of leave or absence entitlement on a voluntary or contractual basis.

Returning to work after the baby's birth

The entitlement to go back to work after the birth of the child is one of five fundamental maternity rights (see page 103). Employer and employee must comply with certain requirements in the case of maternity leave and maternity absence:

- **maternity leave** An employee does not have to tell her boss whether she intends to return to work after maternity leave, or confirm the date of her return. However, if she wishes to return early she must give at least seven days' notice in writing of the date of return
- **maternity absence** Employees who qualify for the longer period of maternity absence are required to provide the employer with written notice as to whether they intend to exercise their right to return to work (see box below). This should be done at least 21 days before the start of maternity leave and at the same time as the employee formally notifies the employer of the pregnancy and the date on which she intends to take maternity leave. Before the employee goes back to work she must give her employer at least 21 days' notice of the date on which she proposes to return.

Ensuring maternity absence eligibility

If you are eligible for maternity absence and wish to preserve your right to return, you must state that you intend to return to work after the maternity absence period, even if you are not sure that you will come back. Keep a copy of the letter to your employer.

The general obligation on employers to inform employees of their benefits extends to their entitlements to maternity leave and pay and the steps they must take to secure them. Failure to notify a female worker of what steps she should take to claim the entitlement could lead to the employer having to pay compensation, as the case history below shows.

CASE HISTORY: Nicky

Nicky worked for a firm of solicitors. She did not have a written contract of employment and when she told her employer she was pregnant the firm failed to give her any instructions as to what procedures she should follow. When she sought to return to work from maternity leave she was told she could not return to her job because she had not followed the correct notification procedures before going on leave. The tribunal ruled that because the employer had neglected to inform her, it could not cite her failure to comply with the regulations as an excuse for the dismissal. Nicky was awarded £7,900 which included £6,000 for injury to feelings.

Ascertaining whether the employee intends to return to work

Employers may write to the employee to ask her to reconfirm her intention to return to work after maternity absence no earlier than 21 days before the end of the maternity **leave** period. The letter must explain that if the employee does not reply, normally within 14 days, she will lose the right to return to work.

Extending maternity absence

The employer can delay the worker's return for a maximum of four weeks following the end of the statutory maternity absence period (see page 105), provided that it has notified her in advance of the reasons for the postponement and the new scheduled date on which she may return.

The employee can postpone her return to work beyond the date she has notified for a maximum of four weeks and only on medical grounds. She must give her employer a medical certificate in advance stating why she is unable to return. After the four weeks, she will be treated as any other worker taking time off due to illness. At this point, she may be eligible for statutory sick pay (see page 65).

Employees' rights on returning to work

Slightly different rules apply for those employees returning to work from maternity leave and maternity absence.

- **maternity leave** Employees who return to work after a period of maternity leave (see pages 104–5) are entitled to return to exactly the same job on the same terms and conditions as if they had not been absent

- **maternity absence** Employees who return after maternity absence are also entitled to return to the same job, terms and conditions. If this is not reasonably practicable, or if the employee's role has become redundant during the maternity absence period, she must be offered suitable alternative employment within the company. Note: if the woman works for an employer with five or fewer employees she may not be able to reclaim her old position (see box, page 118).

Late return to work owing to illness

An employee who has completed maternity leave will be treated the same way as any other worker who is absent due to sickness.

After maternity absence, a woman has the right to postpone her return for four more weeks provided she supplies a medical certificate in advance explaining the reason for the delay. After this, she will have to show that she is too ill to return to work and should be treated as any other sick employee.

Return to work part-time or in a job-share

Many women wish to return to work part-time after having a baby so that they can spend more time with their child. Since the right to return is an entitlement to return to the job in which the worker was formerly employed, a request to work part-time or job-share does not fall within this category and therefore there is no *absolute* right to work part-time or to job-share. However, an employer's refusal to allow a transition to a job-share or part-time arrangement may amount to indirect sex discrimination if there is no justifiable business reason why the post should be full-time.

CASE HISTORY: IPC Magazines

In a case in 1996 involving IPC Magazines, an employee returning from maternity leave was not allowed to work on a job-share basis. In a court hearing IPC subsequently agreed to pay her £35,000, which represented her losses up to the date of the hearing, two years' future loss of earnings plus compensation for injury to feelings.

Source: EOC annual report

Changes to an employee's terms and conditions without consent during maternity leave or maternity absence

If the employer imposes changes to the employee's terms and conditions of employment unilaterally, the employee may have a claim for constructive dismissal (see page 169). This will give rise to a claim for damages for breach of contract (see page 191) and compensation for unfair dismissal (see pages 188–90). In addition, the employee may have a claim for sex discrimination or under the Equal Pay Act (see Chapter 5).

Refusal by the employer to allow the employee to return to work

A refusal to allow an employee to return to work after maternity leave will normally constitute unfair dismissal – regardless of the length of service (see 'The law on pregnancy-related dismissal', below) – since it will be presumed that the dismissal is pregnancy-related. A refusal to allow an employee to return to work after maternity absence will also be treated as automatically unfair if the reason for dismissal is connected with the pregnancy. However, in this case, in order to retain the right to claim unfair dismissal the woman must ensure that she has followed the correct notification procedures (see page 111).

Obviously, if the employer could disprove that the dismissal was connected to the pregnancy – for example, if the worker had committed theft – any claim submitted to an industrial tribunal would not succeed.

Small employers' rights

If the employer has five or fewer employees, he or she does not have to allow the woman to return to work after the maternity absence period (this exception does not apply to maternity leave). The employee's other rights in relation to her pregnancy, such as her entitlement to antenatal care (see page 104), are not affected. Small employers with pregnant staff are entitled to help with SMP payments – see page 110.

Other maternity rights

Protection against discrimination on maternity-related grounds is one of five basic maternity rights (see page 103). An employee who is treated unfavourably because of her pregnancy – being passed over for a promotion she had been led to expect, for example, or denied a pay rise – can take legal action against her employer. Such treatment would enable her to submit a claim for sex discrimination and, if the employment was terminated, for unfair dismissal as well (see Chapter 10).

The law on pregnancy-related dismissal

It is unlawful to dismiss an employee before, during or after the end of her maternity leave or maternity absence, or to select her for redundancy in preference to other employees because she is taking maternity leave or maternity absence. If a woman is dismissed in these circumstances, she will have a claim for unfair dismissal (see Chapter 10). *Note: in such circumstances the employee does not need to have over two years' continuous employment prior to submitting a claim.*

Generally, if an employee is dismissed for a pregnancy-related reason, this will automatically give rise to a presumption of sex discrimination, the rationale being that only women can be pregnant. Unless there are justifiable objective reasons for the dismissal or other mistreatment, the employer's action is automatically discriminatory. The employee may have a claim for sex discrimination under the **Sex Discrimination Act 1975** (see Chapter 5).

Redundancy and pregnancy

Employers are entitled to make employees who are absent during a period of maternity leave or maternity absence redundant, provided that it can be shown that the employee was fairly selected for redundancy. However, if the employee is made redundant for pregnancy-related reasons, the dismissal will be automatically unfair and the employee may have an additional claim for sex discrimination (see Chapter 5).

Redundancy during maternity leave or maternity absence
If the employee is made redundant during the period of maternity leave or maternity absence, the employer is under an obligation to continue to look for suitable alternative employment for her up until the date on which she is entitled to return to work.

Contractual rights

It is quite common for female workers to have enhanced contractual rights granted to them by their employer which supplement the statutory provision and often provide a much better deal. Typically, this might include the right to receive full pay instead of statutory maternity pay (SMP) during the 18-week period, or full pay for x number of weeks followed by half pay for y weeks. The exact entitlement may vary depending on the length of service with the employer.

Another popular benefit is an incentive bonus which is paid to women who return to work for a pre-determined period of time after giving birth – usually six months. This bonus is often repayable to the employer if the employee fails to return to work for the whole of the agreed period.

Other parental leave

Fathers and adoptive parents may want to take time off work when a child arrives.

Male employees

Unlike their counterparts in many other European countries, male employees in the UK are not entitled to paternity leave (time off on the birth of a child). However, some employers do make provision for such leave in their employees' contracts of employment. The average entitlement is by no means as generous as for women: at present the TUC's target when negotiating on behalf of its members is ten days' paid leave, with the option of further unpaid leave.

Adoptive parents

Current legislation does not grant adoptive parents the right to take time off work. Entitlement to leave and pay is therefore dependent on the employer. In most cases, partners planning to adopt will nominate a 'main' or 'primary carer' to receive the equivalent of maternity leave and pay, and a 'secondary carer' to receive the equivalent of paternity leave and pay – what is actually granted will vary. Adoptive parents will be entitled to unpaid time off when the Parental Leave Directive is introduced (see box below).

Parental leave

Following the government's commitment to the Social Chapter in 1997, it is under an obligation to implement the Parental Leave Directive into UK law. This will ensure that employees can take up to three months' unpaid leave at any time in the first eight years following the birth or adoption of a child. This right will apply to both the mother and the father.

Additional help

A useful booklet from the Department of Trade and Industry is *Maternity Rights: A Guide for Employers and Employees* (PL958), obtainable from DTI Publications Orderline.★ The Labour Research Department (LRD), a trade union-based research organisation, publishes a helpful booklet entitled *Maternity – an LRD Guide to the Best Law and Practice*, available from LRD Publications.★

Chapter 7

Protecting the employer's business

All businesses depend to some extent on ideas, creativity and sensitive information. Even when the business is manufacturing a physical product, millions of pounds may have been invested in research and development to market a particular product, and information on the best way to manufacture it would be highly valuable to competitors. Years of expensive research and testing often take place in the pharmaceuticals industry before a new drug can be sold to the public, for example. If a competitor could simply analyse the drug and produce a rival product without having to invest in research, there would be no incentive for the company that formulated the drug to be creative in the first place. Similarly, if computer games writers were unable to prevent other people from selling copies of their programs, no one would bother to write new material.

Even if the business of a company appears to be mundane, it will possess information about its customers and its intended business plans that it regards as highly sensitive and wants to keep confidential.

Statutory protection for the employer's business

A quick look at the job contract of many senior executives will show three areas of critical concern to the employer:

- **intellectual property** The ownership of any ideas or inventions the employee comes up with during the course of employment (i.e. copyright, moral rights, design rights and patents)

- **confidential information and trade secrets** The employee's obligations regarding restricted information, both while in employment and when the employment ends
- **restrictive covenants** Contractual restrictions on what the employee can do when he or she leaves work (e.g. a clause preventing the employee from poaching the former employer's staff and clients).

The law protects the employer's business in all three areas. A range of statutory rights are in place to safeguard what is sometimes called the 'intellectual capital' of a business, in order to ensure that the business is able to reap the benefits of its investment and experience without it being possible for a rival to copy its ideas or put them into practice. The law provides different levels of protection and strikes a balance between the interests of the employee who has had a bright idea, and the employer who is paying him or her to be creative.

Intellectual property rights

Intellectual property rights relevant to the employer–employee relationship are copyright, moral rights, design rights and patents.

Copyright

This right protects:

- pieces of writing (business reports as well as blockbuster novels)
- musical compositions
- pictures, paintings and photographs
- TV programmes
- films and performances
- computer programs (including screen displays and layouts).

Copyright usually comes into existence as soon as a piece of work is recorded, whether on paper, film, computer, audio or video tape or by any other method with some degree of permanence. There is no need to register copyright with anyone; it is not even necessary to add the copyright symbol ©, although it is advisable to do this and to state who owns the copyright and the year of its creation.

Copyright does what the name suggests: it allows the holder to prevent other people from making copies of the work or significant parts of it. It therefore also gives the holder the ability to exploit the right by selling copies of the work or by licensing someone else to do so in return for a fee, usually called a royalty. Copyright is recognised automatically in most countries throughout the world, which makes it an enormously valuable right. Generally, copyright lasts for 70 years following the death of the work's author. Copyright may be transferred but this must be done in writing.

Copyright does *not* give the holder the right to prevent someone else coming up with the same material independently. There have been a number of cases where writers of pop songs have been sued for infringement of copyright by people claiming that the new song is very like an old song which they wrote previously themselves. However, if the writers were unaware of the old song and simply came up with the same tune, the claim will fail because there was no actual *copying* of the original song.

Determining ownership

The owner of the copyright in a new work is usually the person or people who wrote it. (Where a work is a collaborative effort, all the writers will share the copyright and have a say in how the piece is exploited.) Self-employed people will usually own the copyright themselves. However, if an employee creates the work, ownership will turn on whether the work was created in the course of employment.

In order to make a decision as to whether the work was created as part of the employee's job, the true scope of the employee's duties at work and the circumstances in which the work was written must be carefully considered. This can be done by the parties involved or, ultimately, a court.

For example, a journalist who writes an article for the paper he works for will not own the copyright: instead, this will automatically belong to the newspaper company. This is a fairly clear-cut case because neither party could really suggest that the journalist was doing something outside his normal employment. Situations less easy to judge would include: the same journalist writing the article outside working hours with the intention of selling it to another publication; a solicitor in a law firm writing a legal textbook; and a computer programmer devising a new game in his spare time. When determining ownership, the following points must be taken into account.

General duties of employment

As set out in Chapter 4, employees are generally obliged not to compete with their employer's business and not to moonlight. The full-time journalist described above who decides to freelance as well may therefore find that his employer can stake a claim to any articles he writes, even if they are penned in his spare time. On the other hand, the situation would be different if he were employed as a security guard at the newspaper and wrote the article in his spare time.

When the work is carried out

Employees are generally obliged to devote their full time and energies to their employer's interests (see page 71). If the solicitor mentioned above writes his textbook when he should be doing client work, he may find that his law firm has a claim to the copyright. By contrast, in the case of the computer programmer described above it may be far more difficult to point to a time of day when he is supposed to work only for his employer, since computer programmers are well-known for working unstructured hours.

Nature of the job and the relevance of the copyright work

Ownership will depend upon the scope of the employee's duties and to what extent the work touches upon the business of the firm. A solicitor's job may be seen as advising clients on the law. However, the role increasingly involves marketing to bring in new work and clients. If this was expected of the lawyer writing a textbook, a book on a subject directly relevant to the lawyer's practice might be considered to be written in the course of employment, even if he wrote it during his spare time – and his firm might have a claim to copyright. However, if the lawyer wrote, say, a novel or sitcom outside work it would be difficult for the law firm to assert ownership.

A conflict of interests may lead to other problems developing: if the computer programmer devising a new game used up vast computer resources at work on his pet project, for example, this may of itself be a breach of the terms of his job contract.

Practical realities

Some employers may not be concerned about the employee profiting from ownership of a copyright work. In the case of the textbook written by the lawyer, his employers may be perfectly happy to allow him to keep any fee by way of rewarding his initiative and recognising that the book's publication reflects well on the firm as a whole. However, the issue of ownership may be critical in other situations, such as when a research scientist invents something while working for one company but intends to jump ship to a rival employer.

In cases of doubt: steps for employees

If the position regarding ownership is not clear-cut and is likely to be critical, an employee nurturing a bright idea has two alternatives: to speak with the employer in advance and agree who will own the copyright; or to proceed with the project while being scrupulously careful not to use company time or resources.

Moral rights

These are an offshoot of copyright (see above) and allow the author of a copyright work to prevent other people taking credit for it or abusing it in some way: for example, by parodying it. Moral rights apply even when the copyright itself has been transferred to someone else and are intended to protect the reputation of the original author.

Employees may be able to claim moral rights even if copyright is owned by the employer because the work was created in the course of employment (see page 124). However, this right is restricted in order to prevent employees claiming ownership in cases where the work is used only for the purpose for which it was written (for example, an advertising jingle being used to promote a product).

A number of moral rights – for example, the right to be identified as the author – must be 'asserted': in other words, the author must make a formal statement of his or her right. You can often now see a statement to this effect in books, on the imprint page.

Moral dilemma

Employees in creative industries, such as graphic design or advertising, may be asked by the employer to waive their moral rights (this may also be a requirement of the ultimate client). The employer has a real interest in preventing the value of the product being undermined by potential claims from disgruntled employees or ex-employees. If asked to renounce ownership, employees should give the matter careful consideration and preferably should not grant a blanket waiver. See Chapter 3 for information on negotiating terms.

Design rights

The design of three-dimensional manufactured objects can be registered, usually through the services of an agent, provided the design is not merely an inevitable consequence of the function of the object and makes some appeal to the eye (for example, the shape of a garden chair which enables it to be stacked). In other words, if there is only one way of designing the product in order to make it work, that design cannot be registered – although certain rights apply (see box below).

Once a design is registered, the registration holder will be able to prevent anyone trying to manufacture an object that is identical, or very similar, in design. The rights are similar to copyright ownership (see pages 123–4).

As with copyright, an employee who creates a design in the course of his or her employment cannot apply for registration: this right belongs to the employer.

Protection for functional designs

Purely functional designs that are not attractive enough to merit registration may have some protection as unregistered designs, provided the design is not commonplace. Parts designed solely to fit another object will *not* be protected – for example, the inside edge of a contact lens was refused protection since it had to be manufactured a certain way to fit the wearer's eye.

Patents

A patent is a right which applies only to inventions and arises on registration. This is done via a patent agent. Once granted, a patent gives the holder a 20-year monopoly over that invention. After that time, the invention is no longer protected.

Generally, the 'first come, first served' principle applies: whoever registers the right takes precedence over anyone who may have invented a similar item earlier but failed to patent it. The application for the patent then becomes public – part of the price of the monopoly right is an obligation to disclose the secrets behind the invention.

As the rights granted to the patent-holder are so powerful, the criteria for awarding a patent are strict. To meet the criteria, the invention must be:

- new
- inventive (i.e. not an obvious or logical progression from something that has been done before)
- capable of industrial application.

Unlike copyright, therefore, patents reward the invention of something with potential commercial value rather than creative merit.

Protection for projects in development

If a company is researching an invention and wants to keep it under wraps prior to making an application for a patent, the project may come under the category of confidential information until the patent is granted (see opposite).

Determining ownership

The rules for employers and employees regarding ownership are not quite the same as for copyright. Although the 'course of employment' test applies (see page 124), the employer must establish additional criteria in order to be entitled to the patent. It must prove one of two conditions:

- circumstances were such that the invention (in other words, something capable of being patented) could be expected to arise – e.g. the employee's job were to research new compounds for medicinal properties

- owing to the special nature of the employee's duties, he or she owed a greater obligation towards the employer than normal. In other words, the employee's role was senior and/or sensitive – e.g. that of managing director. Someone in this position would be expected to further the interests of the company.

Even if the employer can demonstrate that it deserves the patent rather than the employee, the special status of the employee as the true inventor is still recognised. If no formal arrangement for the employee to share in the benefit of a particularly valuable patent exists, the court can award him or her compensation to reflect his or her contribution.

Whenever a job requires a worker to be creative and inventive, employer and employee would be advised to agree in the job contract how the question of ownership and exploitation of any patentable inventions is to be dealt with between them (see Chapter 3).

Multiple rights

It is important to realise that more than one right can apply to the same thing. For example, a computer program is protected by copyright (see page 123) and in some circumstances is also capable of being patented (see opposite). The intricacies of its source code – the computer language in which the programmer writes the program before it is translated into a binary format – may be seen as confidential information (see below), while the customer list of the licensees may be the subject of a restrictive covenant (see page 135).

Confidential information

Confidential information or 'trade secrets' covers the information and know-how owned by a company which is not necessarily protected by one of the intellectual property rights set out above. The essence of confidential information is that it is secret and that its disclosure to third parties needs to be controlled.

Critical as this information can be while someone is employed at a company, the level of sensitivity multiplies when a worker decides to move on. The existing employer will be anxious to prevent its trade secrets becoming known to a competitor; on the other hand, the new employer may be keen to take on the individual because of his or her inside knowledge. The employee, of course, does not want to find him- or herself unable to exploit the fund of experience built up in the old job. The following section looks at the typical legal and contractual restrictions on the exploitation of valuable information, and how it can be protected.

Exposure to confidential information

Nearly every employee is exposed to confidential information in some shape or form, from a hospital porter carrying medical records to a secretary typing client lists and a butler serving a well-known person.

In many cases it is obvious that certain types of information are confidential. Some documents, and the envelopes in which they are transported, are stamped 'Strictly Private and Confidential' or 'Addressee Only' to make clear the sensitive nature of the contents and the requirement that they remain classified. In some situations, employees are clearly informed that the information to which they will have access, or the conversations to which they will be a party, are confidential. For example, an employer entering into secret negotiations to buy a rival's business, or, indeed, sell his own, may tell certain members of his staff on a 'need-to-know' basis and urge them not to divulge the information.

Establishing the grounds for a case

In order to take legal action against an employee who wrongfully discloses confidential information, or is discovered to be about to do so, an employer must establish a number of facts.

- **The information must be confidential** If the details are already publicly known before the employee discloses them, the courts will not subsequently attempt to close the stable door.
- **The employee must be obliged to keep the information confidential** This could be an express duty contained in the employee's job contract, an office manual or even a separate confidentiality agreement; alternatively, the employer may have disclosed the information in circumstances where its confidential nature was made clear. As explained on page 71, employees are obliged to keep the employer's business affairs secret as a matter of course.

- **The confidential information must be disclosed without authorisation and the employer must suffer a detriment as a result** This might involve financial loss or embarrassment: for example, if a celebrity's butler were to reveal salacious details of his employer's sex life to a newspaper, or an employee at a brewery were to disclose the formula for a new lager to a rival.

If the employer can establish these criteria, it may be able to seek an injunction to prevent the employee from disclosing the information or, in some circumstances, to prevent the recipient from exploiting it (see page 144). The employer may also be able to seek damages if the employee or a third party has already profited from the wrongful disclosure (see pages 143–4).

The range of information that comes under this duty of confidentiality is wide, extending beyond the obvious – such as client lists and marketing strategies – to the more nebulous area of skill and know-how which the employee has picked up; this is not readily fitted into any category (see below). Once employment is terminated, employees are obliged to keep this information confidential only if their contract of employment contains express provisions imposing such a duty and the employer has not itself broken the contract when it ended (for example, if the employer were to dismiss the employee without giving the requisite period of notice, or the employee was to treat him- or herself as having been constructively dismissed as a result of the employer's conduct – see page 169).

Skill and knowledge

Even if they are subject to an express post-termination confidentiality clause, departing employees cannot be prevented from earning a living by exploiting their general skill and knowledge. Distinguishing between this category and confidential information can sometimes be tricky. Broadly, skill and knowledge are the information that an individual carries in his or her head. In the case of an accountant, for example, the application of certain well-known accounting principles to a particular business would be treated as general skill and knowledge rather than confidential information, whereas a company's mail-order sales results, market research and plans for future catalogues would definitely be regarded as confidential information. The skill and knowledge exception does not apply to confidential information which the employee has deliberately memorised.

Protection for highly sensitive material

A narrow category of highly confidential information known as 'trade secrets' exists whereby employees remain under a duty not to disclose details after the employment has terminated, even if the contract does not have an express clause to this effect. Typically this is restricted to secret processes of manufacture, chemical formulae and classified designs. The protection lasts for as long as the information remains highly sensitive and secret.

Considerations for employers

Employers should ensure that their employees' contracts of employment deal specifically and comprehensively with the issue of confidential information. In particular, they should:

- impose clear restrictions on the use and disclosure of confidential information, both during employment and after it ends
- define carefully what is to be treated as confidential
- impose practical security measures to restrict access to confidential information and maintain its secrecy (e.g. marking documents 'confidential' and restricting the number of copies, ensuring secure storage and limiting staff access to sensitive material, whether or not they are employees, as well as ensuring that they have first signed a document promising to treat the information as confidential)
- ensure that the job specifications and contracts of employees handling confidential information make clear whether their duties involve working with such information
- require all employees to return all confidential documents or other materials (such as computer disks), including all copies, either when employment ends or at the end of the project to which they relate.

Employers should bear in mind that the mere inclusion of a clause preventing an employee from disclosing confidential information will not necessarily guarantee that a court will enforce it. Two factors need to be remembered:

- the obligation of confidence will continue only for so long as the information remains confidential. Generally, confidential information or know-how tends to lose its confidential nature over time, and however watertight an express contractual provision may be, the courts will not protect the use or disclosure of material which has become public knowledge
- the enforceability of clauses preventing the use of information obtained by an employee during his or her employment after the end of that employment must be no wider in terms of scope than is reasonably necessary to protect the employer's legitimate interests. Otherwise, such clauses will be considered by the courts to be unreasonable and unenforceable.

Breach of confidentiality by the employee

Employers, particularly if their business interests are threatened, are likely to take a tough line with employees who break the terms of their contracts of employment. In many cases, the employer's main concern is not restricted to preventing employees departing with confidential information: the real aim is to prevent them setting up in competition or poaching employees or customers for themselves or for a rival. Many job contracts provide employers with the right to dismiss employees immediately if they leak confidential information. Even if the contract of employment does not include such a right or the employee does not have a written contract, any of the following types of behaviour by employees which threaten the employer's business interests would probably justify immediate dismissal without compensation:

- disclosure of confidential information
- tendering for business in competition with the employer
- setting up in business in competition with the employer.

The employer may also be able to sue the employee for damages if it can prove that it has suffered a financial loss as a result of the employee's actions (see pages 143–4). In some cases, the court may be willing to grant an injunction to prohibit the employee from, for example, disclosing the employer's confidential information (see page 144).

Employees' obligations during employment

As noted in Chapter 4, every worker owes a duty of loyalty to the employer during the course of employment. So during normal hours of work employees are expected to devote themselves fully to their employer's business and are not entitled to freelance or take time out to pursue their own interests. This duty of good faith and loyalty continues right up until the day the employment ends. Employees who set up on their own are therefore not entitled while still employed or under notice to poach clients or employees, or to copy or memorise confidential information.

Activities employees can pursue

The duty of loyalty does not prevent employees from taking the first steps towards setting up on their own, such as:

- looking for premises
- instructing an accountant
- buying an off-the-shelf company
- buying equipment necessary for the new business.

Likewise, an employee is perfectly entitled to look for a job elsewhere, even with a competitor. Naturally, the employee will want to keep his or her job hunt quiet, rather than risk the existing employer finding out and taking the initiative by dismissing the worker before he or she resigns.

Employees' obligations post-employment

Once the employee is no longer under contract, he or she can compete and even poach customers, if he or she wishes. However, many job contracts contain provisions known as post-termination restrictive covenants, which aim to restrict employees' activities once they have left the employer (see opposite).

Restrictive covenants

Restrictive covenant clauses take a variety of forms, all intended to protect the continuing business of the former employer:

- **non-compete clauses** These are intended to prevent the employee setting up or working for a competing business, usually within a defined geographical area and for a specified period. For example, a hairdresser may have a contract which states that for a period of six months after her employment ends she may not in any capacity be involved with any business that competes with that of her former employer within a defined area (say, within a two-mile radius)

- **non-poaching clauses relating to clients** These clauses are not as restrictive as non-compete clauses, as they do not prevent employees using their skills altogether, but they do attempt to prevent them poaching clients or customers with whom they worked while under the former employer. While a non-compete clause might seek to prevent, say, a hairdresser from working within a particular area for a certain period of time, a non-poaching clause would simply prevent her from trying to persuade customers she dealt with at her old employer's business to come to her new salon

- **non-poaching clauses relating to staff** Some employers are particularly anxious to ensure that a former employee does not poach their remaining staff, especially if much time and effort has been invested in training them and if they have built valuable relationships with clients. Notable cases of employee poaching that have hit the headlines relate to teams of City of London brokers decamping from one large merchant bank to another, generally for significant amounts of money. However, the principles apply equally to poaching a valuable salesman, PA, chef or estate agent. Employers in service industries (such as law, accountancy, banking and advertising) are particularly concerned to put in place every available safeguard against key members of the workforce being stolen

- **non-dealing clauses** Some employers attempt to go a stage further than a non-poaching clause by including this type of clause. The purpose is to prevent the employee from providing any services to customers he or she used to deal with for a set period of time. If a clause of this type were upheld by the courts it would mean that the employee could not serve old customers even if they came to him or her voluntarily and no effort was made to poach their business.

Just because an employee's contract contains post-termination restrictive covenants, it does not necessarily mean that they will be enforced by a court if the employee chooses to ignore them. In deciding whether to enforce such covenants the court will attempt to balance two conflicting views. The first is that employees should not be restrained in any way from exercising their right to earn a living and therefore covenants which seek to enforce such restraints are unreasonable and unenforceable. The second is that the employer and the employee should be free to negotiate the type of job contract that suits them. (See Chapter 3 for advice on negotiating terms of employment.)

Dismissal of the employee in breach of contract

A typical example of this would be instant dismissal of the employee without any notice or justification. It might also occur if the employee elected to treat him- or herself as having been constructively dismissed as a result of unacceptable conduct on the part of the employer (see page 169).

If the employer dismisses the employee in breach of contract, the current view is that any post-termination restrictive covenants will be automatically unenforceable. The reasoning behind this is that if an employer has broken the terms of the contract of employment, it should not be allowed to rely on whatever terms of the contract it chooses.

Enforceability of restrictive covenants

Provided that they are carefully drafted, post-termination restrictions are potentially enforceable. Employers and their solicitors should ensure that they spend sufficient time drafting covenants which address the particular needs of the employer. Certain fundamentals must be satisfied in the process, including the legitimacy of the interest to be protected and the reasonableness of the restriction.

Protection of a legitimate interest

First, the employer must show that it has a legitimate business interest to protect, such as the business's goodwill, clients, confidential information or remaining senior or key employees. If the employer cannot establish that it has a genuine interest to protect, the covenant will not be enforceable.

Further clarification is provided by the statement of a judge in one case:

> The employer's claim for protection is based on the identification of some advantage or asset inherent in the business which can properly be regarded as, in a general sense, his property, and which it would be unjust to allow the employee to appropriate for his own purposes, even though he, the employee, may have contributed to its creation. For while it may be true that an employee is to be entitled – and is to be encouraged – to build up his own qualities of skill and experience, it is equally his duty to develop and improve his employer's business for the benefit of his employer. These two obligations interlock during his employment: after its termination they diverge and mark the boundary between what the employee may take with him and what he may legitimately be asked to leave behind with his employers.

The dividing line between a legitimate interest, which is protectable, and skill and know-how, which are not, is often a fine one. (See the example of the accountant on page 131.)

Clients

Existing clients or customers are capable of constituting a legitimate interest. This is particularly the case where the employer can show that it has built up a good relationship with the client and that the employee has gained influence with the client only through working for the employer. However, this is not always the case.

CASE HISTORY: Recruitment consultancy

A firm of recruitment consultants tried to prevent a former employee from poaching a client, relying on a non-poaching clause contained in his contract of employment. It was established that the client, a firm of solicitors, always used several recruitment consultants when it was looking for staff. The court therefore decided that in these circumstances the employer did not have a legitimate interest to protect because the client did not have any special relationship with that particular firm of recruitment consultants.

Employees

There has been some debate as to whether employees may be considered to be capable of constituting a legitimate interest. One judge took the view that non-poaching clauses in respect of staff were unenforceable as an employer's staff were not 'stock in trade' like 'apples and pears'. Since then a series of court rulings have supported the view that key employees are capable of qualifying as a legitimate proprietary interest capable of protection.

Reasonable restriction of ex-employees

Once employers have shown that there is a legitimate interest to protect, they must then show that the restriction put in place to protect the interest is reasonable – in other words that it is no more restrictive than necessary.

The courts are usually very reluctant to enforce a blanket non-compete clause (see page 135) where they believe that a milder form of restraint would suffice. For example, if the employer has a genuine concern about a former employee poaching its customers for a rival business, the legitimate interest is the client connection and a non-poaching clause (see page 135) should be sufficient to protect the client base. In these circumstances a clause preventing the employee from working for any competitor would be considered too restrictive and would be unenforceable because it would unnecessarily restrict the employee's ability to find another job.

Employers commonly try to prevent their former employees from competing within a certain distance of their business by using non-compete clauses. A typical clause may say that the employee will not, for a certain period of time, work for any competitor within a five-mile radius of the former employer's business. Again, such a clause will be upheld only if it is reasonable and in each case it will depend on the circumstances (see below).

Example A solicitor is prevented from working for a competitor within a five-mile radius of her employer's premises.

If the solicitor's employer's office were based in a remote area where there were few clients, such a restriction might be deemed reasonable. However, if the solicitor's former employers were based in central

London it would not be considered fair. This is because owing to the concentration of law firms in the capital, the clause would effectively prevent the solicitor from working for a very large number of potential employers. In such a case, a non-poaching clause relating to clients (see page 135) would be a more appropriate way to protect the employer's interests.

The restrictive covenant must be reasonable in the light of the legitimate interest the employer wishes to protect (see above).

Compare these typical non-poaching restrictive covenants:

Example A

> The employee will not, for a period of six months from the termination of the employment, solicit custom for a business which competes with a business carried on by the employer at the termination date from any customer whom the employee had material dealings with or responsibility for at any time in the 12 months immediately preceding the termination of the employment.

Example B

> The employee will not, for a period of two years from the termination of the employment, solicit custom from any person who was a customer of the employer at any time in the 12 months immediately preceding the termination of the employment.

Only the first of these clauses would be likely to be upheld by a court. Clause A is potentially enforceable because the interest that it is attempting to protect is quite narrow and the restrictive covenant only has a life of six months. By contrast, clause B would not be enforced by a court – partly because of the over-long duration of the restriction (see box overleaf). In addition, clause B refers to 'any person who was a customer of the employer': unlike the first clause, there has been no attempt to make a connection between the employee and the client. In other words, clause B is attempting to prevent the employee from approaching *any* of the former employer's customers, even those that he or she had never met or formed a relationship with while at work.

Finally, clause A aims to prevent the employee from poaching customers for a competing business while clause B aims more broadly to prohibit the employee from doing business with 'any person who was a customer of the employer'. One interpretation of clause B, then, is that if the employee were to leave employment as, say, a hairdresser and to join, say, an ice-cream company, he or she would be banned from selling ice-cream to his or her old employer's customers. In these circumstances the court would not enforce clause B as it would take the view that the old employer's business and the employee's new activities were totally unrelated.

Hence, *there are no guarantees that a restrictive covenant will be enforceable*. As explained above, restrictive covenants must be reasonable to stand a chance of succeeding, and it is not sufficient for an employer to point out that an employee signed a contract agreeing to the inclusion of such restrictions.

Length of time of restriction
One year is, in normal circumstances, the top limit of what is considered acceptable for restrictive covenants.

Garden leave clauses

Given the uncertainty regarding the enforceability of restrictive covenants, a more subtle form of restriction known as a 'garden leave clause' has become popular with some employers. These clauses are typically seen in the job contracts of sales staff, recruitment consultants, professionals and others workers who have regular contact with the employer's client base and who may attempt to take clients or staff to a new employer.

This type of clause gives the employer the right, during a notice period (given either by the employer or the employee) to require the employee to serve out the notice at home, while avoiding contact with the employer's clients and his or her work colleagues. During this notice period, the employee will continue to be paid in the normal way and to enjoy any fringe perks such as the use of a car, private medical insurance or pension contributions (see pages 48–53).

The advantage for the employer is that this can effectively prevent the employee from working for a competitor during the notice period *or* from poaching employees or clients. This is because the employee remains bound by the duty of good faith and loyalty, which prevents him or her from taking any action which would threaten the employer's interests (see page 71).

Clearly, the longer the notice period to which the employee is subject, the more effective the garden leave clause will be. It is for this reason that usually only more senior employees with longer notice periods are subject to garden leave clauses. (For more on the notice period, see pages 45 and 65.)

To date, only a limited number of cases involving garden leave clauses have reached the courts. The increased use of such clauses has heightened speculation that the circumstances in which they are enforceable will soon be closely examined.

Failure to pay an employee on garden leave

An employer which failed to pay an employee during garden leave would leave itself open to a claim that it was in breach of contract. The worker could decide to treat him- or herself as having been constructively dismissed, in which case he or she could sue for compensation for breach of contract and, if he or she had the necessary qualifying service, unfair dismissal (see Chapter 10). In addition, any restrictive covenants in the contract of employment would be unenforceable as a result of the employer's breach of contract.

Employee joins another employer before the end of the garden leave period

The issue here is whether the employer can enforce the garden leave clause. In considering whether to enforce a clause when an employee wants to leave before the notice period has expired, the court must balance two factors: the real danger posed to the employer's business by a breach of the clause, and the potential damage caused to the employee's career prospects as a result of a period of enforced idleness.

> **The relationship between garden leave clauses and restrictive covenants**
>
> Until recently, it was commonly believed that if employees were placed on garden leave for lengthy periods of time, any post-termination restrictions due to come into play at the end of the employment would either be unenforceable or shortened owing to the duration of the period served out on garden leave. However, in a case involving financial brokers departing to join a rival organisation, it was held that the post-termination restrictive covenants were still potentially enforceable despite the brokers having already served a considerable period of time on garden leave.

Breach of a restrictive covenant or garden leave clause

Exactly how much of a risk an employee takes by failing to comply with the terms of a agreement will depend on a range of factors, including:

- the enforceability of the clauses
- the seriousness of the breach
- the willingness of the employee and the new boss to fight the action
- the old employer's financial resources.

Even if the former employer has been advised that the agreement is unenforceable, its first step is likely to be sending a threatening letter in order to intimidate the employee. The employer is unlikely to resort to court proceedings without first providing the employee with a warning. Workers who receive a threatening letter of this sort should immediately take the issue up with their present employer and, if necessary, try to extract a promise that if the former employer does bring an action, the new employer will meet any legal costs incurred fighting the claim and any damages that may be awarded against the employee. In many cases the issue never gets to court, either because the old employer is relying on agreements that are too widely drafted or because the risks associated with bringing an action do not justify the effort (legal costs can very quickly run into thousands of pounds).

Employees' attempts to circumvent restrictions

One tactic employees intending to poach their old employer's customers sometimes use to good effect is to ask the customers who have agreed to come with them to write to the old employer asking it to confirm that it has no objection to the former employee working for the customer. If the customers agree, the old employer is left with a real practical dilemma, even if the restrictive covenants are enforceable, because it is unlikely that the customers will return to the employer if it takes action to prevent the old employee working for them.

Damages

If an employee breaks the terms of an enforceable restrictive covenant or garden leave clause, he or she will be in breach of contract and the employer will be entitled to sue for damages. Damages are calculated by reference to the loss suffered by the former employer.

CASE HISTORY: Felicity

Felicity worked as a secretary. After being entrusted to secrecy, she leaked confidential information about her boss's bid for a contract to a competitor. As a result of her action, her employer lost the contract. Felicity was dismissed, and her employer sued for compensation equal to the profit that he would have made on the contract.

CASE HISTORY: James

After working for a firm of recruitment consultants for several years, James left his employers to join a rival firm and, in breach of his restrictive covenant, stole some of his former company's clients. His ex-employers were able to sue for compensation equal to the profit that the firm would have achieved had those clients not been poached by James.

The case histories above are straightforward: however, it is often very difficult for the employer to show precisely what loss has been suffered as a result of the employee's breach, and the employee may be unable to pay compensation. This is why some employers are often more anxious to obtain a court order restraining employees from breaking the terms of their contract of employment (see below) than they are to deal with the consequences of breach after the event.

If the employee has already left and/or demonstrated a complete disregard of whatever restrictions the employment contract contained, the employer should consider an urgent application to court for the obligations to be enforced by an injunction.

Injunctions

An injunction is a court order compelling a party to do something (a **mandatory injunction**) or restraining a party from doing something (a **prohibitory injunction**). An injunction can be granted either to rectify an offending activity that has commenced (such as an employee setting up in competition) or to prevent something happening (such as the leaking of confidential information). It is normally necessary to consult a solicitor in order to obtain one (see Chapter 17).

A permanent order will usually only be made once both parties have been heard in court. However, in urgent circumstances the court will sometimes grant an **interim injunction**, while it considers whether there is a case for granting a permanent injunction. Although these interim injunctions are only temporary, in many cases the parties are inclined to accept the court's decision at this stage as an indication of what could happen if the matter were to go to a full court hearing.

If an interim injunction is granted before a full hearing and consideration of the case, the employer must promise to compensate the ex-employee if it later fails to establish its right to the injunction.

Employers cannot get an injunction as of right. The court decides whether it is appropriate to make such an order.

In employment cases, injunctions are primarily used to protect an employer's business in the following situations:

- to restrain a former employee from breaking the terms of a valid restrictive covenant
- to restrain an employee or ex-employee from revealing confidential information or trade secrets.

The court is much less likely to grant an injunction if the employer, once it is aware of some breach of a restrictive covenant, fails to take immediate action.

Applications for an injunction can be made without giving formal notice to the opponent if the matter is urgent and giving notice would delay matters, or if there is a need to maintain the element of surprise. In extreme cases a judge will hear an application for an interim injunction outside court hours, even at his or her home.

Interdicts in Scotland

In Scotland, **interdicts** are court orders used in similar circumstances to injunctions. However, they are only available to prohibit or restrain a party from doing something. In urgent circumstances the court may grant an **interim interdict**.

The 'Anton Piller' order

In England and Wales, an 'Anton Piller' order is the hydrogen bomb in the employer's arsenal. The purpose of an Anton Piller order is to preserve evidence which the employee might otherwise remove or destroy. Such an order allows an employer to enter an employee's premises and search for and seize relevant documents and property. In employment cases, these orders will most often be used where the plaintiff, often an ex-employer, has good reason to believe that a former employee may have stolen documents or other confidential information in contravention of an agreement. Although forcible entry is not allowed because this order is not the same as a search warrant, if an employee fails to comply he or she can be held in contempt of court and liable to a fine or even imprisonment in extreme cases.

Because the element of surprise is vital, the application is usually made without reference to the employee, who may know nothing about it until his employer's solicitor appears on his or her doorstep.

Before a court will grant such an order, it must be satisfied that:

- the employer has, at first glance, a strong case – the order cannot be used as a 'fishing expedition' on the off-chance that something may be discovered
- the employee's activities pose potential or actual harm to the employer's interests
- there is clear evidence that the defendant has the items in his or her possession and there is a real danger that they will be removed or

destroyed before a full hearing can be held with both parties present.

Some of the following are typically contained in an Anton Piller order:

- an order restraining the defendant from warning any third parties that the order has been granted. This would normally be granted when more than one location needs to be searched and the employer does not want the employee to warn accomplices
- an order directing the employee to allow his or her premises to be searched and to reveal the whereabouts of items listed in the order. This also authorises the plaintiff to remove or copy the specified items, including information stored on computer
- a demand that the employee must disclose the names and addresses of any other person who may be involved in his or her activities: for example, customers or suppliers.

Because of the draconian nature of the Anton Piller order, it will granted only in extreme circumstances – where, for example, an employee has secreted highly confidential information in order to set up in competition and is likely to destroy the evidence.

Warrant for delivery in Scotland

In Scotland employers can request a court order obliging the employee to deliver up the relevant property, and can ask that a search warrant be granted to Sheriff Officers, enabling them to search the employee's premises.

Alternative ways for employers to protect their interests

Because of the legal difficulties sometimes associated with enforcing either garden leave clauses or restrictive covenants or both, certain forms of practical restrictions, some of them in the shape of financial incentives, can be used:

- **deferred bonuses** paid half-way through the following year (provided the employee is still employed and not under notice as at the due date of payment). The idea is that the employee will always have an incentive to remain with the employer because another bonus payment will soon become due

- **share option schemes** under which employees who have been with the company for a number of years earn the right to purchase shares

- **'good behaviour' payments** to employees, paid by monthly instalments following the termination of their employment. These payments are dependent on the employee not breaching any of the post-termination restrictions. An arrangement of this type is very effective, if the employee is prepared to agree to it, as the employee has a strong incentive not to break the terms of the restrictive covenants

- **ensuring that no one employee deals exclusively with customers during his or her term of employment** This policy reduces the possibility of one employee being able to entice a valued customer away

- **ensuring tight control over access to confidential information** (see page 132)

- **ensuring the return of property** The employer should ensure that employees have in their contracts of employment an obligation to deliver up all documents, computer disks (together with all copies) and other property on the termination of employment

- **cultivating a happy workforce** For some employers, the best way to protect their business is much simpler – to ensure that the employees are content. If employees feel motivated and rewarded, so the theory goes, they should not want to go elsewhere.

Maintaining effective restrictive covenants

If intending to rely on restrictive covenants in their employees' contracts of employment, employers should be aware that these will only stand a chance of being enforced if they reflect the current state of the law. This means that they should be reviewed regularly by lawyers.

The following chapter deals with what happens to employees on the sale of a business.

Chapter 8

Employees' rights on the sale of a business

Almost every day, an employer decides to sell up its business. In some cases the businesses are multi-billion-pound companies traded on the Stock Exchange. More often they are small, family-owned shops and restaurants. Whatever the size of the business the employees' concerns are usually the same: how will it affect me, and what rights do I have?

There are three distinct forms of business:

- a **sole trader** such as a corner shop or a garage where the employer is the owner of the shop or garage
- a **partnership**: typical examples are firms of accountants, solicitors and surveyors. The employer in this case is every member of the partnership. If an employee is dismissed without justification, he or she can sue each partner individually or all of them together for compensation
- a **company** (represented by a board of directors), which differs from a sole trader or a partnership in that it has a separate legal identity of its own. In other words it is treated as a person. It can sue or be sued. If an employee is dismissed without justification by a company, he or she cannot sue the main shareholder and owner of the company but must instead sue the company itself because it is the 'person' who employed him or her.

Selling a company

A company can be sold in one of two ways.

Sharesale

In a sharesale, some or all of the company's shares are sold, with the result that the identity of the majority shareholder (and ultimate owner) changes. Even though the identity of the shareholder changes, the entity or body employing the employees does not alter. Therefore the employees remain employed on exactly the same terms and conditions of employment.

Business sale

Alternatively, the company's business can be sold as opposed to its shares. Typically, the business will consist of assets such as a lease of premises, the goodwill of clients and stock, machinery or other equipment. As neither a sole trader's nor a partnership's business consists of shares, these businesses can be disposed of only by way of a business sale.

Statutory protection for employees in a business sale

In the past the business sale was a very effective way of dumping responsibility for the employees on to the seller. The buyer was absolved of any responsibility for the employees as they would be left behind in the remaining shell of the company. For example, a buyer which purchased the main components of the business, rather than its shares – its premises, customer lists, goodwill and equipment – would take control of all the important elements of the business. In this situation, although the owner of the shares in the company would remain the same, the firm would cease to constitute a viable business owing to the sale of its significant assets. The company would remain the employees' employer but the continued employment of the workforce would be insupportable and they would be made redundant on the grounds that the company, stripped of its business, no longer needed any employees.

Likewise, on the sale of a sole trader's or partnership business a buyer could purchase a viable business without any obligation to assume responsibility for the employees employed in that business, who remained the seller's responsibility and would invariably be made redundant.

A European law known as the Acquired Rights Directive (ARD) was introduced in 1977 with the purpose of providing employees with the same protection on a business sale as on a sharesale. In other words, a buyer of a business takes over not only the business but also the employees, and is expected to assume the same responsibility for them as it would if it were to buy the shares of a company. The British government was required to pass legislation to translate the ARD into UK law, which was accomplished by way of the **Transfer of Undertakings (Protection of Employment) Regulations 1981 (TUPE)**. A number of decisions by the European Court of Justice have led to TUPE applying not just on a business sale, but also in a range of other situations, including those where employers have outsourced or contracted-out certain business activities to third parties. Many cases have focused on the renewal of outsourcing agreements, particularly cleaning contracts.

Business sales to which TUPE applies

The application of TUPE is a particularly complex area of the law and is subject to frustratingly frequent re-interpretation as a result of decisions of the European Court of Justice (see above). The central issue of these judgments is what needs to be satisfied in order for TUPE to apply. A detailed analysis of these cases and their consequences would take a book in itself. However, it is mostly obvious whether TUPE will apply.

The test is whether the business in which the employee works will retain its identity after the transfer to the new owner or employer. As a result of many court cases, several factors that are significant when deciding whether a business has kept its identity have been established. These include:

- whether any assets are transferred
- whether employees are taken on
- the similarity of the activities carried out by the business before and after the transfer
- the length of interruption to the business's activities, if any.

In the vast majority of cases, the position is very clear.

Example An employer decides to sell a building business. He transfers the lease of the premises and outstanding contracts for work, plus all tools, stock and vehicles to a buyer who takes over the management of the business. The buyer then runs the business in substantially the same way as the former owner.

In this case, TUPE will almost certainly apply because essentially the same business continues: the only thing that has changed is its new owner.

Sale of a business to a third party to which TUPE applies

The new owner of the business becomes the new employer of the people who work for the business. This means that the new owner takes over responsibility for these employees (see 'Terms and conditions following a transfer', overleaf). However, any criminal liability the old employer may have in relation to the employees will not transfer. For example, if the old employer had been fined for failing to inform the Department of Trade and Industry of its intention to make 20 or more employees redundant (see page 186) that criminal liability would not be assumed by the new employer.

Transfer of employees in a business sale

TUPE makes clear that in a business sale (see page 149), certain conditions apply to the transfer of staff.

- **Only employees who are employed in the business immediately prior to the date of transfer will go with the new owner** 'Immediately' means literally hours before the handover. Because of this, employees who are redeployed to another part of the business the day before the sale will not transfer to the new owner. For example, an employer which has a business manufacturing bottles and cardboard boxes decides to sell the bottle-making part of the business. Only those employees employed in that part of the business as at the date when the sale is completed will transfer. Therefore if, prior to the completion of the sale, certain employees are redeployed from making bottles to boxes, they will not transfer as they will not have been employed in that part of the business transferred immediately prior to the date of transfer. Likewise, employees who are dismissed prior to the date of the handover will not be transferred, although liability for those dismissals may be. (See also

'Employees dismissed before the sale or transfer of the business', page 155.)

- **Employees must be employed in the part of the business being transferred** In many cases it is clear which workers satisfy this criterion. For example, if a shop is sold, all the shop assistants will be treated as being employed in the business transferred. However, if an employer which has a business employing 100 employees decides to sell half of it there may be some employees who have business-wide responsibilities which do not neatly fall into one part of the business or another. These employees might typically include receptionists, payroll clerks and members of the personnel department. In such circumstances it is less clear whether such employees are being transferred.

A number of court and industrial tribunal decisions provide some guidance on what constitutes employment in the business transferred. Factors to be considered include:

- the amount of time the employee spends working in different parts of the business
- what the employee's contract of employment says
- the value the employee places on one part of the business or the other.

In practice, both the buyer and the seller will usually analyse each employee's role and then with legal advice will make a decision on whether the employee should transfer.

Terms and conditions following a transfer

Just as in a share sale, employees will transfer to the new owner on exactly the same terms and conditions of employment as they enjoyed prior to the sale, with one exception (see box opposite). Because of this, employees are entitled to receive from the new employer the same notice period, salary and fringe benefits. Any liability for arrears of pay or holiday will transfer to the new employer. The qualifying service period for statutory purposes will also transfer. For example, if an employee has completed two years' continuous employment, this period of continuous service will automatically be added to any time served with the new employer. For more on employees' contractual rights and employers' obligations see Chapters 3 and 4.

Occupational pension scheme exception

If the employees are members of an employer's occupational pension scheme, the new owner of the business does not have to replicate those pension benefits. This exclusion relates only to occupational pension schemes set up by an employer for its employees, and not to personal pension plans taken out by employees to which the employer agrees to make contributions. The obligation to provide an occupational pension does not transfer because TUPE recognises the practical difficulty for new employers in replicating the pension benefits provided by the previous employer. For more details on pension arrangements, see pages 50–3.

New employer's ability to change terms and conditions

The question of whether the new employer can change an employee's terms and conditions is at the centre of an unresolved legal debate. What is clear is that the new owner would require the employee's consent in the normal way before making any significant changes to the contract of employment (see page 70). Failure to obtain such consent may leave the employer exposed to potential claims for constructive dismissal – see page 169.

However, new employers are often keen to buy-out some of the employees' fringe benefits, in order to bring the new, enlarged workforce together on the same terms and conditions of employment. Typically this could be done by offering employees comparable or superior benefits to those they are asked to give up, having first obtained their consent. In the past, it was thought that if employees agreed, following a transfer, to accept such a modified contract, they would not later be able to argue that they were not bound by the new terms. However, the law is in some confusion at present. The current position is that even if employees have agreed to accept changes to their job contracts, they will not be bound by those changes if they can show that the changes were introduced for a reason connected with the transfer of the business. Clearly, the closer changes are introduced to the transfer date the greater the likelihood is that the employee will be able to establish that the changes have been introduced for a reason connected with the transfer.

Example   A mechanic works at a garage. When it is sold, he transfers to the new owner by virtue of TUPE. His contract requires him to work 35 hours a week and he is paid time-and-a-half for any hours worked in excess of that 35-hour week. The new employer decides to increase the mechanic's salary by 20 per cent in return for him agreeing that he will no longer be paid for overtime worked. The mechanic accepts these terms. Two months later he is sacked, but in the interim he has worked on average 42 hours per week.

The mechanic could, in these circumstances, sue to recover the overtime payments he would have received under his old contract, by arguing that as the changes to overtime arrangements were introduced for a reason connected with the transfer, they were not binding.

Date of the transfer

The TUPE provisions are activated *when the person responsible for the day-to-day management of the business changes.* It does not matter what date the buyer and seller say the business should change hands: what is important is the date on which it actually occurs. For example, on the sale of a restaurant the significant date is not the date on the contract stating the completion of the sale, it is the date on which the new owner assumes management control of the workforce. This can be important, bearing in mind that only those employees who are employed in the business immediately prior to the transfer will become employees of the new owner (see page 151).

Employees' objections to being transferred

One of the most difficult concepts to grasp about the application of TUPE is that it happens automatically. So if a trader decides to sell its business, the employees working in that business will automatically become employees of the new owner. There is no legal requirement that employees need to agree to transfer. They may not even be aware that a transfer has taken place because everything happens so quickly that the employer does not have time to inform and consult the workforce (see page 157).

Example The owner of a pub is on the verge of going bankrupt when a buyer appears who is prepared to buy the business, provided the sale is completed within seven days and that negotiations remain secret.

In these circumstances, the business could be sold and the employees' contracts of employment transferred without the employees even being aware that a sale has taken place.

Employees can object to being transferred, however, if they are aware that a transfer is about to take place, but objecting is not advisable unless they have other jobs to go to. If an employee protests, this will be treated as a resignation, and he or she will therefore have no claim for compensation for breach of contract or unfair dismissal against either the old employer or the new owner of the business.

Employees' freedom to leave the new employer

It is worth remembering that those employees who are transferred are not bound indefinitely to the new employer, any more than they were to the previous one. They can resign with or without notice. If they leave without giving notice, technically they are in breach of contract, although in many cases employers are inclined to take the view that it is more trouble than it is worth to take any action against such employees.

Employees dismissed before the sale or transfer of the business

In many cases the new owner of a business may not wish to take over all of the old employer's staff. It may already have employees of its own that it knows and trusts, whom it wants to take over responsibility for the business. At first glance, the simplest policy, for the buyer, is to agree with the seller that the seller will dismiss the employees that the buyer does not want prior to the completion of the sale. The reasoning is that if TUPE applies only to those employees employed in the business immediately prior to the date of transfer, those who have been dismissed will not transfer and therefore the new owner will escape liability for them.

However, the courts have recognised the existence of this loophole and as a result have ruled that if employees are dismissed for a reason connected with a transfer, liability for the dismissal will not remain with the seller of the business but will transfer to the new owner. If the employee is dismissed without notice or justification, the liability will be made up of two parts, the first being a claim for breach of contract. The starting point for calculating this liability will be, basically, a sum equal to the value of the net salary and fringe benefits the employee would have received during the notice period. The second claim, provided the employee has over two years' continuous service with the employer (a limit that is expected to drop to one year as a result of government proposals – see box, page 176), is for unfair dismissal.

Claims for unfair dismissal in TUPE-related circumstances differ from other such claims in so much as, if the employee has been dismissed for a reason connected with the transfer, the dismissal will automatically be deemed to be unfair. At present compensation in respect of claims for unfair dismissal is made up of two parts: the basic award, which is calculated taking into account the employee's weekly salary, subject to a maximum of between £110 and £330 per week (depending on the employee's age), and the number of completed years of employment, subject to a maximum of 20 years; and the compensatory award, which is subject to a maximum of £12,000 (as a result of government proposals it is expected that this ceiling will be lifted – see page 189). See Chapters 10 and 11 for more information.

Dismissal for a reason unconnected with the sale or transfer

In this case, any liability to pay compensation will remain with the seller and the unfair dismissal claim will not automatically be treated as unfair. In other words, the employer will have an opportunity to justify the reason for dismissing the employee.

The issue of whether a dismissal was connected with a transfer of a business can be of immense importance, particularly if the old employer has become insolvent and is not able to pay any compensation. In such circumstances the employee will want to prove that the dismissal was connected with the transfer and that compensation is payable by the new owner of the business (see above).

In many cases it is not always clear whether dismissals have taken place as a result of the transfer. If the business was in financial difficulty prior to the sale, it is arguable that dismissals were inevitable, regardless of the sale. In many cases, ultimately only an industrial tribunal is able to decide on the status of the dismissal. Because of the uncertainty, and in order to protect themselves, employees who are dismissed prior to a sale of a business should submit claims against both the buyer and the seller. The industrial tribunal will then decide which party should assume liability for the dismissals. See Chapter 16 for advice on applying to an industrial tribunal.

Employees' right to information and consultation

Despite the fact that businesses are often sold during a very short time period, TUPE provides that, except where it is not practical (for example, where the business is sold by a receiver at a moment's notice), the seller and the buyer of the business should inform and consult with the employees who will be affected by the sale. Essential information would include, for example, details of when the transfer will take place and its implications for the workforce. The employer should also consult with the workforce on any changes anticipated as a result of the transfer of the business. Where appropriate, the buyer must provide the seller with information in order to enable the seller to inform and consult effectively.

The employer is not expected to inform and consult every employee individually, but is expected to liaise with recognised trade unions and staff associations, if appropriate (see Chapter 17). As an alternative, or where no such body exists, the employer may liaise with employee representatives elected by the workforce for the purpose of consultation. If the workforce has not appointed any employee representatives the employer should offer the employees an opportunity to nominate representatives.

The consultation period should start as soon as is reasonably practicable (this will vary depending on the type of transaction). If the employer fails to carry out its duties to inform and consult, employees will be entitled to compensation. The maximum amount that can be awarded to each employee is a sum equal to four weeks' actual pay (as opposed to the statutory limit of £220 applied to calculations of a week's pay when determining the basic award in unfair dismissal cases or statutory redundancy payments – see Chapter 11). However, the industrial tribunal has the discretion to decide on the precise amount, which will depend on the seriousness of the employer's shortcomings. For example, an employer that fails to inform and consult with its workforce when it has known for a considerable period of time that a transfer is to proceed would be much more likely to be penalised than an employer which has had to dispose of its business at very short notice and therefore did not have an adequate opportunity to carry out its duties to the full. Claims must be submitted to an industrial tribunal within three months of the date of transfer.

Additional help

For further information useful leaflets are: *Employees' Information and Consultation Rights on Transfers of Undertakings and Collective Redundancies* from DTI Employment Relations Directorate;* and *Employment Rights on the Transfer of an Undertaking* (PL699) from DTI Publications Orderline.*

Chapter 9

Termination of employment

The final stage of the employment relationship is often traumatic for the employee and the employer. The employment relationship can be brought to an end in a variety of ways, not all of which will automatically give rise to a claim by one party against the other for compensation. These include:

- by notice (see below)
- by mutual agreement (see page 164)
- on the expiry of a fixed-term or fixed-task contract (see page 164)
- by frustration (see page 166)
- by breach (employer's or employee's) – see page 167.

For details of what happens at the termination meeting, see Chapter 12.

Termination by notice

This is the route by which most contracts of employment are most commonly terminated, in one of two ways:

- the employee resigning (see page 162)
- the employer dismissing the employee (see page 163).

The amount of notice will depend on what the contract of employment provides (see page 45). In most cases the employer and the employee are usually expected to give each other an equal length of notice.

The position may be different where senior executives are involved. They might be entitled to receive a two-year notice period but will try to reduce the notice period they are expected to give to six months. Likewise, those working overseas may want to commit the employer to giving a long period of notice while reserving an early get-out clause for themselves. However, if the contract contains no notice period or the employee does not have a written contract of employment, other factors come into play. The **Employment Rights Act 1996** imposes a statutory minimum period of notice to which both the employer and the employee are subject (see page 65). In addition, if the employee has no contract of employment or the contract contains no notice period, a period of 'reasonable notice' will be assumed by the legal custom known as common law (see page 66).

Form of notice

Contracts of employment will often provide clear rules as to how notice should be served. Typically, a job contract will say that the notice should be in writing and either given personally to the relevant party or delivered by post, in the case of the employee to his or her last known address and in the case of the employer to its main business address. Contracts often state that notices can be sent by fax.

Pay-in-lieu-of-notice clauses

Some employers include a pay-in-lieu-of-notice clause in their contract of employment. This clause provides them with the right, during any notice period given by either the employer or the employee, to pay the employee a sum (usually an amount equal to the value of the salary and fringe benefits the employee would have received during the notice period) as an alternative to requiring him or her to work out the notice period. The advantage for the employer is that in such circumstances the contract can lawfully be terminated early, thereby ensuring that any restrictive covenants contained in the contract which continue to have effect after the employment has ended will remain potentially enforceable. These ongoing obligations typically relate to issues such as the poaching of customers or employees. (See Chapter 7 for more detail.)

In the absence of a pay-in-lieu-of-notice clause, if the employee were dismissed without notice, the employer would technically be in breach of contract – even if the employee were paid an amount equal to the salary and benefits that he or she would have received during the notice period – and any post–termination restrictive covenants would therefore be unenforceable.

Heat-of-the-moment terminations

Many contracts of employment do not say how notice must be served. Usually this is not a problem because employers and employees make their positions clear either by writing a letter, giving notice or simply telling the other party at a meeting that the employment is at an end. But sometimes people express a wish to terminate the employment in the heat of the moment.

For example, in one case an employer, after an argument, ordered his employee out of his office with the words, 'Get out, get out'. Did this amount to a dismissal or was it merely an order to get out of his office? In another case the employer used the words 'You're finished with me'. In both these cases it was held that because of the particular circumstances the employer had not intended the remark to constitute a dismissal.

Likewise, an employee might in a moment of anger say 'I resign' or 'I am leaving'. If an employee clearly and unambiguously resigns the employer is entitled to accept that resignation. However, case law shows that both employers and employees may be excused momentary outbursts. For example, one employee resigned in the course of an argument. After he had calmed down, he tried to retract the resignation but the employer refused to accept it. It was decided that in these circumstances the employee was entitled to withdraw the resignation and that any attempt by the employer to refuse to accept the retraction would be treated as an unjustified dismissal.

The advice, therefore, for both employers and employees, is that if either party says something in the heat of the moment which could be taken to terminate the employment, he or she should, at the earliest possible opportunity, retract the statement if he or she wants the employment to continue. Likewise, the party on the receiving end of the outburst should, when the smoke has cleared and the other party is calm and rational, ascertain whether the relationship is really at an end.

Resignation by the employee

Employees intending to resign should follow the correct procedure for giving notice and try to avoid heat-of-the-moment terminations (see above). By resigning, employees may lose certain rights, as described below.

Effect on statutory rights

Once the resignation takes effect the employee's employment is terminated and the employee will not be able to transfer the period of continuous employment accrued with the old employer to another for the purposes of calculating eligibility for certain benefits, such as the right to a statutory redundancy payment (see page 191), statutory maternity pay (see page 108) or protection against unfair dismissal, unless the employers are associated companies.

Effects on contractual rights

Employees should also consider what impact resigning might have on any contractual benefits they receive from their old employer:

- **bonus schemes** Some employers, particularly in the City of London, operate bonus schemes which require employees to be employed, and not under notice, at the date of payment. Employees who participate in bonus schemes of this type should ensure that the timing of when they serve notice will not prejudice any bonus entitlement

- **commission** Sales personnel often have commission arrangements which pay up long after the order has been secured: for example, recruitment consultants usually receive commission payments only after job candidates have completed a certain period of employment with their new employer. Workers who are entitled to commission should check what the position is in relation to these payments if they leave before payment becomes due.

Withdrawal of a resignation letter

Resignation letters can be withdrawn only with the employer's consent. Once the employee has served notice, he or she has no automatic right to withdraw the resignation and remain in employment. Many employers may be reluctant to agree to withdraw a resignation letter once an employee has shown that he or she is not fully committed to the business in which he or she has been working.

Inadequate notice given by the employee

Often, particularly during an economic upturn, or if the company is short-staffed, the employee's new employer will be keen for the worker to start as soon as possible, even if this means the employee leaving before the end of the notice period.

Technically speaking, if the employee leaves before the notice period runs out he or she is in breach of contract and the employer could sue for damages. The damages would be calculated on the basis of the loss suffered by the employer as a result of the employee failing to serve out the notice. In reality, the loss suffered is often difficult to establish. Typically it might include the difference between the employee's salary for the notice period and the cost of getting in an agency worker to cover until the end of the notice period. In a very few cases the employer, particularly where very senior employees are involved, may be able to establish that it suffered a much greater loss – for example, if it could show that a crucial contract had been lost as a result of an executive's early departure.

However, in most circumstances there is little that employers can do unless they are prepared to go to court and sue for damages. No employer can force an employee to work out his or her notice. Going to court is an expensive option which employers should take only when they are worried that the employee's early departure will damage their business activities.

Prospective employers should not encourage employees to break their contracts: if they do, they commit the wrong of inducing a breach of contract and could be exposed to a claim for damages from the current employer. The practical difficulty for the current employer is that of proving that actual financial loss was suffered as a result of the employee leaving without having given proper notice, and establishing that the employee's new employer encouraged the employee's action.

Dismissal of the employee by the employer

When an employee is dismissed, attention must focus on two separate and distinct sets of rights: contractual claims and statutory claims (see page 173).

If the employer gives inadequate notice to the employee, the employer will, in these circumstances, be in breach of contract (see page 168).

As with a resignation letter, the employer cannot withdraw a dismissal notice without the employee's consent. Once the employer has served a dismissal notice, it has no automatic right to withhold that notice and to require the employee to remain in employment.

Termination by mutual agreement

An employer and an employee can agree that the employment contract will terminate automatically in certain pre-determined situations. For example, in the case of a senior executive this might be a takeover of the company he or she works for.

In these circumstances, executives usually want their contracts not only to say that the employment will end automatically but that it will entitle them to an immediate and generous pay-off. These types of clauses are known as 'golden parachutes'.

These termination-by-agreement clauses are not restricted to senior executives. Some top footballers, for example, reserve the right to terminate their contracts with a particular club if, at the end of a season, the club drops out of a particular league or fails to qualify for a European tournament.

Agreement not to claim compensation

Where the employer and employee mutually agree to an immediate termination of the employment in certain pre-determined situations then neither party will have a claim against the other for compensation unless the contract of employment specifically provides for such a payment.

Expiry of a fixed-term or fixed-task contract

A fixed-term contract is one that is granted for a pre-determined period of time such as three, six or nine months (see page 19). Often, the contract can be renewed if both parties are happy that the relationship is working out – for example, the contracts of teachers and lecturers are reviewed at the end of the academic year. The fixed-term contract differs in this respect from the usual so-called 'rolling contract'. A rolling contract is just another name for the most common type of contract which can be terminated at any time on the service of an agreed length of notice (see Chapter 3).

A fixed-term contract should have a clear start and end date. The employer is under no obligation to give the employee notice when the contract is about to come to an end, but in practice most employers do remind employees, if only to ensure that they return all property belonging to the employer, such as a computer, a uniform or a company car.

The expiry of a fixed-term contract does not constitute a dismissal by the employer for contractual purposes. Provided the employer has honoured all of its obligations under such a contract, such as paying salary, holiday pay and expenses, the employee will have no further contractual claim against the employer.

Statutory claims for unfair dismissal

The coming to an end of a fixed-term contract will constitute a dismissal for statutory provisions and therefore may give rise to a claim for unfair dismissal depending on whether the employee has the necessary period of continuous service (see Chapter 10). However, employees who would otherwise qualify for the right to bring a claim for unfair dismissal will lose that right if they have previously agreed to contract-out of such rights (see page 178). Employers commonly require this when asking employees to sign long-term fixed-term contracts.

Fixed-task contracts

Fixed-task contracts are not very common because it is much more difficult to establish exactly when a task has been completed and the contract thereby terminated, but they do exist. Building contractors, for example, sometimes employ engineers or architects to work on a specific project until its completion. Academics are sometimes recruited to work in art galleries or museums while an exhibition is in progress, and if its end date is extended their contracts may be allowed to continue accordingly. Likewise, some TV companies recruit researchers or presenters to work on a series of programmes until such time as it ends.

On the completion of a fixed-task contract, as for a fixed-term contract, the employee will have no contractual claim. Nor, however, will the employee have a potential claim for unfair dismissal because the coming to an end of a fixed-task contract is not treated as a dismissal for the purposes of the laws governing unfair dismissal. However, if a fixed-task contract was terminated for some reason other than it coming to an end, the employee may have a claim for unfair dismissal (see Chapter 10).

Termination by frustration

Frustration occurs when a contract of employment can no longer continue because of unforeseen circumstances, such as death.

Example An employee commits an offence and is imprisoned.

Broadly, the longer the prison sentence the greater the possibility of establishing that the contract has been frustrated. However, much may depend on the employee's responsibilities and the length of contract. For example, if the employee was a chief engineer employed on a fixed-term contract to work on a project for one year but was sentenced to six months in prison, it could be argued that the contract had been frustrated because he would only be available for half the term of the contract. There would be less scope for arguing that the contract had been frustrated if the employee imprisoned was a casual worker employed on a contract giving him four weeks' notice, because his absence for a period of time would not make it impossible for the contract to be performed. In these circumstances, although the employer could argue that the contract was frustrated he or she could still simply terminate it by dismissing the employee.

CASE HISTORY: Joe

While working as an apprentice in a manufacturing firm, Joe was sentenced by a court to a period of between six months and two years in a young offenders' institution. The court decided that his employer was entitled to treat the contract as having been frustrated.

If a contract of employment is terminated as a result of frustration there will be no breach and therefore no claim for compensation by either employee or employer.

Termination by breach

This occurs in circumstances where the contract of employment is terminated because one of the parties has broken its terms.

Employee's breach

In certain situations the employer may be entitled to terminate the contract of employment immediately, without notice, because the employee has breached the terms of the contract. The contract may state specific circumstances such as:

- gross misconduct or gross negligence (see below)
- conviction of a criminal offence
- persistent breaches of the contract of employment
- conduct likely in the opinion of the employer to bring either the employee or employer into disrepute
- unauthorised disclosure of confidential information.

In the case of types of misconduct not specifically mentioned in the contract, staff handbook or similar document, the employer can still dismiss without notice. The employer needs only to establish that the employee has committed a breach of contract which is so serious that it is sufficient to entitle the employer to terminate the employment. It is not possible to provide a comprehensive list of the type of behaviour that justifies dismissal. The general rule is that the more serious the breach, the more likely it is to justify dismissal without notice. Likewise, dismissal may be the result not just of one incident but of a succession of more minor incidents. In other words, one relatively minor misdemeanour may be the final straw which justifies the dismissal of the employee without notice. If the employee has the requisite qualifying service (see page 176), the employer must be able to show that fair procedure has been followed in selecting the employee for dismissal if it is to avoid an unfair dismissal claim.

Gross misconduct and gross negligence

In an employer's staff handbook the definition of what constitutes gross misconduct will typically include: theft, racial or sexual harassment, drunkenness or drug abuse and assault (see also pages 179–80). Gross negligence would apply in a situation where the employee has, say, completely ignored established safety procedures, resulting in a serious accident.

Delay by the employer in taking action

If the employer procrastinates before dismissing the employee, that employee may be able to argue that the employer has, by virtue of the delay, waived the right to take any action. For this reason, employers are usually expected to act quickly once they have all the relevant facts in order to justify immediate dismissal.

Sometimes employees may be able to delay the employer implementing a dismissal on grounds of misconduct if they can point to a disciplinary procedure which the employer is under a contractual obligation to exhaust prior to dismissing them.

Employer's claim for damages

If the employee is dismissed by the employer as a result of the employee's breach of contract, the employer will have a claim for damages provided that it can establish the loss that has been suffered. In cases of serious misconduct, this may be easily calculated – for example, if the employee has sold confidential information to a rival or maliciously damaged company property. The problem, as always, is that the employer may ultimately have to take legal action to enforce these rights and this will only be prudent where the employee has sufficient money to ensure that any award made against him or her will be honoured.

Employer's breach

The most common breach of contract committed by employers is failure to give the employee adequate notice of the termination of employment. Termination as a result of the employer's breach has three consequences:

- it will give rise to a claim for damages for wrongful dismissal (sometimes known as unlawful dismissal – see Chapter 10)
- it will give rise to a potential claim for unfair dismissal (see Chapter 10)
- it will invalidate any post-termination restrictive covenants contained in the contract of employment such as confidentiality or non-poaching clauses (see Chapter 7).

Constructive dismissal

This term often causes confusion in people's minds. In reality, all it means is a situation where an employee treats him- or herself as having been dismissed as a result of the employer committing (or making clear its intention to commit) a serious breach of contract.

Once the employee has treated him- or herself as having been constructively dismissed, he or she has, like any other employee dismissed without notice in breach of contract, a potential claim for wrongful dismissal and a potential claim for unfair dismissal (see Chapter 10).

The breach of contract *must* be serious: in order for an employee to succeed with a claim of constructive dismissal, the employee must in effect be able to show that the employer has acted in a way that shows that it no longer intends to abide by the terms of the contract.

Behaviour by an employer that would typically justify an employee treating him- or herself as having been constructively dismissed may include:

- imposing a significant pay cut
- demotion
- withdrawing benefits such as a pension scheme or a company car
- humiliating the employee in front of other employees
- suspension without pay
- false accusations of misconduct
- relocation where the contract of employment does not include a mobility clause
- racial or sexual harassment.

The employer does not necessarily have to have breached the contract in order for a claim to succeed. It is enough for the employee to show that the employer had a firm intention to break the terms of the contract. For example, if an executive receives a memo which says that in three months he will lose responsibility for his department, the executive can use this as evidence that the employer no longer intends to be bound by the terms of the contract. In contrast, if an employer proposes the introduction of pay cuts subject to agreement with the affected employees, this would not normally constitute sufficient grounds to establish an anticipatory breach of contract as the employer would not have made an irrevocable decision to proceed.

Establishing a claim for constructive dismissal

Employees should look for and retain any evidence which shows that the employer has broken or intends to break the terms of the contract. Clearly the evidence will vary depending on the circumstances. In some cases it will be obvious: for example, if a waiter in a restaurant were demoted to being a dishwasher or an executive were deprived of her company car, each would have an arguable case. However, in other instances where more serious breaches of contract arise, such as bullying or harassment, the task of gathering evidence may take longer. The employee may need to record the times and places at which the bullying took place together with evidence of any efforts made by the employee to get the employer to deal with the problem. Likewise, copies of all incriminating memos should be retained and notes kept of damaging conversations.

Changes imposed unilaterally by the employer

Employees should not automatically agree to accept any changes detrimental to their position imposed unilaterally by their employer unless happy to do so. This is because if employees do not raise any objection to actions which undermine their position they potentially leave themselves exposed to an argument that they have accepted the changes that have been imposed. As a result, they risk losing the right to treat themselves as having been constructively dismissed.

Employees who decide to treat themselves as constructively dismissed must act within a 'reasonable' period of time. What is reasonable varies depending on the circumstances. In most situations employees would be ill-advised to delay for more than three weeks. However, in some cases, particularly where the employee is long-serving, the courts may consider a longer period of reflection reasonable.

Employees' options following employer's breach of contract

Although employees are allowed a reasonable period of thinking time (see above), ultimately they must decide how to proceed. The options are as follows:

- to stay and accept the changes
- to stay and sue for damages for breach of contract
- to leave and sue for wrongful dismissal (and unfair dismissal if eligible).

Those employees who decide to treat themselves as constructively dismissed (as opposed to staying with the employer) must walk out and sue for damages for breach of contract and, if applicable, unfair dismissal (see Chapters 10 and 11). This means that they immediately cease to be employed and, if the employer refuses to reach a swift settlement, face the prospect of being without any further money until they find another job. Anyone considering taking such action should therefore consider the financial consequences very carefully. No former employer facing potential claims for wrongful and/or unfair dismissal is likely to be very willing to provide the former employee with a reference. Remember that an employer is not under any legal obligation to provide a reference (see page 36).

Employees should also bear in mind that the court may decide that the employer's actions did not amount to a breach of contract or, in the case of a claim for unfair dismissal, an industrial tribunal may decide that the employer acted reasonably in the circumstances.

Employees' ability to challenge changes without losing their jobs

Clearly the employee's options will to an extent depend on the nature of the employer's breach. For example, if the complaint relates to bullying or harassment the employee's first step should be to activate the employer's grievance procedure. If the changes involve a cut in pay or benefits there is nothing to prevent the employee from remaining in the job but at the same time suing the employer for damages (see page 191). The obvious risk with this course of action is that the employer may decide that it is simpler to dismiss the employee.

In many cases the reason for the employer introducing pay cuts or withdrawing benefits is not the employee's poor performance, but because the employer is in serious financial difficulties. Therefore the employee who recognises this and wants to keep his or her job *and* the employer's business alive may want to negotiate a compromise such as a temporary rather than a permanent pay cut or more holiday or reduced hours of work in return for less pay. The key is to be flexible.

However, in some cases, regardless of how flexible the employee is prepared to be, the employer is determined that the employment relationship should come to an end. The issue in such circumstances is what rights the employee has as a result of the employer's decision to dismiss him or her. For more information, see Chapter 10.

Chapter 10

Employees' rights on the termination of employment

The previous chapter looked at the various ways in which a contract of employment could be terminated. Employees who have been dismissed without compensation will first and foremost wish to know what their rights are and how they go about enforcing them.

Employees' rights on dismissal

Employees' rights on dismissal fall into two broad categories: those provided under the contract of employment and those provided by statute.

Contractual claims

Dismissals in breach of contract are known as '**wrongful**' or '**unlawful**'.

Statutory claims

Dismissals in breach of statute (except for dismissals as a result of discrimination – see Chapters 5 and 6) are known as '**unfair**', as provided for under the **Employment Rights Act 1996**.

Interrelationship between types of dismissal

In many situations, dismissed employees will have claims for both wrongful dismissal and unfair dismissal. It is also possible for an employee to have a claim for breach of contract (see page 168), but not for unfair dismissal.

A dismissal may be wrongful but not unfair

If an employee is dismissed without notice or justification, his or her contract will have been breached and the employee will have a potential claim for wrongful dismissal. However, unless he or she has completed a qualifying period of over two years' continuous employment (see below), he or she will not – save in certain limited circumstances (see page 177) – have a potential claim for unfair dismissal.

A dismissal may be unfair but not wrongful

For example, if an employee was given the correct period of notice under his or her contract of employment and worked that notice period out in full, he or she would not have a claim for breach of contract because the terms of the contract would have been complied with. However, were the employee to have completed over two years' continuous employment he or she may still potentially have a claim for unfair dismissal.

A dismissal may be neither wrongful nor unfair

An employee may be given the correct period of notice under his or her contract of employment, but may not have over two years' continuous service (as required before a claim for unfair dismissal can be pursued). Alternatively, the employee may have the necessary two years' qualifying service but the dismissal may be considered to be procedurally fair and justifiable, owing to the employee's conduct or performance.

Qualifying period for unfair dismissal

The two-year qualifying period is subject to challenge in the European Court of Justice and the government has in addition indicated a commitment to reduce the qualifying period to one year. All references to the two-year qualifying period are therefore subject to that qualification (see box, page 176).

Unfair dismissal

Certain employees are not eligible to bring a claim for unfair dismissal. These include:

- those ordinarily working outside Great Britain
- those who are self-employed

- members of the police and armed forces
- employees who have reached a settlement with their employer either through ACAS★ or on the basis of a compromise agreement (see page 213)
- those employed on fixed-term contracts which have expired, where the employee has previously waived his or her right to bring a claim for unfair dismissal (see page 178)
- employees who, before the dismissal date, have reached the employer's normal retiring age or the age of 65 (although this age limit has been the subject of challenges)
- masters and crew members whose pay consists of a share of the profits of a fishing boat.

Eligibility of part-time or agency workers

Provided they are employees, part-time or agency workers have the same rights as their full-time colleagues. The fact that they may work from home or work different or shorter hours is unimportant. There is no minimum number of qualifying hours required in any week for continuous employment.

A number of conditions must be satisfied in order to bring a claim for unfair dismissal.

- **The employee must be entitled to bring a claim** He or she must have been dismissed or be under notice of dismissal (see below) and should not fall within a category of employees excluded from bringing a claim (see above).
- **The employee must have been dismissed or be under a notice of dismissal** Employees who voluntarily resign, for example, will have no claim for unfair dismissal because a resignation is not a dismissal. If the employee could show that the resignation was forced – for example, if an employer gave a worker the choice of being dismissed or resigning and the employee chose resignation – the employee could still pursue a claim for unfair dismissal by arguing that the forced resignation was in reality a dismissal. Likewise, employees treating themselves as having been constructively dismissed (see page 169) could still claim unfair dismissal.

- **The employer must show that it had a 'fair' reason for dismissing the employee** and must prove that it acted reasonably in dismissing the employee (see page 182).
- **The employee must have completed the necessary qualifying period of employment** Except for a limited number of situations (see opposite) employees must, according to the **Employment Rights Act 1996**, have completed over two years' continuous employment as at the date of dismissal before they are able to bring a complaint of unfair dismissal to the industrial tribunal (but see box below).

Proposals to revise the qualifying period for unfair dismissal

The two-year qualifying period is currently subject to an appeal. In July 1995, two women challenged the requirement by arguing that it was indirectly discriminatory to women and as such was contrary to European law, the reason being that at the time when the two women were dismissed, in 1991, it was possible to show statistically that women were likely to change their jobs more regularly than men and that therefore the two-year qualifying period indirectly discriminated against them because they had less chance of gaining statutory protection. The case was initially sent to the House of Lords, which referred it to the European Court of Justice for a final ruling. Following a recent case, it was decided that all applications submitted by employees who have completed over one year's continuous employment will be stayed as opposed to struck off, until a decision is reached by the European Court of Justice. In May 1998 the government produced a White Paper entitled 'Fairness at Work' in which it indicated its commitment to introduce legislation reducing this qualifying period to one year.

Employees with more than one year's service but less than two

Employees in this position at the date of dismissal are advised, following the outcome of a recent Scottish case, to submit a claim to an industrial tribunal – see Chapter 16 – and to await the decision of the European Court of Justice regarding the legality of the two-year qualifying period (see above).

Situations to which the qualifying period of employment does not apply

In a limited number of situations employees are *not* required to have completed over two years' service in order to bring a claim for unfair dismissal. The most important of these are:

- trade union membership or refusal to become or remain a member of a trade union
- assertion of a statutory employment right (such as the right to receive a written Statement of Particulars of employment – see pages 68–9 – or an itemised payslip)
- pregnancy or any maternity-related reason
- refusal to do shop work or betting-related work on a Sunday.

Calculating the two-year qualifying period

The law currently states that the employee must have two years' continuous employment as at the **effective date of termination (EDT)**. The EDT is calculated as follows:

- if the employee is required to work out the notice period, the EDT will be the date on which the notice expires
- if the employee receives pay in lieu of notice instead of working out the notice period (see page 160), the EDT will be the last day on which the employee works
- if the employee is dismissed without notice in breach of contract, in calculating the EDT the employee will be entitled to add on the statutory (as opposed to contractual) notice period he or she should have received (see page 65)
- if the employee is dismissed without notice in accordance with the terms of the contract, the EDT will be the last day he or she works. This differs from the position outlined above in that the employee's contract of employment has been terminated lawfully
- if the contract of employment is a fixed-term contract, the EDT will be the date on which the contract expires.

Example An employee is entitled in his written contract of employment to three months' notice but is dismissed three days before he completes two years' continuous employment.

In this case, the employee would still have the necessary two years' qualifying service as the statutory minimum period of notice that should be added for the purposes of calculating the EDT is one week. (After one month, the employer is required to give the employee not less than one week's notice during the first two years of employment.)

Contracting out of unfair dismissal

An employer and an employee can agree that on the expiry and non-renewal of a fixed-term contract which lasts for at least a year the employee will have no claim for unfair dismissal. The agreement must be in writing, and will be binding only if the reason that the employment has terminated is because the contract has run its entire course.

Example An employee has a three-year, fixed-term contract which includes a waiver clause preventing her from bringing a claim at the end of the three-year term. After two-and-a-half years, she is dismissed by the employer.

Since the employee is dismissed two-and-a-half years into the contract, she will be able to claim unfair dismissal, as she has accrued over two years' of continuous employment. The waiver will therefore be ineffective because the employment did not terminate as a result of the contract reaching the end of its three-year life.

Time limit for submitting a claim

Employees must present any claim to an industrial tribunal within three months of the date of dismissal. For example, if an employee is dismissed on 1 March, the tribunal must normally receive the application on or before 31 May. Claims submitted late are usually time-barred and will only be considered in exceptional circumstances.

Applications are not usually allowed out of time. Applications for an extension of time have been refused where the reason for the delay is caused through:

- general ignorance of the law
- the employee awaiting the outcome of negotiations
- the employee awaiting the outcome of a court case.

Applications have, however, been allowed outside the time limit in certain circumstances, including:

- where inadequate advice was given by a member of the industrial tribunal staff; or
- there was an unreasonable delay in the post.

For advice on applying to an industrial tribunal, see Chapter 16. Employees can also consult *Unfairly Dismissed?* (PL712), a leaflet from DTI Publications Orderline.★

Establishing a successful claim

Once an employee has established that he or she has been dismissed and that he or she has the appropriate qualifying period of employment (see page 176), then unless the employer can show that the dismissal was for a fair reason, it will be deemed unfair.

Fair dismissal

A dismissal will normally be considered to be potentially fair if the employer can show that it was for one of the following reasons:

- the employee's misconduct
- the employee's lack of capability or qualifications for the job
- redundancy (broadly speaking, where the employer needs fewer people to run its business)
- a statutory requirement which prevented the employee from continuing to work (e.g. the lack of a valid work permit)
- some other substantial reason which could justify dismissal.

These categories cover a broad range of dismissal situations, but whatever the employer's reason for the dismissal, it will be carefully scrutinised.

Dismissal on grounds of misconduct

The main difference between dismissal on the grounds of conduct and dismissal owing to lack of capability (see overleaf) is that employees are usually in the position to improve their conduct, whereas they may simply not have the ability to improve their capability. Examples of unsatisfactory conduct can be very wide and typically include:

- theft
- assault
- racial or sexual harassment
- drunkenness
- disclosing confidential information
- abusive language
- refusal to obey orders
- lateness
- absenteeism.

Dismissal on grounds of capability

Typically, this covers circumstances where the employee is incompetent or does not have the necessary qualifications to carry out the job for which he or she is employed: for example, an employee who is unable to master the appropriate software for the company's computer systems in relation to his/her function, despite having been trained, or a salesman who consistently fails to make realistic sales targets set for him.

Redundancy

Contrary to popular belief, redundancy is just one form of dismissal, not a catch-all phrase to describe any dismissal. An employee is, broadly speaking, redundant when the employer requires fewer people to do the type of work the employee was employed to do. This may happen when, as a result of a reduction in orders, the employer cuts back on production, or, more drastically, the business collapses or closes and the entire workforce is no longer required.

See page 185 for information on what constitutes an unfair redundancy.

Dismissal on grounds of a statutory requirement which prevents the employee from continuing to work

Few dismissals are made on this ground. It may include circumstances where an individual does not have a legal right to work in the United Kingdom because he or she lacks a work permit, and it would constitute a breach of the **Asylum and Immigration Act 1996** for the employer to continue to employ that person (see Chapter 14), or where health and safety requirements prevent a pregnant employee from doing a particular job.

Other substantial reason

This catch-all provision is sometimes relied upon by employers who are uncertain as to whether any of the other grounds adequately explain why the employee has been selected for dismissal: perhaps the employee has refused to accept reasonable changes to his or her contract of employment (for example, a scientist who refuses to sign a confidentiality clause prior to starting work on his employer's secret project).

Industrial tribunals have taken the view that if there are good business reasons for the dismissal, a claim for unfair dismissal by the employee may not succeed. For example, if the re-organisation of a company required the termination of some employees' contracts of employment and their re-employment on different terms, a refusal of the new contract by the employees could amount to a fair dismissal. Likewise, if an employer changes an employee's work location, even though the employee may resign and claim damages for breach of contract, if the decision to relocate was taken for good business reasons this would usually be sufficient to prevent a claim for unfair dismissal succeeding. Industrial tribunals have also held that it can be fair to dismiss a worker if an employer's valued customer has threatened to withdraw its business unless the employee is dismissed.

When dismissing an individual on such grounds, the employer must ensure that fair procedure is followed (see overleaf).

Dismissals that are automatically unfair

In certain situations an employee may be able to establish that the dismissal is automatically unfair and the employer will have no defence.

Reasons for dismissals which are automatically unfair would include :

- those connected with the Transfer of Undertakings Regulations (TUPE) – see page 156
- sex, race or disability discrimination
- trade union membership or refusal to belong to a trade union
- pregnancy-related grounds
- action taken by the employee on health and safety grounds
- assertion by the employee of a statutory right
- refusal by certain shop and betting workers to work on Sundays.

Fair procedure for employers

If the dismissal is not automatically unfair and the employer can establish a potentially 'fair' ground for that dismissal (see page 179–81) it must then, in addition, show that it has acted fairly in the circumstances.

Employer's obligation to provide written reasons for dismissal

Employees who have completed over two years' continuous employment can ask their employers to provide written reasons for the dismissal. The employer is under an obligation to do so within two weeks of such a request being submitted and failure to comply can result in the employee being awarded an additional two weeks' pay by the industrial tribunal. The reasons put forward by the employer are admissible in any subsequent industrial tribunal proceedings. In other words, if the matter reaches an industrial tribunal the employer is bound by the reasons provided in the response to the employee's request.

The question of what is fair depends on the situation: for example, did the employer use a fair procedure and, secondly, having used such a procedure, was it appropriate to dismiss the employee rather than taking some other action short of dismissal (such as a warning in the case of misconduct)? In deciding whether the employer acted reasonably in the circumstances the industrial tribunal will take into account the size of the employer's business and what resources it has available.

For example, a large factory owner would be expected to go to greater efforts to find alternative employment for a redundant worker than the owner of a small restaurant. The reasoning is that a larger employer is more likely to find another role for an employee than the owner of a small business.

The burden of showing that the employer operated an unfair or a fair procedure falls equally on employer and employee. However, the employer may well be expected by the industrial tribunal to justify why it has acted in a particular manner.

The need to operate a fair procedure applies regardless of whether the employee is dismissed for conduct, capability or any other substantial reason. Likewise, if the employee is selected for redundancy, the employer will be expected to show that the procedure used when singling out that employee was fair.

Employers must grant employees who have been given notice of redundancy time off work to attend job interviews.

Fair procedure and dismissal for misconduct

Prior to dismissing an employee for misconduct (see page 167), the employer must show that a fair system has been used, first to decide on the employee's guilt and then to select dismissal rather than some lesser penalty (such as a final warning) as the appropriate sanction.

Disciplinary hearings

It is common practice for employers to have a written disciplinary procedure. Employers of more than 20 employees are required by law to provide employees with details of this within two months of their starting work in the Statement of Particulars (see pages 68–9).

The Arbitration and Conciliation Service (ACAS)* provides guidelines of the procedures that should be included in any employer's disciplinary procedure. Although failure to follow the ACAS guidelines does not mean that the employer has broken the law, an industrial tribunal, when considering whether the employer has acted fairly, will take into account the extent to which the disciplinary procedure followed complies with ACAS guidelines. For more information, employers can consult *Discipline at Work*, an advisory handbook from ACAS.

In many cases, the employer will have a procedure set out in the contract of employment which it is obliged to follow. The employee should check carefully that the rules are carefully adhered to. If they are not, the employee will normally have a good chance of convincing an industrial tribunal that the employer has acted unfairly.

Prior to a disciplinary hearing

A number of important steps need to be followed in order for the employee to obtain a fair hearing:

- **The employee should receive, in good time, full details of any allegation made against him or her** The requirement 'in good time' is designed to deter employers from springing disciplinary hearings without warning. If an employer does so, the employee should immediately ask for an adjournment in order to consider the charges made against him or her.
- **The employee should be given full access to all relevant information in order to defend him- or herself properly** For example, if the employer is relying on the evidence of witnesses the employee should be given an opportunity to cross-examine those witnesses or be given their statements. Likewise, it is normal for the employee to be given the opportunity to have a friend with him/her during the hearing. This may be another work colleague or a trade union representative. However, this will not, in normal circumstances, stretch to allowing the employee to have a solicitor or other legal representation at the hearing.
- **An employee should normally be given the right of appeal** against any decision made against him or her.

CASE HISTORY: Simone

Simone worked for a graphic design company which had a surplus of slightly out-of-date computer equipment. She formulated a plan to sell some printers to her friends, but her boss uncovered the deception before she could put the plan into action and dismissed her on the grounds of misconduct for attempting to sell his goods for her own profit. The employer was held to have acted fairly by a tribunal because he had followed correct procedure, even though he discovered Simone's intentions before they could be put into practice.

Fair procedure and dismissal for capability

If an employee were to be dismissed because the employer believed that he or she was not up to the job, the employer would normally be expected to have considered some of the following points in order to avoid a claim of unfair behaviour:

- was the employee given sufficient training?
- did the employee receive warnings about substandard performance?
- if targets were set, were they reasonable in the circumstances?
- would similar employees have been dismissed in similar circumstances?

The same standard of performance cannot be applied to every job. In some occupations where a high degree of skill is required, even the smallest departure from that high standard will make a dismissal fair; in other cases greater leeway can be given to substandard performance. For example, the driver of an express train, or an engineer operating a nuclear reactor, would be expected to maintain a very high standard of performance at all times because even a minor slip could have very serious repercussions. By comparison, an employer would be expected to be more tolerant of a secretary who made minor typing errors.

Fair procedure and redundancy

Redundancies are made when the employer no longer requires the same number of people to carry on the business. Dismissals by reason of redundancy will be treated as unfair if they occur as the result of:

- maternity-related reasons
- assertion of a statutory right such as the right to a Statement of Particulars of employment or an itemised pay statement
- attempted enforcement of health and safety requirements
- reasons connected with race, sex or disability, or with trade union-related activities
- refusal by certain shop and betting workers to work on Sundays.

The employer must operate any redundancy programme fairly. For example, an industrial tribunal has concluded that selecting employees for redundancy on the basis of their age is not a justifiable policy (see page 77). Employers should also normally consult with employees individually regarding the decision to make them redundant, and consider whether there are any other options available short of dismissal, such as redeploying the employee elsewhere in the organisation.

Failure to consult with employees, save in very extreme circumstances, will usually make dismissal unfair.

When an employer is making 20 or more employees redundant it should consult with employee representatives or recognised trade union representatives at least 30 days prior to the redundancies taking effect. If 100 or more employees are being made redundant the time-scale is extended to 90 days. The employer will have a defence if exceptional circumstances make such consultation impracticable. In addition the employer must inform the Department of Trade and Industry* of its intention to make such redundancies.

Fair procedure and dismissal for some other substantial reason

The employer has the burden of proving to the industrial tribunal that the reason for dismissing the employee was substantial – for example, an employer would be justified in dismissing a scientist working on a top-secret project who refused to sign a confidentiality agreement. In other words, the employer cannot simply rely on a trivial reason to justify dismissing the employee.

Dismissal on the grounds of ill health

A distinction needs to be made between situations where employees are genuinely ill and where they are persistently absent for short periods of time without any real justification. Persistent genuine long-term illness may allow the employer to dismiss the employee fairly on the grounds that the employee is no longer capable of doing the job for which he or she was employed. Obviously, the length of absence due to illness which would justify a fair dismissal will vary depending on the job the employee was required to do. In many cases, an absence of six months may be considered reasonable.

If an employee is persistently absent for short periods of time for unexplained bouts of illness this may ultimately constitute grounds for disciplinary action. In the case of genuine illness the employer would normally be expected to take the following steps before dismissing the employee:

- conduct a thorough medical examination of the employee and obtain an opinion on how long it is likely to be before he or she is well enough to return to work. The employer would be expected to arrange and pay for the medical examination that the employee was expected to undergo, using a doctor which it had selected
- consider, in the context of the needs of the business, the employee's likely length of absence from work and his or her ability to return to the same job
- ascertain whether there is any alternative employment available which the employee would be able to do
- discuss the conclusions of the above exercise with the employee.

Clearly, in deciding whether the employer has acted reasonably, much will focus on the employee's state of health, the type of job the employee does, the size of the employer's organisation and the employer's requirements. For example, if the employee is a hod-carrier and as a result of injury the employee is no longer able to do that job, the employer may be able to justify dismissal relatively easily by showing that there is no other suitable work that the employee could be expected to do. However, the position would be different if, say, an employee who worked in a chemical factory were allergic to certain chemicals which made him ill, but could be moved easily to another similar job elsewhere in the factory away from those chemicals.

Additional help

Employers may find it useful to consult a leaflet entitled *Fair and Unfair Dismissal: A Guide for Employers* (PL714), available from the DTI Publications Orderline.★

Chapter 16 provides guidance on how to bring a claim to an industrial tribunal. However, in many cases employers are willing to settle potential claims for compensation that employees may have following dismissal without the employee having to resort to legal proceedings. It is therefore important that employees should have an idea of what compensation may be due to them before entering into negotiations with their employer. See Chapter 11 for full details.

Calculating compensation following dismissal

For most employees, once they have been dismissed the central issue is to establish immediately how much compensation they are entitled to recover from their former employer. Until the employees have established how such compensation should be calculated they will not be able to effectively judge the fairness of any offer of compensation that the employer may propose.

As the previous two chapters have explained, employees' potential claims for compensation fall under two categories: those provided as a result of breach of contract (wrongful/unlawful dismissal – see page 173) and those provided by statute.

The most common statutory claims pursued by employees are for unfair dismissal or a statutory redundancy payment (see page 191). Employees who are dismissed by reason of their sex, race or disability may have additional claims (see Chapters 5 and 6).

Compensation for unfair dismissal

If an industrial tribunal decides that an employee has been dismissed unfairly the compensation award will be made up of two parts: a basic award and a compensatory award.

Basic award

This is calculated by reference to the employee's age and length of service. The basis of the calculation is half a week's pay for each year of service in which the employee is under the age of 21; one week's pay for each year of service in which the employee is under the age of 41; and one-and-a-half week's pay for each year of service in which the employee is over the age of 41. The calculation of a week's pay is capped at a current maximum of £220 per week. This rate is reviewed on an annual basis, but in recent years has increased only marginally. The maximum number of years in respect of which a basic award can be made is 20.

Example   George, aged 53, earns £185 per week and has been working for the same employer for ten years. In his case the basic award would be calculated as follows: £185 × 1.5 × 10 = £2,775.

Example   Anne, aged 28, earns £500 per week and has worked for the same employer for five years. In her case the basic award would be calculated as follows: £220 × 1 × 5 = £1,100.

Example   John, aged 44, earns £800 per week and has worked for the same employer for six years. In his case, the basic award would be calculated as follows: (£220 × 1 × 3 = £660) + (£220 × 1.5 × 3 = £990) = £1,650.

Compensatory award

This is calculated by reference to the employee's loss of salary and benefits from the date of dismissal until he or she finds another job. If the employee finds a new job but at a lower rate of pay, this reduced salary will be taken into account when calculating the loss suffered by him or her. Unlike contractual claims (see page 173), the loss is therefore not confined to what the employee would have earned during the notice period. The compensatory award is currently subject to a maximum limit of £12,000. This compares unfavourably with awards for race, sex or disability discrimination, which are not subject to any upper limit. However, the government has indicated in its White Paper 'Fairness at Work' its intention to introduce legislation to remove this cap to bring it into line with the position when awarding compensation in discrimination cases.

Determining compensatory awards

An industrial tribunal has a general power to award, subject to the £12,000 limit, whatever it considers 'just and equitable' in the circumstances. Usually, the industrial tribunal calculates the compensatory award in two ways: first, by establishing the employee's actual loss, taking into account the extent to which the employee has reduced his or her loss by seeking alternative employment (see 'Mitigation', page 196), then by reducing the compensation to take into account the extent to which the employee's conduct contributed to the employer's decision to dismiss the employee.

For example, an employer might decide to dismiss immediately, without investigating properly or conducting a full disciplinary hearing (see page 183), an employee guilty of bullying other employees. In such a case, the industrial tribunal might find that because of the employer's knee-jerk reaction, the dismissal was technically unfair, but that it would not be right to award the employee any compensation owing to his or her unacceptable conduct.

Once the appropriate level of compensation has been established, the award may then be reduced to give the employer credit for any compensation it has already paid to the employee – although there have been conflicting cases regarding this approach.

Average size of compensatory awards

In 1995–6 the average award for unfair dismissal in the industrial tribunal was £2,499.

Reinstatement or re-engagement of the employee

Some employees who establish that they have been unfairly dismissed are more interested in getting their jobs back than receiving compensation. An industrial tribunal has the power, in limited circumstances, to order employers to take employees back.

The industrial tribunal very rarely agrees to make such an order, and it can be done only where the tribunal believes it to be reasonable and practicable. It would be highly unlikely for such an order to be made if the employer has a small workforce, because if employer and employee have had a violent disagreement it would be unrealistic to expect them to work together again. A reinstatement or re-engagement order is much more likely to be made if the employer has a large staff and it is possible to relocate the employee to another part of the organisation where a future clash of personalities is unlikely to occur.

If the industrial tribunal grants a reinstatement or re-engagement order and the employer refuses to comply with the order, the employer can be ordered to pay additional compensation to the employee.

Statutory redundancy payment

Redundancy is merely one form of dismissal (see page 180). Employees who are made redundant and have completed over two years' continuous employment are entitled to receive a statutory redundancy payment, which is calculated in exactly the same way as the basic award (see pages 188–9).

On being unfairly dismissed, employees cannot receive both the basic award and a statutory redundancy payment: the granting of the basic award cancels out the right to receive the latter. The industrial tribunal decides which payment should be awarded in cases of doubt. A useful leaflet is *Redundancy Payments: A Guide for Employees, Employers and Others* from DTI Publications Orderline.★

Damages for breach of contract

Breach of contract may occur in a variety of circumstances (see pages 167–9). When the courts or industrial tribunals are calculating contractual compensation, the underlying principle is that the compensation awarded to employees should put them in the position they would have been in if the terms of the contract had been fulfilled. In other words, if an employee is dismissed without notice in breach of contract the starting point for calculating compensation is the value of the net salary and fringe benefits that the employee should have received during the notice period. The industrial tribunal's power to award damages for breach of contract is presently capped at £25,000.

Contrary to popular belief, compensation for loss of salary is calculated on a net basis after the notional deduction of an amount in respect of the income tax and National Insurance that would have been deducted from the salary payment. This is because employees should be compensated only in respect of their actual loss. In other words, although an employee may have a salary of £20,000 per annum, the actual amount received by the employee, after the deduction of income tax and National Insurance, is somewhat less than this. The effect is that the employer enjoys a windfall, as it is under an obligation to pay compensation to the employee only to the tune of the employee's net salary, without the obligation to pay National Insurance or income tax on the compensation payment.

> **'Golden handshake' payouts**
> Large compensation payouts to executives sometimes feature in the press. These 'fat cats' enjoy high salaries and long notice periods and the lion's share of any compensation awarded to them is derived not from their statutory rights, but from the rights contained in their job contracts. The large 'golden handshakes' these employees receive are the result of the favourable contracts that they negotiated for themselves when they started work.

Notice period

Those employees who have a written contract of employment will invariably have a notice period contained in the contract. In the absence of an agreed notice period, employees will be entitled to at least the statutory minimum notice period (see page 65). They may be able to argue for a longer period, the common-law period of 'reasonable notice' (see page 66). Note: this period does not apply in Scotland.

Benefits

In calculating compensation for the loss of the benefits the rule is that the benefits should be calculated on the basis of the cost to the employee of replacing them rather than on the cost to the employer of providing them. The difference can be quite substantial (see example below).

Example   An employer is able to provide private medical cover to his workforce at a cost of £500 per annum because he receives a discount for group membership. An employee who is a 40-per-cent taxpayer pays £200 per annum in tax on the benefit and has a twelve-month notice period. When his employment is terminated without notice, he finds that the cost of providing the same medical cover on an individual basis is £1,500 per annum. In this case, the employee's actual loss is £1,300 per annum because this is the amount that he would need to put him in the position that he would have occupied had the terms of the contract had been fulfilled.

The same principle is adopted when calculating compensation for the loss of other benefits such as life insurance cover, subsidised lunches, permanent health insurance cover, or the use of a company car (see pages 48–9).

Pensions

Calculating compensation for loss of pension contributions can be very complicated, and will depend on the type of pension arrangement set up by the employer (see pages 50–3).

Contributions to an employee's personal pension plan
In this case, the actual loss suffered by the employee is the amount that the employer was obliged to pay into the scheme during the notice period. However, the employer would be entitled to make a deduction from any lump-sum payment made to the employee in respect of personal pension contributions, to take into account any additional investment return gained by the employee by early receipt of the lump-sum payment which would not be available if pension contributions were made in monthly instalments over the course of the notice period.

Contributions into a money purchase scheme
In a money purchase scheme, the employer pays an amount, usually a percentage of the employee's salary, into the pension scheme on the employee's behalf. The employee's pension entitlement at retirement age is calculated according to the contribution attributed to that employee. It is therefore relatively easy to calculate the compensation due to the employee because, like contributions into a personal pension plan, the compensation is equal in broad terms to the contributions the employer would have paid into the pension scheme during the notice period (subject to a notional deduction for early receipt of the lump sum – see above).

Contributions to a final salary occupational pension scheme
When calculating compensation for pension rights lost during the notice period in relation to a final salary occupational pension scheme, the employee's pension on retirement is calculated not according to contributions specifically attributed to the employee, as in the case of

personal pension plans or money purchase schemes, but according to the employee's number of years of pensionable service and his or her salary at the date of retirement. The rate of contributions are largely irrelevant to the calculation because some occupational pension schemes which are in surplus often enjoy 'pension holidays', during which time the company does not have to make any contributions in respect of the employees because the pension scheme has adequate finances to fund its commitments. The pensionable salary is usually calculated by taking the average of the employee's salary in the three years prior to the end of the employment.

Example   An employee who was earning £60,000 per annum and is entitled to one year's notice was dismissed without justification. The final salary pension scheme provides a pension equal to 1/60th pensionable salary for each year of service. The employee's pension loss from the normal retirement date will therefore be a pension of £1,000 per annum (£60,000 × 1/60th = £1,000).

In this case the compensation due to the employee will involve a more elaborate calculation: it is not sufficient merely to find out the average amount that the employer pays into the scheme on behalf of each employee. An actuary will be required to work out how much it would cost to provide the employee with a pension of £1,000 per annum as at the date of retirement.

Resolving pension scheme problems

In the first instance, you should consult with the pensions department in your organisation for advice. You may want to take extra advice from an independent pension consultant. The Society of Pension Consultants* will be able to find one in your area. If you have a problem with your employer scheme, try to resolve it through the scheme's complaints mechanism (it must by law have one). If this fails, contact the Occupational Pensions Advisory Service.*

If you have lost touch with the administrators of your employer pension scheme you can contact the Registrar of Pension Schemes,* which runs a free tracing service.

Accrued salary and unused holiday

Employees are entitled to receive their salary, calculated up to the date of dismissal. The right to receive pay in lieu of holiday earned but not taken will depend on the terms of the contract of employment. Generally speaking, employers will pay their employees accrued holiday pay on the termination of employment. Those who are entitled to receive holiday pay but are denied it can bring a claim to an industrial tribunal or a court in order to recover the amount due to them (see Chapter 16).

Bonuses and commissions

Many employees, particularly sales personnel, receive part of their remuneration through bonus schemes and commission payments. For example, recruitment consultants usually receive their commission payments months after they have placed a candidate with an employer, because the recruitment consultancy itself does not get paid until the candidate has completed six months' employment with his or her new employer.

The right to receive bonuses and commission payments which have been earned but not paid as at the date of dismissal will depend on the terms of the contract of employment. Most recruitment consultants' contracts provide that they will receive this commission regardless of whether they are still in employment on the date of payment. By contrast, many brokers in the City of London have contracts that state that they will be entitled to receive bonuses only if they are employed and not under notice as at the date of payment.

If the bonus scheme is a contractual one which is subject to achieving certain pre-determined targets, employees have a right to be compensated for the loss of the opportunity to earn bonuses or commission during the notice period.

In some cases, employers operate discretionary bonus schemes under which any payments made to the employee are paid entirely at the employer's option. In such cases, it is very difficult to establish a right to compensation in respect of the loss of such bonus payments, because they do not constitute a contractual right. However, the employee can argue that if he or she is eligible for membership of a discretionary bonus scheme then even though the precise amount payable may be not be ascertainable, the employee is entitled to assume that the employer would not exercise its discretion in bad faith to deprive him or her of a bonus.

The position would be different if the employee could show that bonuses were paid habitually in each year and therefore, over a period of time, had become a contractual right (see page 68).

Executive share options

Executive share options, as their name suggests, are enjoyed only by more senior employees. The rules of these schemes usually provide that on the termination of employment, the options will automatically lapse and the employee will not have any further legal right to exercise them, save in limited circumstances, such as retirement, illness, redundancy, or with the approval of the board of directors.

In England and Wales, a clause which states that the options will no longer be exercisable will be sufficient to prevent the employee from bringing a claim for compensation for the loss of the right to exercise the options. However, because different laws apply in Scotland employees there may still be able to bring a claim for compensation for the loss of the share option rights.

Injury to feelings

An employee cannot claim compensation for any injury caused to feelings by the dismissal. However, in a case in 1997 a court gave a preliminary view that in theory compensation could be recovered where, because the employer ran a corrupt or dishonest business, the employee experienced difficulty in finding another job on dismissal. This preliminary view of the court should be regarded with caution, as the issue will have to be considered in greater detail at a full trial. However, it seems unlikely that the courts would wish to extend this principle to a significant degree.

Mitigation

Employees are under a duty to attempt to reduce the size of their compensation claim by finding suitable alternative employment. The impression often given is that employees are entitled to compensation even when they find another job immediately; this is wrong. For example, if a secretary who is paid £15,000 per annum and is entitled to three months' notice were to be dismissed without notice or justification and immediately finds a job which pays £17,000 per annum, she would not be entitled to any compensation for breach of contract. This is because her loss would be reduced to nothing as a result of her having found a better-paid job immediately. Clearly, she may still have a claim for unfair dismissal (see Chapter 10).

In the high-profile golden-handshake cases often reported in the press, mitigation is usually the most hotly contested element of the negotiations over the amount of the compensation payable (see page 192).

Employees are under a duty only to take reasonable steps to look for another job. They are *not* expected to take the first job that comes along: an employee would not have complied with his or her duty to mitigate the loss if he or she simply took any job available paying any level of salary, because in this case the employee would have failed to make sufficient effort to obtain a job at the level he or she was capable of achieving. Initially at least, the employee is under an obligation only to find a job which provides comparable benefits. After a certain period of time, depending on their status, employees are expected to drop their sights.

In the vast majority of cases, where employees are entitled only to a modest period of notice – such as three months or less – it would not normally be reasonable to expect them to find a job within the notice period. In these circumstances the employee's compensation should be calculated by reference to the entire notice period.

If the employee takes another job, even if it is not as good as the one he or she had before, his or her claims for damages will be reduced to the extent that he or she actually reduces his or her loss.

Example   An employee is entitled to four weeks' notice and is paid, after tax, £400 per week. The employee gets another job immediately which pays, after tax, £300 per week. In this situation the employee's potential claim on dismissal amounts to £1,600 (£400 × 4) but as the employee found another job immediately, his potential claim is reduced to (£400 – £300 × 4) = £400.

Discount for accelerated receipt

Employers are also entitled to deduct from the calculation of any compensation payment an amount equal to the interest that could be earned on any lump-sum payment made during the notice period.

In other words, if an employee is entitled to receive six months' notice but immediately receives, instead, a lump-sum payment equal in value to six months' salary and benefits, he or she will be able to invest that lump sum and receive interest on that investment. Strictly speaking, the employer is entitled to reduce the compensation payable to take account of the return enjoyed by the employee on this investment. In reality, except in cases involving employees who are entitled to lengthy notice periods, employers usually ignore such interest payments.

Tax on compensation payments

Up to the first £30,000 of any compensation payment can be paid to the employee without deduction of tax if it is made in connection with the termination of employment. (This also applies to statutory redundancy payments – see page 191.) This tax exemption applies whether the payment is made as a result of an unfair dismissal claim or for breach of contract. Because the exemption relates only to payments made in connection with termination of employment, tax and National Insurance must be deducted from accrued salary, bonus payments and holiday pay (see pages 195–6) as these amounts are not treated as termination payments.

In some cases, the first £30,000 tax exemption is not available.

- **Pay-in-lieu-of-notice clauses** Many job contracts include a clause by which the employer may, as an alternative to asking the employee to work out the notice period, require him or her to leave immediately and receive a sum equal to the salary he or she would have received during the notice period (see page 160). The view used to be that because the employer had discretion as to whether to rely on such a clause, the payments were not taxable. However, recently the Inland Revenue has taken the view that where an employee's contract contains a pay-in-lieu-of-notice clause, that proportion of any compensation payment which represents pay in lieu of notice will be fully taxable

- **Compensation payments made in reliance on a term in the contract of employment ('golden parachute')** This will apply where the employer and employee have pre-agreed the compensation to be paid to the employee in the event of dismissal – often known as a 'golden parachute' clause (see page 164)

- **Signing settlement agreements far in advance of the termination date** In some cases both the employer and the employee want to reach an agreement on the employee's terms of departure some time in advance of the actual departure date. The risk for the employee, in such circumstances, is that the Inland Revenue may argue that the compensation payment provided for in the settlement agreement is not a termination payment at all, but instead relates to the services the employee will be obliged to provide between the date on which the agreement is signed and the actual termination date, and as such should therefore be taxed in the normal way. Clearly, the longer the period between the date of signing the agreement and the actual termination date, the greater the risk that the Inland Revenue will seek to tax the payment

- **Payments to employees on retirement** The Inland Revenue is always very suspicious of any payment made to employees who are approaching retirement age. Its view is that in some cases such payments are not really compensation payments at all, but are in reality retirement payments made in recognition of the employee's long service. Payments that fall in this category are not treated as tax-exempt. As a result, many employers are reluctant to make payments to retiring employees free of tax. Instead, they usually do one of two things: they either obtain Inland Revenue clearance before making the payment, or alternatively they tax the payment and leave the employee to take up the argument with the Inland Revenue as to the tax status of the payment

- **Payments made in return for agreeing to abide by post-termination restrictive covenants** These are made to an employee following the termination of employment in return for the employee agreeing to abide by covenants that, typically, prevent him or her from joining a competitor or poaching clients or employees (see Chapter 7). Payments made to an employee under such an agreement will be fully taxable and subject to deductions in respect of National Insurance. Some heated debate has taken place with the Inland Revenue over how wide the interpretation of a restrictive covenant may be, and the dividing line between what is and is not a restrictive covenant, for tax purposes, remains unclear. If an employer insists on imposing restrictive covenants in the settlement agreement, the employee should insist that only a proportion of the payment is attributed to the agreement to abide by the covenants. The employee will thereby maximise the possibility of arguing that the remainder of the compensation can be paid free of tax, on the basis that it is not connected with the agreement to comply with the restrictive covenants.

No tax is payable on the following payments:

- **payments on death** or following **injury or disability**
- **payments by employers into Inland Revenue–approved pension schemes** run by the employer for its employees. Subject to certain limits, an employer can make contributions into its occupational pension scheme, on behalf of its employees, free of tax. This offers employees receiving compensation in excess of £30,000 an opportunity to do some tax planning as the employer will usually be happy to agree to pay any compensation in excess of the first £30,000 into the pension scheme on behalf of the employee. The trustees of the pension scheme should be able to let the employer known exactly how much can be paid into it free of tax
- **counselling** Outplacement counselling is made available to employees to help them in their search for another job. Typically the service will include advice on preparing a CV, interview techniques and other tactics. If the outplacement services are made available to all employees, or employees of a particular category, the benefit will not be taxable
- **legal fees** Contributions made by the employer to employees' legal costs in connection with the termination of employment will not be taxable provided they are paid directly to the employee's solicitors, as part of the settlement agreement, and relate purely to advice on the termination of employment. (Employers would *not* be able to claim this exemption for advice given in relation to unrelated issues such as buying a house or handling a divorce.) The exemption only applies to legal fees, not other professional costs that may be incurred, such as accountancy fees. This tax concession allows those employees receiving compensation in excess of £30,000 an oppor-

tunity for further tax planning. As part of the settlement agreement, the employer can be asked to pay the employee's legal fees out of the agreed compensation payment, directly to the employee's solicitors. By this route the employee's legal fees can be paid free of tax rather than out of post-tax income.

Tax treatment of termination payments in excess of £30,000

If an employee receives a compensation payment in excess of £30,000, that excess will be subject to tax. If the employer has issued a form P45 it is obliged to deduct tax only from the excess, at the basic rate, leaving the employee to make up the remainder of the tax in his or her annual tax return. In effect the employee enjoys a short-term cashflow advantage as the tax will not have to be paid until the end of the tax year.

Employees who do not normally receive a tax return should request one from their local tax office* in order to make the necessary declaration. Failure to declare tax on compensation payments may lead to a fine and interest penalties.

Grossing up the compensation payment

Because the compensation payment itself is subject to tax, in calculating the employee's compensation entitlement, the court will gross up at 40 per cent that proportion of the compensation in excess of the first £30,000. This is because the purpose of the compensation awarded is to put the employee in the position he or she would have been in if the terms of the contract had been fulfilled and, therefore, if the compensation awarded is itself subject to tax the court must take this into account.

CALCULATION OF COMPENSATION

Name: John Smith
Position: Managing Director
Age: 54
Commencement of employment: 1 May 1986
Date of dismissal: 2 May 1998
Notice period: 12 months

CONTRACTUAL CLAIM

(1) **Gross value of annual benefits**[1]

Salary	£86,000	
Private health insurance cover	£2,500	
Car	£8,000	
Fuel	£1,700	
Car phone	£300	
Permanent health insurance cover	£1,500	
Gross total =		£100,000

(2) **Taxable value of annual benefits**[2]   (say) =   £89,531

(3) **Deduct tax and National Insurance**

Exemptions: single person's tax allowance (£4,195)
Total income subject to tax = £85,336

Tax at 20%	£1–£4,300	£860	
Tax at 23%	£4,300–£27,100	£5,244	
Tax at 40%	£27,100–£85,336	£23,294	
	Total tax =	£29,398	
	Employee's NI =	£2,255.76	
	Total deduction =		-£31,653.76

(4) Subtract total deductions from gross total £100,000
loss   -£31,653.76
Total actual loss =   £68,346.24

(5) Adjusting the compensation for tax

(i)	deduct tax-free amount of £30,000	-£30,000
(ii)	balance attracting tax	£38,346.24
(iii)	gross up the £38,346.24[3]	£63,910.40
(iv)	add back in first £30,000	£30,000
	TOTAL CONTRACTUAL CLAIM =	£93,910.40

STATUTORY CLAIM

(1) **Basic award**

Total no. completed years' service   = 12
Weekly pay (maximum) = £220
Basic award payment = £220 × 1.5 × 12   £3,960

(2) **Compensatory award** (maximum)   £12,000
TOTAL STATUTORY CLAIM   =   £15,960
TOTAL COMPENSATION (STATUTORY
+ CONTRACTUAL CLAIM)   =   £109,870.40

[1] Actual replacement cost to employee of salary and fringe benefits
[2] For the purposes of calculating tax, the Inland Revenue gives some benefits a lower value than their actual value. Benefits with a lower taxable value would include, for example, a company car
[3] This £38,346.24 will itself be subject to tax and therefore needs to gross up at 40 per cent to take into account the tax that will be paid on it

> **Note**
> The compensation calculation opposite assumes that:
> - the employee cannot find another job within the 12-month notice period
> - the industrial tribunal awards the maximum amount of compensation.

Tax treatment of the cash compensation and benefits received in following tax year

In some cases, employees receive compensation payments in stages over a number of months, while continuing to receive benefits such as private medical cover or the use of a car over the same period of time. In the past, all these payments and benefits were treated for tax purposes as having been received in the tax year in which the employment terminated. However, such payments and benefits are now taxed in the tax year in which they are actually received.

If the employer is insolvent

If an employer goes out of business owing to insolvency, the employee, like any other creditor, should submit a claim as soon as possible to the employer for anything he or she is owed. If no payment is received and no liquidator or receiver has been appointed, the employee can apply to an industrial tribunal (see Chapter 16). If after this no payment is made, the employee can apply to the National Insurance Fund armed with the industrial tribunal decision (see box overleaf).

Preferential debts

Some employees' claims rank as preferential debts, which means that those debts will be paid ahead of unsecured creditors' claims. Employee claims such as holiday pay and pension contributions are treated as preferential claims, subject to certain limits. Claims for arrears of salary, overtime and commission will also be treated as preferential although only to an aggregate maximum of £800.

The mere fact that a claim is categorised as a preferential debt does not guarantee payment. Such debts are paid only after the costs of the insolvency have been met, and debts paid to those with fixed charges, such as banks holding mortgages over the business. Often, however, the employer will have spent every last penny trying to keep the business going, and at the end there may be nothing left.

A useful leaflet is: *Your Rights if your Employer is Insolvent: A Guide for Employees, Employers and Others* (PL718), from DTI Publications Orderline.*

National Insurance Fund

This state-operated fund will pay up to six weeks' holiday pay, and eight weeks' arrears of salary. In addition, depending on the length of service, a further 12 weeks' pay can be claimed where the employer has failed to give adequate notice. Unfortunately this does not mean a week's actual pay. In each case, the maximum figure permitted when calculating a week's pay is currently £220. In certain circumstances the state will also make good a proportion of any arrears in an employee's pension contributions if the employer is insolvent. To claim with the NI Fund, the employee should first approach the insolvent employer via the employer's representative, who will submit forms on the employee's behalf. Alternatively, the liquidator or receiver can apply to the NI Fund on behalf of the employee. The Department of Trade and Industry, which processes the claims, usually aims to deal with such claims within 12 weeks of receiving the application. For more information, contact the Contributions Agency.*

The NI Fund will also guarantee the payment of any statutory redundancy payment due to the employee when the employer is insolvent (see page 191). In this case the employee should make a claim directly to the Redundancy Payment Office – contact the Redundancy Helpline* for details.

In order for employees and employers to negotiate a termination settlement effectively, it is essential that both understand their rights and obligations regarding compensation, as discussed in this chapter. However, negotiating a settlement requires not just an understanding of the legal rights but also an appreciation of both parties' objectives and the strength of their negotiating positions. The next chapter deals with reaching a satisfactory settlement.

Chapter 12

Negotiating an out-of-court settlement

In its 1997 annual report, ACAS* reported that the number of applications submitted by disgruntled employees to industrial tribunals had risen from 100,399 in 1996 to 106,912 in 1997. However, in the vast majority of disputes the parties stop short of legal proceedings (whether in an industrial tribunal or in court) and agree on a settlement between themselves. Litigation, which is both expensive and time-consuming, should be seen as only a last resort for employer or employee.

This chapter outlines the usual pattern of negotiation following the termination of employment.

The termination meeting

Some termination meetings are carefully planned by the employer and follow a set procedure. In other cases such meetings are hastily convened. (The employer is not obliged to issue the employee with a warning, but if the dismissal is not justified it will be liable to pay compensation.)

Often, employees are given little indication of what is about to occur. The range of emotions experienced by employees stretches from shock to anger, disappointment and disbelief. In many cases, employees' recollections of what happened at the meeting are vague owing to the suddenness with which they heard the news.

At the termination meeting the employee's manager will usually be accompanied by a member of the human resources or personnel department. The employee will either be told that his or her employment has been terminated with immediate effect or that he or she is under notice of the termination of employment.

- **Termination of employment with immediate effect** In this situation, the employee is usually escorted from the building immediately. Typically, those who have access to highly confidential information are dismissed immediately. Alternatively, they are placed on garden leave and are required to serve out the notice period at home (see page 140). On other occasions, employees are dismissed justifiably – because they are guilty of gross misconduct, for example (see page 167).
- **Employee given notice of termination** Some employers require their employees to work out the notice period they are entitled to under the terms of their contracts. This might happen when the employer becomes aware, for example, that an order the employee has been working on will not be renewed but his or her services are needed during the notice period to fulfil the outstanding order.

A short letter is normally produced to confirm the conversation at the meeting (see samples below).

Sample letter from employer terminating employment immediately

Mr Smith
[Address]

[Date]

Dear Mr Smith,

This is to confirm our discussion today when I confirmed that your employment with XYZ Ltd would terminate with immediate effect.

Yours sincerely

Sample letter from employer giving notice of termination

Mr Jones
[Address]

[Date]

Dear Mr Jones,

This is to confirm our discussion today when I confirmed that your employment with XYZ Ltd would terminate with effect from [Date].

Yours sincerely

Sometimes the employer will provide detailed reasons as to why the decision has been taken to dismiss the employee in the letter confirming the dismissal; in other cases the employer may be reluctant to do so. Employees who have completed over two years' continuous employment with the employer have a right to receive written reasons as to why they have been given notice or dismissed (see page 182). (This two-year qualifying period may be reduced in line with the qualifying period required to bring a claim for unfair dismissal – see page 176.)

Proposals for compensation

Following the employee's dismissal at the termination meeting, the manager or personnel officer may move on to discuss any proposals for compensation. The words 'without prejudice' may be used and normally appear on any letter containing compensation proposals: they indicate that the compensation proposals discussed, for the purposes of reaching a settlement, cannot be used as evidence in any future court proceedings, should the attempt to reach an agreement fail. The employee likewise should also mark any correspondence relating to the settlement proposals and sent to the employer as 'without prejudice'.

The words 'subject to contract' are often marked on the correspondence in addition. This usually occurs when the employer sets out only the main elements of the financial offer at the outset while reserving the right to produce an agreement subsequently which includes those elements and any additional protection it feels is necessary to ensure a clean break is achieved.

Employees' strategy when proposals are issued

The golden rule for the employee is not to agree or disagree with any compensation package put forward at the termination meeting. If the offer is made verbally, the employee should ask to have the details confirmed in writing and request sufficient time to consider them (hence avoiding the danger of being stampeded into accepting an offer). The employee should ensure that the thinking time asked for is sufficient for seeking legal advice from a solicitor, if necessary.

Resignation

Some employees believe that it is better to resign rather than be dismissed because of the impact that dismissal may have on the search for another job (see page 162). However, employees should not agree to resign prior to agreeing terms of compensation as this may prejudice their right to receive compensation. The danger with resigning, even if it is forced, is that the employer may try to argue subsequently that, as the employee resigned and the resignation was accepted, the employee has no right to compensation from the employer (see page 175). In terms of unfair dismissal, a forced resignation is a dismissal.

Resigning as a director

Some senior employees are directors. This is a status quite separate and distinct from their role as an employee. An employer may be anxious for the employee to resign his or her directorship at the earliest opportunity. This is because, even if the individual has been dismissed as an employee, for as long as he or she remains a director he or she has the right to receive notice of board meetings and may attend such meetings at will. If the director does not receive such notice, the business conducted at the board meetings will be invalidated. Ultimately, if the employee refuses to step down as a director, procedures of varying degrees of complexity can be followed for the purpose of removing him or her. However, it is an inconvenience that the employer would normally prefer to avoid, therefore the agreement to resign can be used by the employee as a negotiating tool.

No loss of compensation

Resignation under normal circumstances can mean the surrender of the employee's right to compensation (see above). If the employee resigns as a director, he or she should not lose this right. The office of director and the position of employee are two separate and distinct relationships and provided that the employee has not voluntarily resigned from his or her employment, he or she should still be able to claim compensation on its termination. In any resignation letter, the employee should make clear that the resignation as a director is 'without prejudice' to his or her rights as an employee, and that the resignation should not be treated as a resignation from employment.

Agreement to supply a reference and avoid derogatory statements

Instead of resigning, the employee's best policy is to negotiate a reference or announcement as part of the settlement agreement which addresses any concerns that a potential future employer may have regarding the reasons for dismissal. The employee could agree with the employer that the dismissal will be explained to any outsider as having occurred because the employee wanted to pursue other opportunities (even if this was not true). A settlement might also involve both parties agreeing not to make derogatory statements about each other.

After the termination meeting

The employee should make a careful note of what was said at the termination meeting; in particular, the reasons (if any) given for the dismissal. If the employer were to suggest that the reason for the dismissal was connected with pregnancy or race, for example, the employee would have a strong discrimination claim.

If an offer of compensation is made, the employee should check it against the legal entitlement (see Chapter 11).

Counter-offers

In most settlement negotiations, an exchange of correspondence takes place. Employers do not usually adopt a take-it-or-leave-it approach. However, employees should be aware of the risks of making a counter-offer. Legally speaking, the effect of a counter-offer is to rescind the employer's original offer. In other words, if the employee makes a counter-offer and the employer rejects it, the employee does not have the right to then accept the employer's original offer unless the employer renews it. In practice, of course, the employer normally does renew the offer – though not always. For example, the employer may refuse to renew the offer if it becomes clear that the employee has found another job, or if it has come to light, since the employer made the original offer, that the employee was guilty of gross misconduct. This would entitle the employer to dismiss the employee immediately without compensation.

The employee should consider carefully how best to respond to the employer's offer: for example, if the employer's offer of compensation is very generous and is more than the employee could hope to recover by suing in either the industrial tribunal, the court or both, the best policy is usually to adopt a non-confrontational approach. If the offer is generous, an employee who makes excessive demands runs the risk of irritating the employer and prejudicing the offer already made.

Using a solicitor

A solicitor or other legal adviser, such as a Citizens Advice Bureau*
case worker, can fulfil a number of roles, including explaining employees' rights, calculating compensation and negotiating with the employer on behalf of the employee. (See Chapter 17.) However, careful thought should be given to the best way to proceed. If the employee has a reasonable relationship with the employer, negotiations are probably best carried out directly between the employer and employee. A legal adviser could be better deployed in the background doing things such as vetting letters before they are sent, say, or preparing scripts to be used in negotiations.

The risk of bringing the solicitor out into the open when the employee has a reasonable relationship with the employer is that this may alienate or frighten the employer, which will then hand over responsibility for the negotiations to its own solicitor. If this happens, the employee may lose the ability to exploit to the full any goodwill that the employer may feel towards the employee.

If negotiations with the employer are acrimonious, the best policy is often for the employee to let the employer know that he or she is serious about enforcing his or her rights, by suing if necessary. This message is best delivered by way of a letter, addressed to the employer from (as appropriate) a Citizens Advice Bureau, law centre or firm of solicitors.

In some cases, employers will respond only if they know that the employee is not prepared to be pushed around. However, employees should not make threats that they are not prepared to follow through. For example, if an employee says that he or she will commence proceedings in an industrial tribunal if a suitable offer is not made by a particular date, he or she should be prepared to carry out that threat (see

Chapter 16). If the employee backs down, his or her credibility will be damaged in any future negotiations with the employer.

Emotional pressure

On being dismissed, it is very important for the employee to focus on the main objective. In some cases, this aim may be restricted to obtaining a good reference, or ensuring a smooth handover. However, in most cases the objective is to negotiate the best financial package possible. If the employer feels badly about the dismissal the employee should be willing to use that discomfiture to get the best deal possible – for example, by stressing the impact that dismissal will have on his or her family, career and confidence.

Few employers enjoy dismissing any of their workforce, particularly if they recognise that those they have to dismiss are decent and hardworking. Therefore, exploiting that feeling of guilt can improve any financial offer.

Improving the employer's offer

Too often in negotiations, parties make simplistic assumptions about what the other wishes to achieve. Employees typically assume that the employer's prime concern is to pay as little as possible and the employer usually believes that the employee's objective is to walk away with as much as possible. In many situations this is a true reflection of the position – but not always. In the light of this, the employee should spend a little time thinking about what might be important to the employer.

The employer's concerns may include the desire to:

- be seen as a fair employer
- avoid adverse publicity and court proceedings
- ensure that the employee does not poach clients, leak confidential information or bad-mouth the employer
- be able to obtain help when needed on matters in which the employee was involved: for example, a court case or negotiations with an important client
- ensure that the employee resigns from any directorships he or she holds.

There are certain things that an employee can ask for to which the employer may well be prepared to agree, as long as they do not significantly increase the cost of the compensation package. In order to improve the deal, employees could:

- ask the employer to continue private medical insurance cover or life assurance cover (see page 49) to the next renewal date. Employers often pay for group cover for their employees by means of a yearly premium and therefore no additional cost is incurred by keeping the dismissed employee covered by the scheme until the renewal date
- ask whether they can keep company equipment, such as a fax machine, computer or mobile telephone. These have a limited resale value but may be useful to the employee when trying to find another job
- if they have the use of a company car, ask whether the company is prepared to sell their company car to them at its book value. The book value for company accounting purposes is usually less than the car's market value
- if they have share options (see page 50), explore with the employer the possibility of extending the right to exercise the options to the maximum period of time permitted under the rules of the share option scheme.

Considerations for employees before accepting the employer's offer

Every employee has different objectives and ultimately the employee must gauge how much scope there is to improve the deal. However, certain factors are worth considering:

- how closely does the offer of compensation represent the employee's legal entitlement? (See Chapter 11.) A crucial factor here could be how long it will take the employee to find another job. For example, a 28-year-old computer programmer is much more likely to find another job than a 58-year-old miner
- if a reference is important, has the employer agreed to provide a reference and, if so, is it sufficient to help in the search for another job?
- what are the alternatives to accepting the offer? Starting legal proceedings can be very expensive and the outcome is uncertain.

The settlement letter

Once the period of negotiation is completed the employer will usually produce a settlement letter for the employee to sign (see sample on pages 215–18). This letter will invariably contain a waiver clause.

Waiver clause

The purpose of the waiver clause is to achieve a clean break between the employer and the employee. Typically, it will state that the employee, under the terms of the agreement, abandons all claims he or she has against the employer relating to his or her employment or its termination. This means that the employee will be prevented from bringing any further contractual claims, including those for personal injury, unless expressly included.

However, statutory claims are another matter. Even if the employee signs a waiver confirming that he or she accepts a payment in full and final settlement, he or she will not be prevented from subsequently bringing certain statutory claims, including for unfair dismissal, in respect of race, sex or disability discrimination or for unauthorised deductions from pay. These statutory claims can only be excluded if the employee signs a compromise agreement or ACAS is involved in brokering the agreement (see below).

Compromise agreements

Compromise agreements are the most common route by which employees are subsequently prevented from bringing statutory claims, but they must satisfy certain statutory requirements. The most important of these is that the employee obtains independent legal advice as to the effect of signing such an agreement. The employer will usually agree to pay towards the cost of this legal advice. The fee agreed is usually about £200 plus VAT.

ACAS★ will act as an honest broker between the parties for the purposes of negotiating a settlement. If the ACAS officer is able to broker an agreement under which the employee agrees to withdraw his or her application to an industrial tribunal, the terms of the settlement will be drawn up on a form known as COT3, which will be signed by both the employer and the employee. Once this form has been signed and the application withdrawn, the employee will no longer be able to make a statutory claim in an industrial tribunal.

Considerations employees may want addressed in the settlement letter

In addition to the points above, employees may wish to cover the following issues:

- date of payment of compensation and confirmation of how it will be taxed (see page 198)
- confirmation that accrued salary and holiday entitlement will be paid (see page 195)
- agreement by the employer to provide a reference in an agreed form (see page 209)
- a statement of pension entitlement (see page 193)
- confirmation that the employer will allow the employee to exercise share options within a pre-agreed time
- confirmation that certain benefits such as private health care and life assurance cover will be kept in place until the renewal date
- agreement on the part of the employer not to make any derogatory statements about the employee to prospective employers
- payment of any outstanding expenses claims
- confirmation that any waiver of claims (see page 213) will not extend to claims for personal injury or accrued rights under the employer's pension scheme.

Considerations for employers when drawing up the settlement letter

Employers may wish to address the following issues:

- the employee's resignation from any directorships (see page 208)
- return of all company property, including company car, computer, printer, fax machine, mobile phone, company credit cards and all documents plus copies of them
- a confidentiality agreement, to prevent the disclosure of confidential information (see Chapter 7)

- post-termination restrictive covenants, to prevent the employee approaching clients or employees (see Chapter 7)
- agreement by the employee not to make derogatory statements about the employer or its employees (see page 209)
- a tax indemnity to cover any tax that the Inland Revenue may argue should have been deducted from payments but was not (see pages 198–201)
- an agreement to waive all claims against the employer, including if necessary a compromise agreement (see page 213)
- the repayment of any loans or parking tickets.

Sample settlement letter

Set out below is a standard form of settlement letter which employees would normally be asked to sign on termination of employment to ensure that a clean break is achieved, by which the employee is precluded from bringing any future claims against the employer.

Mr A.N. Other
[Address]

[Date]

Without prejudice

Dear Mr Other,

I refer to my letter of [Date] in which I confirmed that your employment with XYZ Limited ('the company') had terminated by reason of redundancy with effect from [Date] ('the termination date'). A form P45 has been issued to you. The following terms have been agreed between us:

1 You will be paid your accrued salary and any outstanding holiday pay calculated up to the termination date. Income tax and National Insurance contributions will be deducted in the usual way.

2 The company will provide you with a fair reference and will deal with all oral enquiries in a manner consistent with that reference.

3 You should submit your final expenses claim made up to the termination date to the company within seven days of receipt of this letter. Your expenses will be reimbursed in the usual way.

4   Subject to the fulfilment of the condition set out in paragraph 5 you will receive a payment of [£], within seven days of your countersigning this letter, by way of compensation for the termination of your employment. The first £30,000 will be paid without deduction of tax; tax will be deducted at the basic rate from the remainder.

5   By countersigning this letter you hereby warrant that you have received independent legal advice as to the terms and effect of this letter and the fact that you will be precluded from bringing before an industrial tribunal claims for: unfair dismissal; unauthorised deductions from wages; a statutory redundancy payment; sex, race or disability discrimination. You further warrant that your adviser [name and address] holds a current practising certificate issued by the Law Society, and that your adviser's firm holds a current policy of insurance covering you in respect of loss arising in consequence of their advice to you.

You should deliver a letter from your adviser's firm in a form satisfactory to the company confirming that this advice has been given.

It is agreed that your acceptance of the terms of this letter constitutes a compromise agreement satisfying all the conditions relating to compromise agreements under s203 Employment Rights Act 1996, s77(4) Sex Discrimination Act 1975 (as amended), s72 Race Relations Act 1976, and s9 Disability Discrimination Act 1995.

6   The company shall pay directly to your solicitors your legal fees relating to matters arising out of and concerning the termination of your employment up to a maximum of [£].

7   You confirm that you have returned in good condition all books, documents, papers (including copies), computer equipment (including disks), credit or charge cards, keys or other property of or relating to the business of the company.

8   You will be wholly responsible for the payment of tax of any nature and for liability for National Insurance contributions (if any) arising by virtue of any payment set out in this letter (save for the deduction made by the company in respect of the payments referred to in paragraphs 1 and 4 above), and you will indemnify the company and keep the company indemnified on a continuing basis against all and any liability to taxation which the company may incur in respect of or by reason of such payment.

9 In consideration of a further payment by the company to you of [£], to be made within 14 days after the date hereof, less such tax and National Insurance contributions as the company is required by law to deduct, you hereby agree:

a. not to divulge or make use of (whether directly or indirectly and whether for your own or another's benefit or purposes) any trade secrets or confidential information including but not limited to such information relating to: business plans or dealings; technical data; existing and potential projects; financial information dealings and plans; sales specifications or targets; customer lists or specifications; customers; business developments and plans; research plans or reports; sales or marketing programmes, policies or plans; price lists or pricing policies; employees or officers; source codes; computer systems; software; designs; formula; prototypes; past and proposed business dealings or transactions; product lines; services; or research activities belonging to or which relate to the affairs of the company *or* any document marked 'confidential' (or with a similar expression), any information you have been told is confidential or which you might reasonably expect the company would regard as confidential, and information which has been given in confidence to the company by a third party. This obligation shall apply from the termination date and without limitation in time, but shall not apply to any information in the public domain other than by way of unauthorised disclosure (whether by you or another person)

b. not to make or cause to be made (directly or indirectly) any derogatory or critical comments or statements (whether orally or in writing) about the company, its officers or employees

c. not to disclose (directly or indirectly) to any person or organisation the existence or contents of this letter except to your professional advisers, the Inland Revenue and your partner, *provided always* that disclosure to your professional advisers and partner shall be on terms that they agree to keep the same confidential

d. not to make or cause to be made (directly or indirectly) any statement or comment to the press or other media concerning your employment with the company, its termination or your resignation from any directorships or other offices with the company without the prior written consent of the company

e. you accept the terms of this letter and any sum paid hereunder in full and final settlement of all and any present and future claims or rights of action whatsoever and howsoever arising in all jurisdictions that you have or may have against the company or any employees, officers or agents of the company arising out of or in respect of or relating to your employment or the holding of any office, the termination of your employment or relating to your loss of any office or any other matter whatsoever or howsoever arising including any common-law or statutory claims whatsoever that you have or may have against the company (including without limitation claims under the provisions of the Employment Rights Act 1996, the Sex Discrimination Act 1975, Article 119 of the Treaty of Rome, the Race Relations Act 1976 and the Disability Discrimination Act 1995), and you will refrain from instituting or continuing and will forthwith withdraw unconditionally any legal proceedings or complaint before or to an industrial tribunal in relation to any such matters as are referred to in this paragraph 9.

This letter, and any agreement concluded in relation to it, is to be construed in accordance with and subject to English law. The proposals contained in it are made without any admission of liability.

Please sign, date and return the enclosed duplicate of this letter confirming your agreement with the foregoing.

Yours sincerely

Position ....

For and on behalf of XYZ Limited

I hereby agree to and accept the terms set out in the letter of which this is a duplicate.

Signed ....
A.N. OTHER

Dated ....

Termination letter commentary

Clause 2   The employee has obtained a commitment from the employer to provide a reference.

Clause 5   The document has been drafted as a compromise agreement in order to achieve a clean break, thereby preventing the employee from bringing statutory claims at a later date.

Clause 6   The employer has agreed to pay the employee's legal fees direct to his solicitors rather than as an additional sum to the employee. The payment of these fees by the employer on behalf of the employee will not, in these circumstances, cause the employee to be charged income tax.

Clause 8   The employer has insisted on a tax indemnity. In reality a tax indemnity is only effective if the employee has assets against which it can be enforced. If the employer is concerned about the tax position it should either play safe and deduct tax at source, or obtain prior Inland Revenue clearance on the tax treatment of the payment.

Clause 9   A payment has been attributed to certain restrictions. Payments made in return for entering into post-termination restrictions are subject to tax and National Insurance contributions. The objective of apportioning a sum to these restrictions is to maximise the possibility of the remainder of the payment being paid free of tax.

Clause 9(c) It is not unusual for employers to want employees to keep the terms of settlement confidential in order to avoid other employees who have been dismissed demanding similar treatment.

Clause 9(e) This waiver clause is drafted very widely to exclude any future claim the employee may have against the employer. The employee would usually want to restrict its impact to matters connected with the employment and its termination. In addition, he may want to exclude from the waiver claims for personal injury or accrued pension rights, if he is a member of the employer's pension scheme.

Failure of the parties to reach agreement

Ultimately, if an agreement cannot be reached, the employee must make a decision whether or not to start proceedings in the court or industrial tribunal, or both. Before doing so the employee should think about the following:

- it may be a long time before the claim is heard, and the process may be long, stressful and frustrating
- he or she has a duty to look for suitable alternative employment and any earnings received from this employment will be offset against the compensation claim (see 'Mitigation', page 196)
- substantial legal fees may have to be paid before a settlement is reached, and costs cannot be recovered from the losing party in an industrial tribunal
- although in court the successful party may be awarded costs or legal expenses, it is almost unheard of for an industrial tribunal to award anything meaningful by way of expenses – and even then only in exceptional circumstances
- the employer is likely to have much greater financial resources with which to fight a claim
- the employer can usually re-claim the VAT charged on its legal bills, whereas the employee usually cannot
- the employer is unlikely to provide a reference to help in the search for another job.

For information about applying to an industrial tribunal, see Chapter 16.

Chapter 13

Working overseas

Opportunities for UK citizens to work overseas have increased markedly over recent years, with bankers, engineers, construction workers and many more heading for the Middle East and Far East. Meanwhile, job mobility within Europe has greatly improved (see box below).

Working within the European Economic Area

UK nationals can now work without the need for a work permit anywhere within the European Economic Area (EEA). This zone consists of the 15 European Union states: Austria, Belgium, Denmark, Finland, France, Germany, Greece, Ireland, Italy, Luxembourg, the Netherlands, Portugal, Spain, Sweden and the United Kingdom, together with Norway, Liechtenstein and Iceland. This means that construction workers are free to work on Berlin building sites and students can seek out jobs in Greece without risk of deportation on the grounds that they are working illegally. However, some countries still require foreign workers to register with the local police.

Regardless of which country they work in, all employees share the same concerns when it comes to negotiating the terms of employment. How much will I be paid? What fringe benefits will I receive? Where will I be expected to work? (See Chapter 3.) Whether bankers or bricklayers, people who work overseas must address some other common issues. One of the most important is tax planning.

Tax planning and your financial arrangements

Tax planning is a must for those who decide to work abroad. Employees usually fall into two categories for United Kingdom tax purposes: **resident** and **non-resident**.

Resident in UK

You will be considered resident if, in any tax year (6 April to 5 April):

- you spend more than 183 days (six months) in the UK. It does not matter if this period is continuous or made up of several trips
- you come to the UK to work for a period of at least two years – in which case you will be resident from the date of arrival
- over a four-year period, you visit the UK for an average of 91 days (three months) or more each year – in which case you will be considered **ordinarily resident** in the UK from 6 April of the fifth year.

It is possible to be ordinarily resident in the UK but not resident in a particular year, if, for example, you live abroad for the entire tax year.

If you are resident and/or ordinarily resident you will be taxed on all salary, fringe benefits and other perks (known as 'emoluments') you earn both in the UK and abroad.

If you are resident but not ordinarily resident you will be liable only for tax on emoluments from services carried out in the UK and tax on those emoluments from services abroad which are brought into the UK.

Domicile

You will generally be considered to be **domiciled** in the UK if your permanent home is in the UK and you will probably end your days there. Registering to vote and voting overseas are not normally taken into account in determining whether you are domiciled in the UK.

Non-resident in UK

You will not be treated as resident for tax purposes in the UK if:

- you spend more than 183 days (six months) outside the UK during the tax year
- you work abroad full-time for at least one complete tax year, and have carried out all your duties abroad
- you do not visit the UK for more than an average of 91 days (three months) in any year (the average is taken over the period of absence up to a maximum of four years).

If you are non-resident, you pay UK income tax on only your UK earnings, the profits of a trade or profession carried on wholly or partly inside the UK and UK pensions. You may get relief under a double taxation agreement (see overleaf).

Enquiries about residency may be addressed to the Immigration and Nationality Directorate.*

Calculating the number of days
The day of your departure and the day of your arrival do not normally count as days spent in the UK.

CASE HISTORY: Stewart

Stewart left for Saudi Arabia to work as a foreman on an oil rig on 5 April and returned on 10 April the following year. During this time he came back to the UK for a total of 90 days. Under the terms of his employment, his duties as foreman were restricted entirely to the rig he worked on in Saudi Arabia. Since Stewart's duties were all carried out overseas, he was absent for more than a complete tax year and he did not spend more than a total of 91 days in the UK during that tax year, he was treated as non-resident for tax purposes. Because of this, the earnings he received abroad were not subject to UK tax – although they were of course taxed in Saudi Arabia.

Stretching the rules

Sometimes, employees remain resident in the UK for tax purposes even though they are working overseas – for example, if you worked in a foreign country from May one year to November the following year, owing to the fact that the tax year begins and ends in April, you would not have been employed outside the UK for a complete tax year or have spent over 183 days outside the UK in each relevant tax year. If you do not meet the prescribed criteria for non-residency, you are potentially liable to pay UK tax on your foreign earnings.

Foreign earnings deduction

Prior to the Budget of March 1998, all emoluments arising from duties performed overseas were charged to UK income tax, subject to a possible deduction of 100 per cent – the foreign earnings deduction – for emoluments in respect of duties performed abroad in a 365-day qualifying period. This relief has been abolished by the government.

Tax facts for those working overseas

- The earnings you receive for work overseas are not subject to UK tax provided you are non-resident. However, UK tax will still be payable on earnings from UK sources such as share dividends or interest on a building society account.
- An EU or Commonwealth citizen can set his or her personal allowances against such tax.

Double taxation treaties

The United Kingdom has entered into a large number of so-called double taxation treaties. The purpose of these treaties is to ensure that income earned overseas is not taxed twice, once in the UK and a second time in the country in which the employee is working. Therefore, if for tax purposes your income could be taxed twice, the double taxation treaty will operate to ensure that your earnings are taxed only in the country in which you are working, and that your UK tax liability is reduced by the amount of foreign tax you pay. Each individual treaty has precise rules for deciding which country should have the right to tax the employee. Under this sort of arrangement, one country agrees to give up or reduce its tax in certain circumstances. For example, individuals who are sent to the United States by British employers and lack a permanent home there are exempt from paying the federal taxes, provided they do not stay more than 183 days in the relevant US tax year (1 January to 31 December).

CASE HISTORY: Richard

Richard, an organist, frequently travels overseas to perform in concerts. He pays UK tax but on some payments for concerts abroad, where the country has a double taxation treaty with the UK (for example, in Sweden), he pays tax: in other words, his fee is paid with tax deducted. When preparing his tax return in the UK, Richard is obliged to identify and document those concert fees on which he has already paid tax. The foreign tax paid reduces his UK tax liability on those fees.

Even where no treaty exists, relief from UK tax will generally be available if you are a UK resident paying foreign tax on your earnings abroad. For more information, consult your local tax office.★

Letting the authorities know

If you plan to work abroad, you should inform your local tax office prior to going overseas. You should use Form P85, available from your local tax office, to give the Inland Revenue the following information:

- your National Insurance number
- your employer's name and address abroad
- your date of departure from the UK
- your expected date of return
- the dates of any anticipated visits to the UK during the period abroad.

This should be done as soon as possible. Once you have submitted the form, the Inland Revenue will decide whether it is in a position to authorise the payment of your salary without any deduction of tax. Payment is usually made by the foreign employer.

For more information on the tax position of employees and employers, see *Which? Way to Save Tax* from Which? Limited.★ Two useful leaflets from the Inland Revenue★ are *Residents and Non-residents: Liability to Tax in the United Kingdom* (IR20) and *Income from Abroad? A Guide to UK Tax on Your Overseas Income* (IR139).

Social security contributions

Another issue which needs to be addressed when you go overseas is that of social security contributions and state benefits such as sick pay, pension provision and maternity benefits.

If you choose to work abroad the issue of where you should make contributions and what social security protection is available to you will depend primarily on three factors:

- the country where you will be working
- that country's social legislation
- the relationship between the UK and that country over the provision of social security protection.

EU countries

When employees work in the European Union for a period of less than 12 months and continue to be paid by a UK employer while overseas, both parties will generally continue to pay UK National Insurance contributions during that period.

The employer should obtain a certificate known as Form E101 from the Contributions Agency International Services.* This confirms the obligation of employer and employee to continue making National Insurance contributions and exempts both parties from making social security contributions in the country where the employee is working. It is also possible for self-employed workers overseas to obtain Form E101.

The 12-month period can be extended for a further 12 months and, in certain circumstances, with the agreement of the relevant authorities in the EU country where the individual is working, can be extended beyond this 24-month period for a further three years.

Non-EU countries which have treaty arrangements with the UK

A large number of countries outside the EU have entered into reciprocal agreements with the UK under which employees can avoid having to make social security contributions in two different countries at the same time. The rules of individual treaties differ; however, as a general rule they allow employees to continue to make contributions in the United Kingdom for up to the first 12 months abroad. The United States will allow employees to continue to make UK National Insurance contributions for up to five years after leaving the UK. The employer must apply for the necessary exemption certificate, Form E101, from the Contributions Agency International Services (see above).

Non-EU countries without treaty arrangements with the UK

In this case the employee must continue to pay National Insurance contributions in the UK for the first 12 months if the employer has a place of business in the UK, the employee is ordinarily resident in the UK and was resident in the UK immediately before he or she took the job (see page 222). The employee may in addition be under an obligation to make social security contributions in the country in which he or she is working.

Exemption from paying UK contributions

If the employee is recruited while working abroad to work for an overseas employer, there will be no liability to pay UK National Insurance contributions. However, the employee would be obliged to make contributions in the country in which he or she is working.

Employees can, after leaving the UK, continue to make certain voluntary contributions to the DSS in order to preserve their entitlement to certain state benefits such as the state pension.

Additional help

The Contributions Agency International Services★ handle enquiries regarding the obligation to make National Insurance contributions for all overseas destinations. *Living or Retiring Abroad? A Guide to UK Tax on your UK Income and Pension* (IR138) is a helpful leaflet from the Inland Revenue.★

Renting out property in the UK

Often, employees who decide to go overseas for a considerable period of time opt to rent out their flat or house. In these circumstances the rental income is subject to UK tax regardless of whether the employee is treated as resident or non-resident for tax purposes (see pages 222–3).

The taxable amount of any rental income is calculated by deducting from the rent received the cost of any repairs to the property, agents' fees and mortgage interest. In order to be entitled to make this deduction, the property must be available for renting for at least 26 weeks out of any 52-week period. Those who rent out property while overseas can consult an Inland Revenue★ leaflet: *Non-resident Landlords, Their Agents and Tenants* (IR140).

Negotiating the contract of employment

Expatriates – those living outside their native country – are usually in the strongest negotiating position at the outset of the contract (see Chapter 3).

If you intend to work overseas, you will need to consider the following points.

Notice period

Regardless of the type of work you do, try to negotiate an initial guaranteed period of employment to reflect the risk you have taken in coming overseas (a period of two years is advisable). You could also argue that you need a longer notice period in order to adapt to new surroundings. Obligation to give a long notice period should be restricted to the employer – you should have the right to terminate the contract at short notice if you decide that the project is not to your liking.

Making provision for the end of employment

Make sure that the employer's obligations are clear if the employment is terminated. Typically, the employer should be under an obligation to repatriate the employee and his or her family to the UK or another country of their choice, and should pay any travel costs. You should also ensure that the employer will meet the cost of shipping any belongings home. If possible, try to negotiate a termination bonus.

The extent to which the employer is able to meet your demands will depend on the strength of your negotiating position (see Chapter 3).

Currency of payment

Some currencies are subject to violent fluctuations. To avoid this problem, you should insist that you are paid in stable currency such as UK sterling or US dollars. If your employer wishes to pay you in the host country's currency, you should agree at the outset a minimum rate of exchange.

Law governing the contract of employment

The law that is to govern the contract of employment should be clearly stated on the contract itself. Contracts drawn up overseas are enforceable in the UK; however, it is advisable to have your contract governed by the laws of a legal system that is likely to treat you fairly and based on language you understand.

If you intend to return to the UK, you should insist that the contract is governed by UK law. If any dispute does arise and you are forced to return early, it will be much easier for you to obtain advice on your legal position.

Contracts not governed by any law

In the absence of any agreement to the contrary, the contract will be considered to be governed by the laws of the country in which the employee habitually works. If you have been working overseas, this could prove disadvantageous as the host country's laws will almost certainly apply.

Advantage of UK law

If your contract of employment is governed by UK law, this makes possible the quick calculation of any damages you may be entitled to if the contract is suddenly terminated without justification.

Bringing a statutory claim for unfair dismissal

Workers who are fully employed overseas cannot, even if their contracts are governed by UK law, obtain statutory protection against unfair dismissal (see Chapter 10). You must ordinarily be employed in Great Britain in order to be eligible for this. However, overseas employees may acquire additional protection under the host country's laws, in addition to any rights contained in their contracts of employment. The extent of these rights varies from country to country. Some European countries, such as Germany and France, provide extensive safeguards for employees when they are dismissed, while other locations – including certain American states – are not so generous. The best way to check your rights is to contact a local lawyer.

Fringe benefits

Employees should typically be paid an accommodation allowance, and the contract should include the offer of a certain number of paid flights home in each year. Where possible, particularly on long flights from Australia or Hong Kong, employees should press for business or first-class travel. Many employers will also bear the cost of, or make a contribution to, employees' children's school fees. Again, the precise terms of any arrangement should be carefully recorded.

Work permits

If you require a work permit before departing overseas – to the United States, for example – you should ensure that your prospective overseas employer has applied for and obtained all the necessary immigration clearance before you resign from your job. If you intend to apply for a work permit yourself or are self-employed, contact the embassy of the relevant country at least six weeks in advance to obtain an application form.

Safety and security overseas

If you are planning to travel abroad for work purposes, certain practical considerations must be taken into account.

Before you go

- Arrange passports, visas and work permits six weeks in advance if possible. Allow two to three weeks to obtain the visa (more if a sponsor is required, e.g. to visit Saudi Arabia). Note: to obtain a visa for a trip to Saudi Arabia of over one month, employees must take an AIDS test. This policy is being adopted by some other countries.

- Ensure that you have had the correct vaccinations. Consult your GP or the Medical Advisory Service for Travellers Abroad (MASTA).★

- Find out whether there are import/export restrictions – for example, India, parts of Africa and most communist states prohibit local currency being taken out of the country – and what the allowance is for duty-free goods both to and from your country of destination.

- Try to discover as much as you can about local customs regarding clothing, shop opening hours, taxi fares etc. and check whether there will be any local holidays during your stay (i.e. if you are going to a Muslim country, will you be there during Ramadan?). If a colleague has visited your destination already, ask him or her for advice.

- Check the driving conditions and how local traffic regulations differ. Many countries have more severe drink/driving laws than the UK.

- Provide your UK employer and/or next of kin with contact numbers in case of emergency. You should also leave the numbers of your credit cards and travellers cheques in case of theft.

- If you do not already have a will, it is recommended that you write one. Consult your solicitor or read *Wills and Probate* from Which? Limited.★

- Hand in your NHS medical card to the immigration officer at your port of departure if you are leaving the country for over three months.

On your arrival

- Register with the British Embassy/Consulate as soon as you arrive, if you are staying for more than a short period or where there is local unrest.

- Keep expenses claim sheets up to date and collect receipts.

Checklist of essential items

International driving licence (if appropriate), extra passport photos for use during your visit (e.g. for ID cards, local driving licences, etc.), electrical adaptors, local phrase book, first-aid kit and water purification tablets (if working in a remote area), blood group identification (if working in an area where AIDS is particularly prevalent, e.g. Africa).

On your return

- Have a medical examination in the UK as soon as you return if you feel at all unwell, telling your doctor where you have been.
- Carry on taking preventive medicine as prescribed (e.g. malaria tablets).
- If requested to do so, write a debriefing report for the UK employer.
- Submit any expenses claims.

The Foreign and Commonwealth Office (FCO) Travel Advice Unit* offers information on the risks to travellers in different countries through a helpline and a web site. The information comes from British embassies and consulates and is updated as necessary.

Safety standards at work

In the developed Western and Eastern Bloc countries, health and safety at work standards will in many respects be similar to those found in the United Kingdom. However, even in these countries there will be regions or sites where standards will be substantially lower. In developing countries, standards will most likely be lower than in the UK because resources for maintenance and operation are often scarce. This will be the case even in those countries which are members of the International Labour Organisation and subscribe to the international health and safety guidelines produced by that body.

Local safety procedures

Where local safety procedures are less stringent than in the UK, the overriding safety guideline is: never jeopardise your own personal safety by adopting a method of working which would result in a safety risk greater than you would experience in the UK. In the unusual event of local safety procedures being more stringent than in the UK (for example, in the United States), it is advisable to follow local regulations.

Insurance

If you intend to work overseas, you will need travel insurance to cover yourself against the costs of emergency medical treatment abroad plus a host of other potential mishaps. The sort of insurance you will need will vary according to whether you are taking short business trips or working overseas for long periods, the nature and extent of the work you will be doing and the type of arrangement the employer has in place.

Check what is on offer from your employer first. It is probable that your company will be able to fix cover for you: it may have an arrangement with an insurance company. Alternatively the employer may have an emergency telephone number, for example.

Most standard travel policies include cover against the following eventualities:

- medical expenses
- personal liability
- cancellation and curtailment
- loss of money and personal belongings (including passport and tickets)
- personal accident (including accidental death or bodily injury)
- legal expenses
- delayed or missed departure.

It is important to ensure that the policy covers repatriation in the event of death or serious illness.

Generally, travel insurance will not cover:

- certain business activities (for which you may need specialist professional indemnity insurance)
- hazardous activities (e.g. hang-gliding, bungee jumping)
- claims as a result of driving abroad (covered by your car insurance policy)
- claims as a result of war
- women in the last three months of pregnancy
- HIV-related illnesses and AIDS
- detainment by Customs or government officials and confiscation/ destruction of baggage
- loss owing to exchange rates moving against you.

Pay-as-you go policies cover you for one specific trip and are the best choice if you go abroad infrequently for less than 21 days at a time, while annual policies cover foreign travel for a whole year. If opting for an annual policy, make sure that it covers you for the country or countries that you are planning to work in and that you are covered for the total length of your stay – some annual policies limit the number of days for which cover is provided. (People planning to live abroad for a considerable length of time should inform their insurers in the UK since this may affect buildings and contents policies, for example.)

You may already have insurance for some of the elements travel insurance aims to cover: for example, if you have top-of-the-range private medical insurance you may already be covered for emergency medical expenses worldwide, while if you are a member of your company sick pay scheme you may be entitled to financial compensation in the event of suffering a disability. If you are not already covered, you should aim for minimum medical expenses cover of £1 million.

Insurance for medical expenses will cover bills for a hospital stay, out-patient treatment, emergency dental care and consultations with a doctor, as well as the cost of prescriptions. Because of the expense of treatment in some countries and the poor medical conditions in others, many insurance companies would rather you were treated in the UK and will pay to bring you back, by air ambulance if necessary.

If you are self-employed, the contractor who has commissioned you may be willing to pay for cover for you. Otherwise you should make your own arrangements following the guidelines above. For more information on travel insurance, see *The Which? Guide to Insurance* from Which? Limited.★

Form E111

Form E111 (available from post offices) entitles you to free or reduced-cost treatment in EEA member states (see box, page 221). If you require treatment while staying in one of these countries you must present Form E111 together with proof of UK residency. Depending on the arrangements that the UK has with the country in which you fall ill, you may still need to pay for the treatment (keeping all receipts for any drugs or treatment that you receive) and then claim a refund either abroad or when you return to the UK. The E111 can be useful but is no substitute for the medical expenses part of travel insurance if you want cover for other possible costs such as emergency repatriation.

Death overseas

The travel insurance policy usually covers the cost of burial or cremation overseas or of bringing the body back to the UK.

When a British subject dies abroad, whether as a resident or as a visitor, the death must be registered where the individual has died in accordance with local regulations and customs. The British Consul can offer advice in these circumstances. For more information, consult *What to Do When Someone Dies* from Which? Limited.*

Chapter 14

Employing overseas nationals

As the flow of British employees working overseas increases (see Chapter 13), likewise overseas nationals continue to come to the United Kingdom. American bankers and lawyers have flocked to the City of London, while refugees from the former Yugoslavia, Russia and other former Eastern Bloc states have also headed for Britain. Some of these employees, such as IT specialists, have skills that are in short supply. Others, who are unskilled, are prepared to take low-paid jobs that resident nationals are less willing to do, such as factory or cleaning work.

Illegal working: a growing problem

According to the Home Office Immigration and Nationality Directorate,* the number of people detected by the Immigration Service while working in the UK either illegally or while prohibited has risen significantly in recent years. (There is a difference: the first term describes an immigrant who has unlawfully entered the country through a breach of immigration laws or by deception, while a prohibited individual may have the right to enter the country but is not allowed to pursue employment.) The result of this increase was the introduction of the **Asylum and Immigration Act 1996**, which aims to punish employers for employing people who have no legal right to work in the United Kingdom.

Until January 1997, when sanctions on employers with an illegal workforce were introduced as a result of the Act, the penalties for employers were minimal. Although employees were liable to be deported or imprisoned for breaches of the immigration rules, action was rarely taken against their bosses. Today, an employer who employs someone who does not have the legal right to work in the UK commits a criminal offence and is subject to a fine of up to £5,000.

Typically, employers who take on employees as casual labour – in restaurants or hotels, or on building sites, for example – are most at risk from hiring people without realising they are illegal because of the high availability of casual staff.

The law on illegal working

Section 8 of the Asylum and Immigration Act makes it an offence for an employer to employ a person aged 16 or over unless that person has lawfully entered the UK and has the right to work there.

People exempt from immigration control

The following groups can freely enter the UK and are entitled to live and work there:

- British citizens
- nationals of European Economic Area countries and their families (see page 221)
- Commonwealth citizens entitled to live in the UK and their families. The position for Commonwealth citizens is complex and varies according to where their parents or grandparents were born.

For advice on entry to the UK and immigration rules, contact the Migration and Visa Division of the Foreign and Commonwealth Office.*

Preventing illegal working

If there is any doubt as to the status of an individual the employer should try to ensure that the person has the right to work *before* employing him or her.

If it comes to light that an employer has employed someone who is working illegally, he or she will have a defence against prosecution provided that he or she has seen, and taken a copy of, a document which appears to show that the individual in question has the right to work legally (see below). This defence will hold good unless it can be proved that the employer knew that the person was not entitled to work in the UK at the time that he or she was employed.

The employer is obliged to check whether an employee has the right to work legally in the UK only if that employee was taken on after 27 January 1997. In other words, employers are under no obligation to check whether employees taken on prior to 27 January 1997 have the necessary permission. However, this protection extends only to employers; by contrast, illegal workers hired before this date remain liable to deportation or imprisonment. Police and immigration officers have full powers to enforce the Asylum and Immigration Act, and it is advisable that employers check the rights of all their employees to work in the UK.

The employer needs to have seen only one of a wide range of documents to establish a defence against prosecution. The most common include:

- any document produced by the Benefits Agency, Contributions Agency or Employment Service with the employee's National Insurance number on it
- a form P45
- a form P60
- a valid work permit
- a passport or national identity card issued by a European Economic Area state.

The vast majority of workers who can produce a National Insurance number will either be British citizens or have the right to work in the UK, and in most cases workers should be able to produce valid credentials.

The employer should make a copy of the document produced. If the document is a passport or other travel documents, it may be necessary to photocopy the relevant pages (including that bearing the entry stamp). Normally the employer should not retain the original document unless it is a P45. However, it is important to keep copies while the worker is in employment, and for at least six months after he or she has left employment.

If the employee cannot provide any of the specified documents

In these circumstances the employer would be ill-advised to employ the individual until satisfactory evidence of his or her legality can be produced. If it came to light that the person was working illegally, the employer would not have a valid defence and might be liable to prosecution.

Employers are obliged to check only the credentials of their employees – in other words, they would not be expected to check the status of self-employed freelances or agency temps employed by a recruitment agency. However, if an employer took on staff recruited on its behalf by a recruitment agency, the ultimate responsibility for carrying out the checks would rest with the employer rather than the agency.

Avoiding racial discrimination

Under the Race Relations Act 1976 it is unlawful for an employer to discriminate against employees on the basis of their race, colour, ethnic or national origin, or nationality. In the light of this, when checking whether potential employees have the right to work in the UK, employers should ensure that the same procedure is applied to every job candidate: for example, job applicants from racial minorities should not be asked to produce their passports if other applicants who look or sound British are merely asked to produce evidence of their National Insurance number. If such a policy were pursued, applicants from racial minorities would potentially have a claim for racial discrimination against the prospective employer (see Chapter 5).

Work permits for overseas nationals

For many employers, from football clubs to advertising agencies and newly established companies, the best way of getting key personnel into the UK is by way of a work permit. During 1997 the demand for work permits increased by 36 per cent, according to the Overseas Labour Service* of the Department for Education and Employment.

Work permits are in demand for various reasons. One is that British companies are now beginning to take seriously the year 2000 computer time-bomb known as the Millennium Bug. Systems may become unreliable due to the date change, and Britain's banks alone plan to spend £1 billion on averting a computer breakdown. The result is a surge in demand for IT experience. Many IT support service organisations are now importing the necessary IT skills from overseas, particularly India, in order to meet demand. Employers are increasingly making multiple applications for workers because winning a particular IT support contract is often dependent on ensuring that the necessary foreign labour will have the right to work in the UK for the duration of the contract. Other areas of the UK economy are also booming and registering an increased demand for workers – not just the IT sector.

Finding the right employee for the job can be a time-consuming exercise, and it is not made any easier in a booming economy. The task will be even more frustrating if it transpires that the employee does not have an automatic right to work in the UK. Commercial pressures and tight deadlines increase the temptation to set the employee to work immediately and sort out the paperwork later. However, this sort of approach is risky as well as illegal, and hence it is strongly advisable to follow the correct procedure as outlined below.

The work permit scheme

The purpose of the work permit scheme is to safeguard, where possible, the resident EEA labour market (see page 221). In broad terms, before obtaining a work permit for an overseas worker, employers must first satisfy the Overseas Labour Service that there is no other employee in either the UK or the rest of the EEA capable of doing that particular job.

To this end, any post must be advertised within the UK and the EEA before the employer can consider candidates from outside this area. This requirement can be waived where the position is very specialised or there are other mitigating factors, for example:

- senior board appointments
- posts that are essential to attracting jobs and capital to the UK (e.g. individuals whose leadership is a key factor in getting outside backers to invest in the UK)

- occupations acknowledged by the relevant industry to be in short supply nationally – e.g. the medical profession, particularly nursing
- employees brought to the UK on inter-company transfers from overseas – in particular, senior employees with badly needed skills, and junior employees who need experience before returning overseas.

Applying for a work permit

Prospective employers are obliged to apply for the required number of work permits. Note: this is *not* necessary for EEA nationals or non-EEA workers married to EEA citizens. A non-EEA husband or wife can work even if his or her spouse is not working.

Employers who need permits for overseas nationals should request application forms as soon as possible. These are obtainable from the Overseas Labour Service★ within mainland Britain, and from the Training and Employment Agency★ in Northern Ireland. Several categories of permission are available, including training and work experience permits plus those for entertainers and sportsmen and -women. The most popular is the full work permit known as a 'WPI', which covers most types of employee. In the case of the 'keyworker' permit category, the employer must satisfy the Overseas Labour Service that the individual it wishes to employ has a unique range of skills whether or not he or she is not highly qualified.

Non-transferability of work permits

A work permit is specific to a particular job. For example, if an employer is granted a work permit for an IT consultant and that consultant decides to leave and accept employment with another IT firm based in Britain, his or her new employer will have to apply for and obtain a work permit for the consultant before the employee is free to start work with that employer.

The amount of time it takes the Overseas Labour Service to process an application varies according to the section the application is allocated to. When confirming receipt of the application, the Overseas Labour Service will indicate the likely length of time before a decision can be reached. Depending on the type of permit required, processing may take between four to eight weeks. In exceptional circumstances –

typically where the employee involved is very senior: for example, the chief executive of a major listed company or a high-flying merchant banker – the Overseas Labour Service may fast-track an application within a week.

When processing an application, the Overseas Labour Service may require evidence that the post has been advertised and that no suitable EEA nationals have been located. If this requirement is not satisfied, there is a real risk that the application will be rejected.

Careful scrutiny will be given to any application which requires an employee for longer than four years in total. This is because once the employee has completed four years' continuous employment on a work permit, he or she can apply for indefinite leave to remain in the UK free of work-permit restrictions.

Business visitors

Because of the delays often associated with preparing, submitting and processing work-permit applications, some employers slip their employees in under the guise of being 'business visitors'. A business visitor is legitimately entitled to carry out certain duties whilst in the UK; however, this does not stretch to working full-time for a prospective employer. Any employer which allows an overseas national to start work before a work permit has been obtained is committing a criminal offence under the Asylum and Immigration Act. For further information see *Business Visitors*, a leaflet from the Immigration and Nationality Directorate* of the Home Office.

Making the job offer conditional

Any employer that makes a job offer to an individual who requires a work permit should ensure that the offer is subject to both the procurement of a permit within a reasonable period of time and the employee's compliance with all the necessary immigration requirements. If the employer fails to make the offer conditional and allows the employee to start work and the application is subsequently refused, the employer may be left with a worker lured on the offer of a generous relocation package who cannot be employed in the position for which he or she was recruited. This could lead to the employer dismissing the employee and having to pay substantial compensation, depending on the terms of the contract – in addition to any relocation costs incurred in enticing the employee to the UK in the first place.

Once overseas nationals who are entitled to work in the UK start employment, they are entitled to the same treatment as British workers and have the same the rights at work (see Chapter 4).

Additional help

The Overseas Labour Service★ is willing to meet employers to discuss prospective work-permit applications and to discuss its current approach and thinking. This can be useful for employers whose future plans are dependent on receiving guidance as to whether they will be able to import the necessary overseas expertise. In the case of an employer involved in IT support services work, for example, the Overseas Labour Service might want to see a letter of intent with the official application, or preferably a contract setting out the details of the project on which the foreign workers will be deployed. Usually, the Overseas Labour Service will try to ensure that contracts of this type are not open-ended but relate to a project with a finite timescale.

The Overseas Labour Service provides a useful guide on filling in work-permit forms entitled *Guide for Employers: Work Permit Applications*. Further information on employers' obligations under the Asylum and Immigration Act can be obtained from the Home Office★ Employer's Helpline. Employers who contact the Helpline can also request guidance notes entitled *Prevention of Illegal Working*.

Chapter 15

Health and safety at work

Health and safety at work is an issue of concern for all employers and employees, from coal miners who contract chest infections caused by working long periods underground (see case history below), to builders and decorators using scaffolding and ladders, to office workers suffering repetitive strain injury after working long hours at computer keyboards, to anyone in employment who suffers injury due to, for example, trailing cables, faulty electrics *or* machinery, insecure fixtures and fittings, lack of guards on dangerous equipment, lack of warnings about dangerous substances, or being required to drive or travel in an unfit motor vehicle. According to a 1990 Labour Force survey, 1.6 million workplace injuries occur annually, while 2 million cases of ill health are caused or worsened by conditions at work.

Over the decades several Acts of Parliament have been passed to regulate safety in the workplace for both employees and visitors to the employers' premises. Increasingly, legislation is being generated by the European Union. Some of it is designed to deal with specific areas of concern such as the use of visual display units.

CASE HISTORY: British Coal

In January 1998 the High Court ruled that British Coal were negligent because they had failed to take reasonable steps to minimise dust levels during the 1950s and 1960s, despite the availability of dust suppression techniques. As a result, former miners developed debilitating lung diseases such as emphysema and chronic bronchitis following retirement. British Coal has not admitted liability but 10,000 claims have been lodged and compensation payouts may equal £1 billion.

Employers' health and safety obligations

The main duty for employers is set out in the **Health and Safety at Work Act 1974**. The aim of the Act is to raise the awareness of health and safety and to involve everybody, both employers and employees, in ensuring that the workplace is safe. The Act applies to everyone involved in employment, whatever their status, and also seeks to protect members of the public from work-related dangers.

The Act states that it is the duty of the employer to ensure, as far as is reasonably practicable, the health, safety and welfare at work of its employees. This means that in deciding whether the employer has fulfilled its duty, account should be taken of the degree of risk in a particular job or workplace and this should be balanced against the time, travel costs and difficulty involved in taking measures to avoid that risk. In other words, if the risk to which the employees are subjected is very small and the cost involved in avoiding it is substantial, the employer would be justified in not taking steps to eliminate that particular risk. However, if the risk were minimal but the consequences could be potentially far-reaching – for example, if a nuclear plant were to leak radioactive material – then precautions would need to be taken, whatever the cost.

What the Act requires in practical terms is that the employer should assess the risks and take sensible measures to tackle them. What is reasonable will vary widely depending on the individual workplace and its inherent dangers. A leaflet from the Health and Safety Executive (HSE)* entitled *Advice to Employers* outlines employers' rights and obligations.

The Health and Safety Executive

The Health and Safety Executive (HSE) is a statutory body appointed by the Health and Safety Commission. The HSE offers an advisory service and can prosecute employers which fail to meet legal standards: the maximum fine for most offences is £2,000. Local offices of the HSE, which include HM Factory, Quarries, Agriculture, Mines and Nuclear Inspectorates can advise on the requirements of individual premises.

Risk assessment

In addition to the Act, the **Management of Health and Safety at Work Regulations 1992** (Management Regulations) require employers with five or more employees to carry out a risk assessment of the workplace. The risk assessment exercise may be straightforward in premises such as an office or warehouse, but if it is a mine or a nuclear power station the procedure is much more complex. For more information, employers may consult a leaflet entitled *Five Steps to Risk Assessment* from the HSE.★

Rules with which employers are expected to comply

Various measures have been introduced by Parliament which relate to specific areas of concern. Some of the relevant obligations, which are derived from European law, require employers to do the following.

- **Take out insurance against accidents to employees and work-related illness suffered by employees** Employers should ensure that the liability cover extends to self-employed workers and contractors.
- **Observe recommendations regarding VDU usage** (see 'VDU safety', opposite).
- **Provide the appropriate protective equipment and clothing for employees** in accordance with the environment in which they work. Employees likely to come into contact with hazardous substances (anything that is toxic, harmful, corrosive or an irritant) should be given proper instruction.
- **Ensure that equipment provided for use at work is safe** Equipment should meet the legal safety requirements and be regularly tested.
- **Observe recommendations concerning the manual handling of heavy equipment** Correct lifting techniques should be followed in order to avoid the likelihood of back injury.
- **Observe first-aid requirements** The statutory requirement is for provision 'suitable' to the conditions on the premises. In other words, the training for first-aiders must cover the injuries likely to be met on site.

- **Observe recommendations concerning the work environment** This means providing and maintaining adequate ventilation, heating, lighting, work stations, seating and welfare facilities.

Employers must appoint safety officers from among their staff, whose job it is to monitor safety standards and report all accidents, illness and dangerous occurrences within their area of control to their supervisor. Employers must supply training for all safety officers, first-aiders and fire wardens in the workforce. In addition to implementing internal safety policies, employers often have separate directives for contractors and service staff, such as cleaners.

Preventing health problems at work

Many common problems can be alleviated by good organisation. The design of the workplace is important, as is efficiency on the part of staff and managers in respect of how work is done – for example, a worker could vary his or her tasks in order to avoid spending long hours in front of the screen. Musculoskeletal problems, visual fatigue and mental stress tend to affect desk-based office staff. To help combat symptoms, employees should perform stretching exercises (possibly at their desks) and take regular breaks.

Working environment
Lighting levels should be carefully assessed and natural lighting made use of wherever possible. Glare should be minimised by shielding light fittings and providing anti-glare screens for monitors. Chairs should have adjustable backs for correct lumbar support and should provide support for the upper arm.

VDU safety
Employees using visual display units should rest their eyes frequently. If experiencing dry or sore eyes or focusing difficulties, they should request an eye test (see below). Screens may be placed at right angles to windows and between rows of lighting to minimise the amount of glare experienced by workers.

Employees whose jobs cannot be done without the use of visual display units (VDUs) are entitled to an annual eye examination. The employer is obliged to pay for the check-up, which may take place on the premises. If the results of tests show that the employee is required to wear glasses for VDU use only, the employer must contribute to the price of the glasses. The Eye Care Information Service* can provide more information.

Pregnant employees and VDUs

According to the HSE, despite considerable public concern scientific studies to date have not shown a link between VDU use and miscarriage or birth defects. If pregnant employees are concerned about working with display screens they should consult their human resources or personnel officer.

Repetitive strain injury

Repetitive strain injury (RSI), also known as 'work-related upper limb disorder', can cause pain, inability to use the hand or arm properly and swelling of the joints. The symptoms are caused by performing a set of repetitive movements (for example, typing). The condition is made worse by having a heavy workload, unvaried tasks, insufficient rest periods and poorly designed office equipment. For employees to avoid suffering this kind of work-related damage, they should be allowed to take short rest periods and a lunch break of at least 30 minutes.

CASE HISTORY: Midland Bank

Several computer workers at a branch of Midland Bank were given a greater workload. As a result, all experienced considerable pain throughout their necks, shoulders and arms. Their condition was held to be repetitive strain injury. In May 1998 a court ruled that the bank had been in breach of its duty of care towards the workers. Each employee was awarded £7,000 as well as compensation for loss of earnings.

Unsafe conditions at work

The following conditions may give rise to a hazard:

- inadequate lighting/ventilation
- unguarded dangerous parts of machinery
- badly maintained power services
- provision of makeshift plant and equipment
- gangways/stairs obstructed.

Whenever an incident occurs at work, it should be fully reported in accordance with whatever procedures the employer has in place – even if the event constitutes a 'near miss' causing no injuries or damage, correctional measures may need to be taken.

Accident prevention

The three main measures employers can take are:

- training staff at all levels and increasing their awareness of health and safety issues
- providing staff with protective equipment that complies with legal requirements. Note: this may not guarantee safety owing to unpredictable behaviour on the part of individuals
- providing and maintaining environmental and physical safe-guards to meet the needs of individuals at risk (and cope with unpredictable behaviour).

Injury at work

If an employee is injured at work, he or she should notify his or her immediate superior right away and ensure that the incident is noted in the company's accident book. If the injury is serious, an ambulance should be summoned. In the case of some injuries – head injuries, for example – the full extent is not always immediately apparent and taking such action can help to pinpoint the cause of a health problem. The employee should have a medical examination as soon as possible so that evidence to show that the injury was work-related can be gathered to establish how serious it was. This is particularly important in cases where there is a long time lapse between the date when the injury was suffered and that of the court hearing. If the employee does nothing, his or her employer may try to argue at a future date that the injuries suffered were not work-related.

Liability of the employer

Employees should not be deterred, through fear of the company suffering financial hardship, from suing their employers for injury caused at work. The common misapprehension is that if the employee sues the employer, the employer will suffer directly. However, all employers must have insurance against injury suffered by employees at work; so long as the employer has appropriate insurance cover then it is its insurers who will ultimately settle the claim.

Time limits for submitting a claim

Employees have up to three years from the date when the injury occurred, or three years from the date on which they were first aware of the injury in which to submit a claim to the court.

Example   If an employee suffers burns to his leg at work as a result of the employer's failure to provide adequate protective clothing, the employee would have three years from the date on which the injury was sustained in which to bring a claim.

Example   If an employee were to contract a disease as a result of working for the employer and it was some years before the extent of that disease became apparent, the three-year period would start from when the employee was first aware of the disease, and *not* from the date on which it was first contracted.

The laws have been relaxed to enable employees to get help in bringing legal action in personal injury cases (see 'Conditional-fee arrangements', page 275).

Stress at work

Normally when people think about injury at work they think of an instantly recognisable injury such as a broken leg, a burnt arm or a shattered toe. Since the 1980s a growing number of employees have claimed to be suffering from work-related stress.

Some common symptoms of stress and anxiety are:

- feelings of fear and panic
- headaches
- anger or irritability

- altered eating habits
- disturbed sleep
- poor concentration.

The employees who suffer the most stress tend to work long hours, be poorly paid and often have little variety in their working life or control over their jobs: for example, supermarket check-out staff and those doing routine clerical work. By contrast, senior employees suffering 'executive stress' tend to work long hours but enjoy a more varied workload and better pay. Often, specific circumstances may trigger stress: relocating for business purposes ranks as a notably stressful event, and worries about redundancy can also take their toll.

Until the case described below (see 'Steve' case history), there was no recorded incidence of an employee successfully suing an employer for stress-related illness. In the past, fortunate employees might be retired early on ill-health grounds while the less fortunate ones were simply forced to look for a less stressful job. However, after Steve's case in 1995 it was established that employees who suffer illness or injury as a result of stress at work can succeed with claims for personal injury against their employer.

CASE HISTORY: Steve

Steve, a social worker, had an employer who imposed impossible deadlines. As a result of work-related stress, Steve suffered a breakdown. Following his return to work, the employer insisted that Steve deal with the same heavy workload as before. Unable to cope, Steve had another breakdown as a result. It was established in Steve's case that the employer's duty to provide a safe place of work extended not only to physical but to mental injuries as well.

Establishing the grounds for a case

In order to succeed with a claim for stress-related injury, employees must negotiate the same hurdles as for any other personal injury case. They must establish that:

- the employer had a duty of care which was broken
- the injury was caused as a result of the employer's breach
- in the circumstances, the injury was reasonably foreseeable.

The success or failure of stress-related claims usually hinges on two points:

(1)   was the risk of a stress-related illness reasonably foreseeable?
(2)   was the injury caused as a result of the employer's actions?

Steve's case meets both of these criteria. Point 1 is satisfied because after Steve's first breakdown it was reasonably foreseeable that an excessive workload would expose him to the risk of injury once more. His employer's decision to overload him with work following the breakdown meets point 2.

Future treatment of stress-related claims

The European Working Time Directive will soon be part of UK law. This will regulate the number of hours worked by employees and the periods of rest to which they are entitled. Since Steve's case made the news, the HSE* has published guidelines on how to deal with stress at work. These include *Stress at Work: A Guide for Employers* (HSG116) and *Mental Distress at Work* (INDG129L).

These changes, coupled with increasing awareness of stress-related problems, may make it less easy for employers to argue that they cannot reasonably be expected to foresee a health risk for employees who are obliged to work long hours in order to meet tight deadlines. However, even if it becomes easier to demonstrate that stress-related injuries are foreseeable, proving that any mental illness suffered by employees is caused by work-related stress remains a problem. Stress-related illness is often the result of a combination of problems, some of which may not be work-related, such as relationship difficulties or a bereavement. Some employees may be unusually susceptible to stress-related illness because they possess certain psychological characteristics. In cases where a specific cause cannot be easily pinned down, employers will have stronger grounds for arguing that any injury caused by working conditions was not reasonably foreseeable.

Actions for employees suffering from stress

Employees who are subject to excessive levels of stress should inform their employers at the earliest opportunity about the problems they are facing. They should ensure that they make a careful note of the date and the name of the person with whom they have spoken. The more carefully the employee documents the incidence of stress and draws the employer's attention to the extent of the pressure that he or she is under, the less likely it is that the employer will be able to establish that stress-related illness was not unforeseeable. If the employee becomes ill, he or she should obtain a medical report to use as evidence.

A few companies have in-house counsellors who can offer assistance with personal problems and work-related issues. Some firms have an Employee Assistance Programme (EAP) in place. Under such schemes, employees may be referred to a counsellor retained by the company. The service is likely to be confidential and paid for by the employer. Alternatively, the human resources or personnel officer should be able to put the employee in touch with someone reliable. Those suffering from stress can contact the British Association for Counselling★ and Relate,★ which deals with individuals as well as couples.

Statutory sick pay

Provided that they meet the qualifying conditions, employees who are absent from work due to illness are entitled to receive statutory sick pay (SSP) from their employer (see page 65). Their contracts of employment may provide for enhanced sickness benefits (see page 47). In normal circumstances, employers are not able to recover SSP payments from the state (unlike statutory maternity pay – see page 109). However, there is an exception for employers which experience a large degree of absenteeism due to sickness. In such cases, the employer can recover a proportion of its SSP payments. Note: small employers are not exempt from making payments. For more information, employers can consult a booklet entitled *Recovering Statutory Sick Pay* from the Benefits Agency,★ which gives a detailed explanation of the system.

Additional help

For guidance on the state benefits available if you are sick or disabled, see Social Security leaflet FB28 or phone the Benefits Enquiry line.★ The HSE★ Information line provides advice on a wide range of issues; alternatively you can contact your local HSE office. Chapter 10 outlines the position when an employee is dismissed on the grounds of ill health.

Chapter 16

Bringing a case to an industrial tribunal

If you have a claim for breach of contract because you have been dismissed without notice or justification (see page 174) you can choose whether to bring a claim in either the **county court** or **high court**, or alternatively at an **industrial tribunal**.

Advantages of the courts

- Victors get at least a proportion of their legal costs back.
- You may be eligible for legal aid (see pages 275–6).

Where your case is heard will depend on the amount of compensation claimed. Generally, the county court considers cases in which the claim for compensation is under £25,000 (under £15,000 in Northern Ireland), while the high court deals with claims of over £50,000. Either court can deal with claims of between £25,000 and £50,000. Sometimes the high court handles complex cases involving less than £25,000.

The **small claims court** is part of the county court. It hears claims of £3,000 or less (£1,000 or less in Northern Ireland), and is designed for use by litigants in person without legal representation. The judge will arbitrate any matter that proceeds to a hearing without a formal trial. Unlike other court actions, no legal costs are recoverable by the successful party.

In order to bring an action in the county or small claims court, the claim must be set out on a summons. Blank summons forms are available from any county court for this purpose. A fee of between £10 and £500, calculated according to the level of the claim, is payable to the court. The county court must issue the summons before it can be served on the defendant – by either the plaintiff (the person bringing the action) or the court itself. The defendant must then acknowledge the claim and state whether he or she admits it, admits part of it, or wishes to defend it. If the matter is not settled before the date of the trial, the plaintiff may appear at the trial or instruct a solicitor or barrister (see Chapter 17). The matter will be heard by a judge sitting alone. The successful party will normally receive a contribution towards the costs he or she has incurred.

The courts in Scotland

In Scotland, claims for breach of contract are normally brought in the **sheriff court** – which deals with small claims (under £750) and summary causes (between £750 and £1,500) – or the **court of session** (for claims over £1,500).

Advantages of an industrial tribunal

* An industrial tribunal is less formal than a court.
* The industrial tribunal team will explain the procedures in a sympathetic manner to those who bring a claim without the aid of a lawyer and will not treat their arguments any less seriously.
* Cases are usually heard more quickly at an industrial tribunal than court cases. Applicants can expect to get a hearing date of four to six months after submitting the application while a high court case could, for example, take up to 18 months to come to court.

The downside is that legal aid is not available and even if you win the case you will not normally recover any costs you have incurred. In England, Wales and Scotland the tribunal's power to award compensation for breach of contract is currently capped at £25,000 (£12,000 in Northern Ireland). However, in Northern Ireland there is no limit for claims involving religious discrimination (see page 77).

Statutory claims that must be brought at an industrial tribunal

These include claims for:

- unfair dismissal (see Chapter 10)
- statutory redundancy payments (see page 191)
- sex, racial and disability discrimination (see Chapter 5)
- equal pay (see Chapter 5)
- unauthorised deductions from wages.

Function of the industrial tribunal

Industrial tribunals were in operation from 1964, albeit with limited powers of jurisdiction. In 1971 they came into their own, with the aim of providing a less formal environment than court in which employees' claims could be heard.

Industrial tribunals usually consist of a panel of three people, one of whom will be a chairman who is legally qualified. One of the other two will be an employer and the other a trade union representative.

Proposed changes to the tribunal system

When the **Employment Rights (Dispute Resolution) Act 1998** comes into force in 1999, industrial tribunals will be renamed 'employment tribunals'. Regulations will also be introduced whereby tribunals may determine proceedings without a hearing – in other words, in reliance on written evidence. In addition, both parties will have the option of submitting their case to binding voluntary arbitration instead of to an employment tribunal.

Applying to an industrial tribunal

The first step is to get an application form – an IT1. (See sample sent to applicants in England, Wales and Scotland on pages 258–9.) These can be obtained from job centres, law centres, Citizens Advice Bureaux★ and the industrial tribunal Enquiry line.★ The booklet accompanying the application form will indicate the regional tribunal office to which the individual should return the form (this is determined by reference to the employer's postcode). In Northern Ireland, applicants can contact the Office of the Industrial Tribunals and the Fair Employment Tribunal★ or training and employment offices.

While negotiations are under way between the parties, employees may be tempted to withhold submitting an application in the hope that matters will be settled amicably or may be wary of antagonising the employer by returning the form. In addition, some employees are afraid of tangling with officialdom. The action of submitting a claim may seem a grave step from which there is no way back. In fact, employees can withdraw an application at any time. However, if they submit a late application it is only in very exceptional circumstances that the industrial tribunal would hear it (see below). Furthermore, once an employer knows that the employee has lost the ability to bring a claim because the time limit has expired, it is surprising how quickly many of them lose interest in negotiating a settlement.

Time limits for submitting a claim

Different claims are subject to different time limits. For example, a claim for a statutory redundancy payment must be submitted within six months of the date of dismissal, while claims for unfair dismissal or sex, racial or disability discrimination must be submitted within three months of the date on which the act of discrimination was committed. Late claims are usually time-barred.

However, the industrial tribunal may hold what is called a 'preliminary hearing' to consider why the application was late. There, it will decide whether to allow the application to be heard. Industrial tribunals will not normally consider the fact that negotiations were continuing a sufficient reason for not submitting an application.

Safeguarding the employee's position

It is always better for the employee to protect his or her bargaining position and submit an application in good time rather than simply ignoring the time limit and hoping that the employer will continue to negotiate in good faith. The application form needs only to contain brief details of the case. Its purpose is to reserve the employee's right to pursue the claim if negotiations break down.

Once the industrial tribunal has received an application, it will provide the employee who has completed it (described as the **applicant**) with a case number which should be quoted in all correspondence. A copy of the application is then sent to the employer (known as the **respondent**), together with a form known as the **notice of**

Sample application form

INDUSTRIAL TRIBUNALS

Received at ITO	FOR OFFICE USE	
	Case Number	
	Code	
	Initials	ROIT

Application to an Industrial Tribunal

- If you fax this form you do not need to send one in the post.
- This form has to be photocopied. If possible please use BLACK INK and CAPITAL letters.
- Where there are tick boxes, please tick the one that applies.

1 Please give the type of complaint you want the tribunal to decide (for example: unfair dismissal, equal pay). A full list is given in Booklet 1. If you have more than one complaint list them all.

UNFAIR DISMISSAL

4 Please give the dates of your employment

From 6 MAY 1993   To   3 MARCH 1998

2 Please give your details

Mr [X]   Mrs [ ]   Miss [ ]   Ms [ ]

First names   IAN

Surname   JONES

Date of birth   20TH JULY 1961

Address
4 RAPID ROAD
FULHAM
LONDON
Postcode   SW6

Telephone

Daytime Telephone

Please give an address to which we should send documents if different from above

AS ABOVE

Postcode

5 Please give the name and address of the employer, other organisation or person against whom this complaint is being brought

Name of the employer, organisation or person
ANOTHER WAREHOUSE LTD

Address
60 RAPID ROAD
FULHAM
LONDON

Postcode   SW6

Telephone

Please give the place where you worked or applied to work if different from above

Address
N/A

Postcode

3 If a representative is acting for you please give details

Name   N/A

Address   N/A

Postcode

Telephone

Reference

6 Please say what job you did for the employer (or what job you applied for). If this does not apply, Please say what your connection was with the employer

WAREHOUSE MANAGER

IT1(E/W)

7 Please give the number of normal basic hours worked each week	9 If your complaint is NOT about dismissal, please give the date when the matter you are complaining about took place
Hours per week	
40	–

8 Please give your earning details
Basic wage/salary
£ 20,000 : per ANNUM
Average take home pay
£ 900 : per MONTH
Other bonuses/benefits
£ OVERTIME : £40 per WEEK

10 Unfair dismissal applicants only
Please indicate what you are seeking at this stage, if you win your case.

- [ ] Reinstatement: to carry on working in your old job as before (An order for reinstatement normally includes an award of compensation for loss of earnings.)
- [ ] Re-engagement: to start another job or new contract with your old employer. (An order for re-engagement normally includes an award of compensation for loss of earnings.)
- [X] Compensation only: to get an award of money

11 Please give details of your complaint
If there is not enough space for your answer, please continue on a separate sheet and attach it to this form.

1. On 3 March 1998, the HR Manager of the Respondents informed me that I was being dismissed forthwith from my job as a warehouse manager on the ground that my work was unsatisfactory. I was given 4 weeks' pay in lieu of notice.

2. Until my dismissal, I had never received any warning or indication that the Respondents were unhappy with my job performance. On the contrary, I had been praised by my manager on several occasions on the quality of my work. Last year I was given an award for being the best time-keeper in the Company.

3. In addition, the Respondents failed to specify the reasons why they considered my work was deficient, and failed to give me any opportunity to improve those aspects of my work which they considered were below standard.

4. For the reasons set out above, I consider that my dismissal was unfair.

12 Please sign and date this form, then send it to the address on the back page of this booklet.

Signed	Date
M. Jones	30th March 1998

IT1(EW)

appearance and an explanatory booklet. The employer is required to fill in the notice of appearance and return it within 21 days, explaining whether it intends to oppose the application. If the respondent does not reply, judgment can be entered against the employer.

Time extensions for returning the notice of appearance

Usually, the industrial tribunal will be prepared to grant a 14-day extension to employers: this can be done over the telephone. The tribunal will be reluctant to grant a longer period of time unless there are compelling reasons for doing so. If an extension is granted, the employer should then confirm in writing what has been agreed.

In England and Wales the attitude of the various regional tribunal offices can differ. Some are prepared to grant an extension of time for submitting a notice of appearance if it looks likely that the parties will reach a negotiated out-of-court settlement in the near future; others are more strict, and demand that the notice of appearance is submitted on time. In Scotland extensions of time are not generally granted.

If a respondent does not reply, it will not be allowed to defend the application. However, if a notice of appearance is sent in late the tribunal can still exercise its discretion to allow the employer to defend the claim. In practice, this discretion will be exercised in most cases.

ACAS

ACAS* (the Arbitration and Conciliation Advisory Service) attempts to act as the broker between the employer and the employee. Once an application has been submitted to the industrial tribunal an ACAS officer will be appointed who will liaise with both parties in order to achieve a mutually acceptable compromise settlement.

If an agreement is brokered through ACAS both parties will be asked to sign a form recording the deal agreed. Once this has been signed the employee will then be unable to pursue his or her claim in the industrial tribunal, and the employer will be under an obligation to honour the terms of the agreement reached with ACAS's assistance.

Role of the Labour Relations Agency in Northern Ireland

The Labour Relations Agency* in Northern Ireland provides advice and guidance on all matters relating to employment law and industrial relations. Once an application has been submitted to an industrial tribunal, a labour relations officer will contact both parties in an attempt to find terms of settlement acceptable to both of them. If the deal is brokered through the Labour Relations Agency, both parties must abide by the same terms that apply to ACAS-brokered agreements (see above). If conciliation fails, the complaint will be heard in the normal way by the industrial tribunal.

Procedures before the hearing

Once the notice of appearance is filed, the tribunal will write to both parties telling them what they are requested to do in order to prepare for the hearing. This will vary but usually each party will be asked to send to the other copies of the documents it intends to rely on at the hearing. These may include:

- contracts of employment
- medical reports
- correspondence
- payslips.

Employers are often reluctant to make public documents containing sensitive details of their business activities. However, if either party possesses relevant documents that it refuses to disclose to the other, that party can write to the industrial tribunal and ask it to make an order to release the document.

Both parties are usually required to produce written statements summarising the testimony of any witnesses, but may not be obliged to disclose this information before the hearing.

The industrial tribunal usually needs five sets of these documents for use at the hearing. The parties normally agree which of them will provide copies.

If a party refuses to comply with the industrial tribunal's order, the industrial tribunal may strike out an application or, in the case of employers, refuse them the right to defend an application.

Fixing the hearing date

The industrial tribunal will write to both parties at least 14 days before the day of the hearing to tell them when the hearing will take place (in Scotland, a letter specifying a window of time during which the hearing is to be fixed will be sent). If either party cannot attend the hearing on the day proposed, it should write to the industrial tribunal within 14 days explaining why and let the industrial tribunal know of any other dates when it cannot attend. Both parties should also let the tribunal know if, in their consideration, the hearing is likely to take longer than a day. This will depend on the complexity of the case, the number of witnesses that need to be heard and the amount of other evidence that must be consulted.

If neither party objects to the hearing date within the 14-day deadline the industrial tribunal will not, save in exceptional circumstances, subsequently re-schedule the date but will proceed with the hearing on the appointed day.

The industrial tribunal will normally consider the inability of any key witnesses to appear on the scheduled hearing date a justifiable reason for delaying the hearing.

If an application for postponement of a particular date is turned down by the tribunal, the frustrated party can appeal. The appeal should be submitted as soon as possible.

Treatment of discrimination claims

The industrial tribunal is aware that discrimination can be difficult to prove. In accordance with special rules, applicants in such cases can send their employers questionnaires. Typically these ask for details of the employer's organisation and anti-discrimination policies: for example, a questionnaire in a racial discrimination case asks for statistics of the number of employees from ethnic minorities and requests details of steps taken by the employer to ensure equal opportunities. If the employer does not reply it will face censure by the tribunal.

In racial or sex discrimination cases the chairman of the tribunal may request a preliminary hearing for the purpose of reviewing the case.

The Equal Opportunities Commission★ and the Commission for Racial Equality★ will fund some applications, particularly if it is felt that the application raises a point of general concern (see page 96).

In Northern Ireland, the Fair Employment Tribunal determines complaints concerning discrimination on the grounds of religious belief and/or political opinion. The Labour Relations Agency★ offers advice on bringing a claim at the Fair Employment Tribunal.

Considerations for employees before a hearing

If the employee is, for example, seeking compensation following dismissal, he or she will need to show evidence of the loss suffered. Typically, he or she should be able to provide copies of:

- payslips from the relevant period of employment showing former earnings
- job advertisements or applications for new jobs
- proof of earnings in any new employment.

If the employee has suffered discrimination in any form he or she should bring as many credible witnesses as possible to support his or her case. (See Chapter 5 for information on gathering evidence of discrimination.) The stronger the employee's case looks and the greater the determination shown, the more likely it is that the employer will decide to settle the claim before the hearing date, usually by making an offer of compensation (see Chapter 12). It is worth the employee's while to try to find out who the employer's solicitors are (if there are solicitors acting this will usually be apparent from the notice of appearance) because employers facing substantial legal fees may be prepared to settle out of court. However, employees should not be surprised if the employer ignores any offer to settle the matter until the last minute.

Considerations for employers before a hearing

Often employers and employees continue to negotiate right up to the door of the industrial tribunal. It is quite common for matters to go quiet for a period of time after the employee has submitted the application and the employer has responded with the notice of appearance. Employers often delay as long as possible in the belief that the employee, particularly if he or she is not legally represented, will lose his or her nerve and either not turn up on the day or settle for a much lower sum.

A lot of the employer's work in preparation for a hearing is carried out quite close to the actual hearing date. Therefore, if the employer wants to settle the matter (as most do unless there is a point of principle involved), it will want to do so before incurring significant legal fees.

If the employer is using a big commercial firm such fees are likely to be substantial in comparison to the employee's potential claim. In the light of this, the employer may find a settlement attractive.

The industrial tribunal hearing

If the matter proceeds to a hearing events unfold as follows. At the hearing both parties are given an opportunity to state their case and to cross-examine any witnesses who give evidence against them. When all the evidence has been presented, the two parties or their representatives will be given the opportunity to address the industrial tribunal. The industrial tribunal aims to keep the procedure as informal as possible and will take into account an unrepresented party's inexperience.

The length of the hearing will depend on factors such as the complexity of the issues involved and the number of witnesses who need to be called. Hearings typically last between one and three days.

Decision and appeals

The industrial tribunal will normally give its decision at the close of the hearing, often after a short adjournment. It will be written, signed by the chairman and given to both parties. Occasionally decisions are delayed owing to the fact that the tribunal members require more time before they can formulate a joint written decision. In Scotland, it is unusual for the tribunal's decision to be given at the close of a hearing. Most parties are subsequently informed in writing.

The industrial tribunal's decision may be challenged in one of two ways. It can be reviewed by the same tribunal, or alternatively referred to the Employment Appeal Tribunal (see below).

Review procedure
The review procedure is normally activated when minor mistakes in procedure have occurred prior to or on the hearing date. The review procedure is not appropriate when a full review of the case is needed.

Employment appeal tribunal
Appeals to the Employment Appeal Tribunal* will succeed where the industrial tribunal is considered to have misinterpreted the law. In other words, the case must have raised a question on the interpretation

of the law and an appeal will not normally be granted simply because one party does not like the result. Notice of appeal must be submitted within 42 days of the frustrated party receiving the industrial tribunal's written decision of its judgment.

Appeals in Northern Ireland

In Northern Ireland, the tribunal may be requested to review the decision it has reached, or the case can be taken to the Court of Appeal.

There are certain grounds on which a tribunal may consider a review. One of these is that the 'interests of justice' require it. However, the tribunal usually requires substantial grounds for permitting a review and a review would not be granted simply because one of the parties demanded it. Alternatively, the aggrieved party may request an appeal on a point of law. Any such request should be submitted in writing to the tribunal office within 42 days of receipt of the tribunal's written decision.

Additional help

Employers and employees in England, Wales and Scotland can consult the industrial tribunal Enquiry line★ for advice. Leaflets from the DTI Publications Orderline★ include *An Introduction to Industrial Tribunals* (CC3), *How to Apply to an Industrial Tribunal* (ITL) and *Hearings at Industrial Tribunals* (ITL). In Northern Ireland, a handbook entitled *Jurisdiction/Procedure on Industrial Tribunals* is available from training and employment offices and local DSS offices.

Chapter 17

Getting help in an employment dispute

Often situations occur in which either the employer, the employee, or both, feel that insurmountable differences have arisen. In such cases external assistance – from a voluntary organisation, a trade union or a solicitor – may be called for in order to help resolve the problem.

Voluntary organisations

In many employment disputes it is possible to obtain good advice and assistance from voluntary organisations such as local law centres or a Citizens Advice Bureau.* In addition, trade unions have representatives who are willing to help members, and who will usually have access to legal advice (see page 269).

All of these organisations will provide employees with an initial assessment of the strength of their legal position and should be prepared to write to the employer on the employee's behalf. In many cases, this initial correspondence is sufficient to resolve the dispute. If it is not and it becomes necessary to take legal action at an industrial tribunal, these organisations can be expected to provide guidance in preparing the application and during the conduct of any negotiations that arise prior to the hearing date (see Chapter 16).

The first step is to contact one of the advice centres mentioned above and make an appointment. At the meeting you should bring along any relevant documents (for example, the contract of employment, staff handbook, etc.). Some law centres and Citizens Advice Bureaux will, subject to the resources available, present the case at an industrial tribunal on behalf of the employee. In London an organisation known as the Free Representation Unit (FRU) takes referrals of cases from local law centres, high-street solicitors and Citizens Advice Bureaux. FRU, which has achieved some notable successes, cannot respond to enquiries from the public.

The drawback with using voluntary organisations is that their resources are often stretched. An alternative is to seek the advice of a solicitor who has the necessary knowledge and expertise (see pages 274–9).

Trade unions

Despite the decline in trade union membership in recent decades, the TUC claims that almost seven million people in the UK belong to a trade union (1998 figure). This figure represents almost a third of the UK's estimated 23 million people in employment.

Trade unions represent workers in particular industries, trades and professions. Their main purpose is to negotiate and consult with employers on pay and other working conditions. Provided that they meet the membership criteria, almost every worker has the right to join (or not to join) a union. However, in some companies certain staff and managers may be represented by a union but not recognised by the employer for the purposes of certain negotiations – for example, pay bargaining (see page 271). There are no longer any 'closed shops' – in other words, workplaces in which only union members are allowed to be employed. Trade unions offer legal advice to any member who is refused a job, selected for redundancy or dismissed on the grounds of being a union member. Generally, membership is transferable when you move jobs, but the ability of a particular union to represent an employee in negotiations on certain issues at a new workplace will depend on whether it is recognised there (see page 271). If you already work at a place which does not recognise a union, joining one in the event of a dispute may not give you any specific advantage in dealing with your employer – although you may be able to get legal advice (see page 269). You would be better advised to try a voluntary organisation (see opposite) or a lawyer (see page 274).

Organisation of the trade unions

Over 70 unions, many of which were formed in the nineteenth century, exist in the UK. The largest, UNISON,* has over a million members. UNISON's members mostly work in health care, the water, gas and electricity industries, further education, the voluntary sector, transport and housing associations.

Among the largest unions are:

- **Transport and General Workers Union★ (TGWU)** Membership includes dockers, agricultural workers, road transport workers and car builders
- **Amalgamated Engineering and Electrical Union★ (AEEU)** This union's members are drawn mainly from the manufacturing utilities, construction and energy supply sectors
- **GMB Union★** Membership covers the private and public sectors and includes the hotel and catering trades as well as the textile, food production, chemicals and energy industries
- **Manufacturing, Science and Finance Union★ (MSF)** Membership includes scientists, engineers and academics as well as members of the health service and finance sectors.

The Trades Union Congress (TUC)★ is a voluntary association of trade unions which is funded by fees paid by the affiliated unions. Its main role is to encourage co-operation amongst trade unions for the purpose of developing a common approach on matters affecting their members. The TUC's policies are debated at the organisation's annual conference.

All union members can get involved in the organisation of their union. Shop stewards are elected by the workforce to represent them in negotiations with the employer. Most unions have local branches which have a secretary elected by the local members. The branch representatives meet with other branch members at a district or regional level. The regional offices are often managed by full-time officials who provide advice to local members. At the highest level, the union will have a national headquarters where the general secretary and the national executive (elected by the union's membership) are based. Many unions hold an annual conference.

Unions are financed by their members' contributions. Each union sets its own subscription rates. The average amount in 1998, according to the TUC, was £5–£8 a month per member.

Trade union services for members

Unions offer a wide range of services for their members. These include:

- **negotiating with the employer over pay and terms and conditions of employment** This process is known as collective bargaining. The process can benefit both employers and employees. The employer can restrict negotiations to appointed representatives of the workforce, thereby avoiding the need to negotiate with each employee individually, while the employees usually enjoy a strengthened negotiating position as a result. According to the TUC, productivity is greater in economies that have high levels of collective bargaining, such as Germany and France, where productivity levels are 20–30 per cent higher than in the UK. ACAS★ also supports the case for collective bargaining, commenting: 'Our experience has shown the value of constructive joint work in providing a greater commitment to change, longer-lasting solutions and overall improved industrial relations'

- **helping members bring cases to industrial tribunals or to court** For example, UNISON brought a successful equal pay claim on behalf of two female speech therapists in 1997 (see page 98)

- **providing individual members with personal legal advice, financial services, discounts on holidays and insurance** Among other things, UNISON allows members to use its holiday club and holiday centre as well as providing discounts on certain insurance cover

- **lobbying the government and other groups** to support the union's policies

- **advising and representing members who have problems at work** This typically happens when the employee faces either a grievance or a disciplinary hearing

- **consulting with employers** in relation to redundancies involving 20 or more employees and in relation to TUPE transfers (see Chapter 8)

- **countering discrimination in the workplace** Unions have been active in promoting equal opportunities programmes.

Advantages of joining a union

The main advantage for employees of joining a union is that their interests will be represented, whether in pay negotiations or in the event of a disciplinary or grievance hearing. Clearly if an employer has a reputation for exploiting employees, sacking them without justification or flouting health and safety rules, employees may be able to gain greater security and protection by asking a union to look after their interests.

Disadvantages of joining a union

The main disadvantage is the need to pay the weekly or monthly subscription fee (see page 268).

Trade unions *vs* staff associations

Most trade unions (and all the unions mentioned in this book) are independent: in other words, 'not dominated by an employer, not controlled by an employer and not liable to be unduly influenced by an employer', according to the **Trade Union Labour Relations Act 1992**. Independent trade unions receive a certificate confirming their independent status and are free to represent their members' interests without interference by the employer. By contrast, in staff associations the employer may be represented. However, some employees may prefer to join their staff association because it is not likely to take as confrontational an approach as some trade unions.

Like trade unions, staff associations exist to represent the views of members, promote their interests and protect their rights in all matters affecting their working conditions. They should be able to provide advice on all aspects of industrial relations and to offer members support in disputes relating to disciplinary and grievance procedures and negotiations concerning terms and conditions of employment. Usually representatives are appointed among the workforce and working parties may be set up over issues such as health and safety procedures and equal opportunities.

Staff associations develop strategies specific to the particular workplace and enter into discussion with management over issues affecting members. Members of staff associations pay subscriptions, but they are likely to be considerably cheaper than trade union dues. Where a trade union is recognised by the employer a staff association will generally have the same access for the purposes of recognition (see below).

Recognition agreements

Many employers have entered into formal recognition agreements with unions for the purposes of negotiating on issues such as pay. The level of recognition can vary and can be at different levels for different purposes. Unions which are recognised by the employer have the right to:

- information for the purposes of collective bargaining
- information and consultation on health and safety issues
- information and consultation on occupational pension schemes
- time off work for members and officials
- information and consultation on redundancies and TUPE transfers (see Chapter 8).

According to the TUC, in 1995 an estimated 10.2 million employees reported that unions were recognised by the management at their workplaces for the purposes of negotiating on issues such as pay and working conditions.

In larger workplaces more than one union may be recognised. The advantage with this sort of arrangement for employers is that with assistance from the unions, difficulties can be identified and resolved at an earlier stage than would have been the case if they were simply left to management to deal with.

At present an employer can simply de-recognise a union for the purposes of negotiation at any time.

Advantages for the employer of union recognition

- Dealing with union representatives may be an efficient way of negotiating pay and conditions for groups of employees.
- Improved morale may develop among the workforce as a result of confidence on the part of the employees that they have a voice in their dealings with management.
- Changes of management could run more smoothly under a union/ employer partnership.

- Where unions have negotiated proper health and safety procedures, fewer days may be lost through sickness and injury. (According to the TUC, where union safety representatives and a joint safety committee exist, the annual rate of serious injuries falls from 10.9 per thousand workers to 5.3 per thousand.)
- Firms with union recognition are more likely to have training programmes for staff.
- Unions are likely to have negotiated better terms and conditions for employees, and thus discourage wasteful staff turnover.

Disadvantages for the employer of union recognition

Disadvantages for the employer are likely to arise in circumstances involving particularly militant and obstructive union officials. Although at the time of writing the employer can simply de-recognise the union (see opposite), such a move is unlikely to lead to an instant improvement in industrial relations.

Proposed changes on union recognition

It is proposed under the government White Paper 'Fairness at Work' that employers should be compelled to recognise unions for the purposes of negotiating where the majority of those balloted support such recognition and the majority voting in favour consist of at least 40 per cent of the workforce.

Collective agreements

Some employers and trade unions enter into collective agreements which can cover the treatment of a wide range of issues, including hiring and firing, suspensions, terms and conditions of employment, discipline and other machinery of collective bargaining. The purpose is to sort out between the parties the procedures that will be followed to deal with particular problems. For example, the employer and the union may agree when negotiating a rate of pay to be bound by the decision of an external third-party pay review body, or the union could agree not to strike until certain pre-agreed procedures had been exhausted. Collective agreements are not normally legally enforceable unless the terms of the collective agreement have been incorporated into the individual employee's contract of employment.

Health and safety issues

Where unions are recognised by the employer they have the right to appoint health and safety representatives. Employers have a duty to consult with them about health and safety matters including training programmes and information for employees and the health and safety consequences associated with the introduction of new technology.

Health and safety representatives are usually trained either by their own union or by the TUC. They can play an important and useful role in minimising the risks of an accident in the workplace. See also Chapter 15.

Industrial disputes

Disputes between the employer and the workforce can occur, for example, over the implementation of new working rotas, redundancies, changing rates of pay or the introduction of new equipment.

When such a dispute does occur the employee's first action is usually to approach the shop steward, who will take up the issue with the appropriate member of management. If necessary, full-time trade union officials may become involved. The issue can usually be resolved: on occasion, unions may resort to industrial action. The first stage of this process is usually to call an overtime ban followed by a work-to-rule or a one- or two-day stoppage. An all-out strike should be called only as a last resort.

Sometimes the employer and the unions will refer the dispute to ACAS.★ This independent body will attempt to broker a deal which is acceptable to both parties.

Strikes

Certain complicated procedures must be followed before a union can authorise a strike or other industrial action. These include giving the employer at least seven days' notice as well as carrying out a postal ballot of all members. The range of lawful industrial action is restricted in broad terms to matters affecting pay and working conditions.

Additional help

The TUC★ publishes a range of booklets and leaflets. If you want to become a union member, contact the TUC's Join a Union Campaign at the Head Office address.

Choosing a solicitor

Many high-street solicitors have a wide range of experience, from debt recovery and conveyancing to drawing up wills and handling divorces. It is highly advisable that the solicitor selected has the necessary employment law experience and is not simply going to refer to the textbooks for an answer.

The best route is to seek a personal recommendation. Friends or local advice centres may be able to help. Another way is to approach the Law Society,★ which should be able to refer you to a solicitor who specialises in employment law. In addition, various directories list recommended firms of solicitors in all parts of the country: these include Chambers' and Partners' *Guide to the Legal Profession* and the *Legal 500*. These books can be ordered from your local library and many advice centres also keep copies.

Steps to take before consulting a solicitor

The first step is to get together any relevant documents, such as the contract of employment, a job-offer letter, staff handbook, payslips, pension details or other documents relating to the problem. You should make a spare set of copies for the solicitor (you will probably be able to arrange cheaper photocopying than the solicitor).

Another useful preparatory step is to set down a summary of all the details relating to the problem. For example, an employee claiming to have been bullied, harassed or undermined should set out the background and list the dates on which incidents took place. Any correspondence should be arranged in date order. It may be useful to give this summary to the solicitor: part of the purpose of preparing the summary is to vent pent-up frustration and help the client to think logically and clearly about how events have unfolded.

Your objectives should be clear. Everyone has different goals and it is important that the solicitor does not make an assumption about what you wish to achieve. For example, for some employees who have been, or are likely to be, dismissed the prime concern is to ensure that they receive the maximum pay-off possible; others are most concerned to obtain a good reference or to be able to join a competitor at the earliest possible moment.

You should make a list of all the points you want covered at the first meeting with the solicitor. It is wise to ask about costs at the outset and to check whether any insurance policy you hold will provide legal cover before the meeting (see page 276).

Conditional-fee arrangements

The main advantage of these is that they allow people who use solicitors to minimise their financial exposure. Before entering into such an arrangement, the solicitor will consider the strength of the client's case with him or her. If the solicitor is satisfied that the individual has a good chance of winning, a 'success fee' will be negotiated (in other words, the solicitor gets paid if the case is won). If the solicitor loses the case, the client is not liable to pay his or her fees.

However, the arrangement does not constitute a licence to go to law. This is because the solicitor will require the client to take out insurance cover against the risk of losing the case and becoming liable for the opponent's costs. The insurance company will need to be satisfied that the policy-holder has a good chance of winning the case and will agree to underwrite the client's legal expenses only if the solicitor has entered into a success-fee arrangement with the client.

At time of writing, conditional-fee or so-called 'no-win, no-fee' arrangements are not available in Northern Ireland and are restricted to cases relating to personal injury, insolvency and human rights in England and Wales. This situation may change. The success of the proposed extension of the conditional-fee arrangement will depend largely on how willing the insurance companies are to offer policies to cover a broad range of actions. Note: these arrangements relate to the costs of bringing an action in the courts. In the industrial tribunal both parties – save in exceptional circumstances – bear their own costs, whether they win or lose.

Help with legal expenses

Assistance with legal costs may be available, as detailed below. Trade union members may also qualify for help (see page 269).

Legal aid

If you have limited means or are on state benefits you may qualify for legal aid on a claim involving breach of contract, provided that this is brought in the courts (legal aid is not available for claims brought to an industrial tribunal). To qualify for civil legal aid to bring a civil case (as opposed to criminal law proceedings) there must be a reasonable chance that you will be successful and generally your disposable income (or that of you and your partner) must be less than £7,595 a year (£8,370 for personal injury cases) and your total capital (excluding your house) must be less than £6,750 (£8,560 for personal injury cases). When making the first appointment with a solicitor, it is advisable to check whether the firm takes legal aid cases. The solicitor will help in the preparation of any legal aid form.

Green form scheme

This scheme enables those who are eligible to receive two hours' free legal advice from a solicitor. (This would not include representation but could include writing a letter.) To qualify, the client must have a disposable weekly income of less than £80 and less than £1,000 disposable capital. For more information, consult a leaflet entitled *How to Get Free or Local Legal Help* from the Legal Aid Board.★

Insurance cover

You should check what your insurance policy covers: many household insurance policies provide for some degree of cover. For example, contents insurance may cover solicitors' expenses and possibly barristers' fees and expert reports, such as a doctor's opinion. Alternatively you could take out legal expenses insurance. If you are covered by insurance, you should check what conditions need to be satisfied. It is possible that the insurance company may require you to use their own solicitor. For more information, see *The Which? Guide to Insurance*, from Which? Limited.★

Solicitors' charges

When choosing a solicitor, it is worth shopping around. You should check the solicitor's reputation and success rate by asking for recommendations or checking the directories listed on page 274. The solicitor offering the best success-fee deal (see page 275) may not necessarily be the one best equipped to achieve a satisfactory result.

Solicitors are expected, in accordance with their professional code of conduct, to give clients at the outset an estimate of their likely charges. If this is not possible (for example, where a dispute might develop into a full court hearing), the solicitor should tell the client how the fee will be calculated. Typically, solicitors charge by the hour and rates fluctuate depending on the solicitor's experience, speciality and location. Average rates are between £100 and £300 per hour. High-street firms will charge less than others, but even so it is worth being prepared for the meeting in order to save time.

If the solicitor does not volunteer an estimate of charges you should ask for one. If it is not possible for an estimate to be provided, an alternative is to set a cap on the level of fees that can be incurred by the solicitor. This will give you an opportunity to review progress before chalking up further costs.

How to complain about solicitors' charges

If you think that your legal bill is too high, you should take the issue up with your solicitor – usually firms of solicitors have a partner assigned to investigating complaints of this type. Those who remain unhappy can have their bill checked again, in one of two ways (see below).

Obtaining a remuneration certificate

This route is available only when the legal work does not involve court proceedings. In this process, the Law Society★ examines the solicitor's file on the matter free of charge and then reviews the client's bill to ensure that the fee is fair. Two conditions must be satisfied before a remuneration certificate is granted: first, when the request is made, the bill must remain unpaid. If the solicitor has already deducted his or her costs from funds held on account for the client (typically this happens when a solicitor acts on the sale of a house), the bill will be treated as unpaid unless the client has given permission for the deduction. Second, the request must be made by the client no more than one month after the solicitor has informed the client of his or her right to a remuneration certificate. If the solicitor has *not* informed the client of this right, the client can apply provided that no more than three months have passed since he or she received the bill and the solicitor has deducted costs from money held on the client's behalf.

Clients should write to their solicitors to ask them to apply for a remuneration certificate. Once the client has asked for a remuneration certificate, the solicitor must complete an application form and forward it together with the relevant file to the Law Society. A client's demand for a remuneration certificate is a nuisance for a busy solicitor: complying with such a request is a time-consuming exercise for which a bill cannot be submitted.

The advantage for the client who opts for a remuneration certificate is that he or she has nothing to lose, apart from the solicitor's goodwill. The Law Society cannot authorise an increase in the bill, even though it has the power to reduce it. The solicitor's only comfort is that after the client has been informed of the right to obtain a remuneration certificate, interest can be charged on an outstanding bill, backdated to one month after the date on which the bill was delivered.

In Scotland there is no process whereby a remuneration certificate can be taxed. However, it is possible to require the account to be taxed by an auditor of court.

Asking for the bill to be taxed

The alternative method of checking whether a bill is reasonable is to ask for it to be 'taxed' at a hearing presided over by a court official. This procedure is the only way by which legal fees incurred in court proceedings can be vetted and it can also be used for work that did not involve court proceedings.

At the hearing, the solicitor's aim is to defend the bill, by convincing the official that the time spent on the matter was reasonable and that any specific items of expenditure incurred were justifiable. The advantage of taxation is that, unlike remuneration certificates, bills incurred in court proceedings can also be queried. The disadvantage is that if the bill is reduced by less than a fifth, the client must pay the solicitor's taxation hearing costs.

Other complaints about solicitors

If you are dissatisfied with the service you are receiving (for example, because you are not being kept informed regarding progress or have lost confidence in the solicitor handling the case) you should, in the first incidence, use the solicitor's firm's internal complaints procedure.

After the first meeting, the solicitor should send you a letter setting out his or her understanding of the task and, if relevant, the likely costs for completing it. This letter should also give the name of the person at the firm who handles complaints. If the letter does not contain this information, telephone the firm and ask to speak to the relevant person.

After the person responsible for dealing with complaints has heard the problem, he or she should carry out an internal review and report the findings to you. If you remain unhappy with the outcome you should, in England and Wales, contact the Office for the Supervision of Solicitors* (OSS), which investigates such complaints. If appropriate, the OSS will take disciplinary action against solicitors who fall short of the standards expected of them. In Scotland and Northern Ireland, complaints should be addressed to the relevant Law Society.*

Employment legislation

The main UK statutes and regulations and European directives relating to employment law covered by this book are listed below.

UK statutes and regulations

Asylum and Immigration Act 1996
Employment Rights Act 1996
Employment Rights (Dispute Resolution) Act 1998
Equal Pay Act 1970
Disability Discrimination Act 1995
Health and Safety at Work etc Act 1974
Race Relations Act 1976
Sex Discrimination Acts 1975 (as amended)
Trade Union Labour Relations Act 1992
Transfer of Undertakings (Protection of Employment) Regulations 1981

European directives

Acquired Rights Directive
Equal Treatment Directive
Working Time Directive

Addresses

This section contains details of organisations giving general advice. You may also be able to contact specialist helplines for your professional area.

ACAS
Brandon House
180 Borough High Street
London SE1 1LW
Web site: www.acas.org.uk
Look in the phone book for your local office

Amalgamated Engineering and Electrical Union (AEEU)
Hayes Court
West Common Road
Bromley
Kent BR2 7AU
Tel: 0181-462 7755
Fax: 0181-315 8234
Email: j.staples@headoffice.aeeu.org.uk
Web site: www.aeeu.org.uk

Benefits Agency
Look in the phone book for your local office

Benefits Enquiry Line
(0800) 882200

British Association for Counselling (BAC)
1 Regent Place
Rugby, Warks CV21 2PJ
Tel: (01788) 578328 (*Information line*)
Fax: (01788) 562189
Email: bac@bac.co.uk

Citizens Advice Bureau
Look in the phone book for your local office

Commission for Racial Equality (CRE)
Elliott House
10–12 Allington Street
London SW1E 5EH
Tel: 0171-828 7022
Fax: 0171-630 7605
Web site: www.open.gov.uk/cre/crehome.htm

Confederation of British Industry (CBI)
Centre Point
103 Oxford Street
London WC1A 1DU
Tel: 0171-379 7400
Fax: 0171-240 0988
Web site: www.cbi.org.uk

Contributions Agency
Look in the phone book for your local office

Contributions Agency International Services
Longbenton
Newcastle-upon-Tyne, NE98 1YX
Tel: 0191-225 4811 (*Helpdesk*)
Fax: 0191-225 7800
Email: a.moy@new040.dss.gov.uk

Department of Trade and Industry
Advance notification section
Redundancy Payments Offices
Hagley House
83–85 Hagley Road
Birmingham BI6 8QG
Tel: 0121–456 4411
Fax: 0121–454 7881
For giving advance notice of redundancies

Disability Alliance (DAERA)
Universal House
88–94 Wentworth Street
London E1 7SA
Tel: 0171–247 8776
0171–247 8763 (*Rights advice line*)
Mon, Weds 2–4pm
Fax: 0171–247 8765

DTI Employment Relations Directorate
1 Victoria Street
London SW1H 0ET
Tel: 0171–215 5985
Fax: 0171–215 2635
Web site: www.dti.gov.uk

DTI Publications Orderline
1 Victoria Street
London SW1H 0ET
Tel: (0870) 1502500
Fax: (0870) 1502333
Email: dtipubs@echristian.co.uk
Web site: www.dti.gov.uk

Employment Agency Standards Office
Department of Trade and Industry
1 Victoria Street
London SW1H 0ET
Tel: (0645) 555105 (*Helpline*)
Fax: 0171–215 2636

Employment Appeal Tribunal
Central Office
58 Victoria Embankment
London EC4Y 0DS
Tel: 0171–273 1041
Fax: 0171–273 1045

Equal Opportunities Commission (EOC)
Overseas House
Quay Street
Manchester M3 3HN
Tel: 0161–833 9244
Fax: 0161–835 1657
Web site: www.eoc.org.uk

Eye Care Information Service
PO Box 3597
London SE1 6DY
Send an SAE marked
'VDU information' for leaflets

Fair Employment Commission (FEC)
Andras House
60 Great Victoria Street
Belfast BT2 7BB
Tel: (01232) 240020
Fax: (01232) 331544

Foreign and Commonwealth Office (FCO)
1 Palace Street
London SW1E 5HE
Web site: www.fco.gov.uk

FCO Migration and Visa Division
Tel: 0171–238 4633/4664
0171–238 4639 (*Leaflet orderline*)

FCO Travel Advice Unit
Tel: 0171–238 4503/4504

GMB Union
Head Office
22–24 Worple Road
Wimbledon
London SW19 4DD
Tel: 0181-947 3131
Fax: 0181-944 6552

Health and Safety Executive (HSE)
Information Centre
Broad Lane
Sheffield S3 7HQ
Tel: (0541) 545500 (*Information line*)
Look in the phone book for your local office

HSE Publications
PO Box 1999
Sudbury
Suffolk CO10 6FS
Tel: (01787) 881165
(*Publications orderline*)

Home Office
Tel: 0181-649 7878
(*Employers' helpline*)

Immigration and Nationality Directorate
Lunar House
Wellesley Road
Croydon
Surrey CR9 2BY
Tel: 0181-686 0688
(*Immigration and residency enquiries*)
Fax: 0181-760 1181
Web site: www.homeoffice.gov.uk/ind/hpg.htm

Industrial tribunal
Tel: (0345) 959775 (*Enquiry line*)
Mon to Fri 9am–5pm

Industrial Society
Peter Runge House
3 Carlton House Terrace
London SW1 5DG
Tel: 0171-479 1000
Fax: 0171-479 1111
Email:
infoserve@indusoc.demon.co.uk
Web site: www.indsoc.co.uk

Inland Revenue
Web site: www.open.gov.uk/inrev/inhome.htm
Look in the phone book for your local office

Jobcentre
Look in the phone book for your local office

Labour Relations Agency
2–8 Gordon Street
Belfast BT1 2LG
Tel: (01232) 321442
Fax: (01232) 330827

Law Society
113 Chancery Lane
London WC2A 1PL
Tel: 0171-242 1222
Call for relevant fax number
Web site: www.lawsociety.org.uk

Law Society of Northern Ireland
Law Society House
98 Victoria Street
Belfast BT1 3JZ
Tel: (01232) 231614
Fax: (01232) 232606

Law Society of Scotland
26 Drumsheugh Gardens
Edinburgh EH3 7YR
Tel: 0131-226 7411
Fax: 0131-225 2934
Email: lawscot@lawscot.org.uk
Web site: www.lawscot.org.uk

Legal Aid Board
85 Gray's Inn Road
London WC1X 8AA
Tel: 0171-813 1000

LRD Publications
78 Blackfriars Road
London SE1 8HF
Tel: 0171-928 3649
Fax: 0171-928 0621

Manufacturing, Science and Finance Union (MSF)
Head Office
MSF Centre
33–37 Moreland Street
London EC1V 8BB
Tel: 0171-505 3000
Fax: 0171-505 3030
Web site: www.msf.org.uk

Medical Advisory Service for Travellers Abroad (MASTA)
1 Pier Street
Lee on the Solent
Hampshire PO13 9NG
Tel: (01705) 553933
(0891) 224100
(*Travellers' healthline – premium rate*)
Fax: (01705) 553936
Web site: http://dspace.dial.pipex.com/masta

Occupational Pensions Advisory Service (OPAS)
11 Belgrave Road
London SW1V 1RB
Tel: 0171-233 8080
Fax: 0171-233 8016
Email: opas@iclweb.com
Web site: www.opas.org.uk

Office of the Industrial Tribunals and Fair Employment Tribunal
Long Bridge House
20–24 Waring Street
Belfast BT1 2EB
Tel: (01232) 327666
Fax: (01232) 230184

Office for the Supervision of Solicitors
Victoria Court
8 Dormer Place
Royal Leamington Spa
Warwickshire CV32 5AE
Tel: (01926) 820082
Fax: (01926) 831532

Overseas Labour Service
Department of Education and Employment
W5 Moorfoot
Sheffield S1 4PQ
Tel: 0114-259 4074
(*General enquiry line*)
(0990) 210224 (*To obtain work-permit application forms*)
Fax: 0114-259 3728

Racial Equality Council
Look in the phone book for your local office

Redundancy Helpline
Tel: (0500) 848489

Registrar of Pension Schemes
Occupational Pensions Regulatory
Authority
PO Box 1NN
Newcastle upon Tyne NE99 1NN
Tel: 0191-225 6393
Fax: 0191-225 6390

Relate
National Headquarters
Herbert Gray College
Little Church Street
Rugby, Warks CV21 3AP
Tel: (01788) 573241
Fax: (01788) 535007
Web site: www.relate.org.uk

Royal Association for Disability and
Rehabilitation (RADAR)
12 City Forum
250 City Road
London EC1V 8AF
Tel: 0171-250 3222
Fax: 0171-250 0212
Web site: www.radar.org.uk

Society of Pension Consultants
St Bartholemew House
92 Fleet Street
London EC4Y 1DH
Tel: 0171-353 1688
Fax: 0171-353 9296
Email: j.mortimer@virgin.net
Web site: www.spc.uk.com

Tax Office
Look in the phone book under 'Inland
Revenue' for your local office

Training and Employment Agency
Work Permits Branch
Adelaide House
39–49 Adelaide Street
Belfast BT2 8FD
Tel: (01232) 257777
Fax: (01232) 257468

Transport and General Workers
Union (TGWU)
Transport House
16 Palace Street
London SW1E 5JD
Tel: 0171-828 7788
Fax: 0171-963 4440
Email: tgwu@tgwu.org.uk

TUC
Congress House
Great Russell Street
London WC1B 3LS
Tel: 0171-636 4030
Fax: 0171-636 0632
Email: info@tuc.org.uk
Web site: www.tuc.org.uk

UNISON
1 Mabledon Place
London WC1H 9AJ
Tel: 0171-388 2366
Fax: 0171-387 6692
Web site: www.unison.org.uk

Which? Limited
Which? Books
Castlemead
Gascoyne Way
Hertford X, SG14 1LH
Tel: (0800) 252100
Web site: www.which.net

Index